THE MUSICIAN'S GUIDE
TO AURAL SKILLS

THE MUSICIAN'S GUIDE TO AURAL SKILLS

Sight-Singing

THIRD EDITION

Paul Murphy
Muhlenberg College

Joel Phillips
Westminster Choir College of Rider University

Elizabeth West Marvin
Eastman School of Music

Jane Piper Clendinning
Florida State University

W. W. NORTON & COMPANY
NEW YORK · LONDON

W. W. Norton & Company has been independent since its founding in 1923, when William Warder Norton and Mary D. Herter Norton first published lectures delivered at the People's Institute, the adult education division of New York City's Cooper Union. The Nortons soon expanded their program beyond the Institute, publishing books by celebrated academics from America and abroad. By mid-century, the two major pillars of Norton's publishing program—trade books and college texts—were firmly established. In the 1950s, the Norton family transferred control of the company to its employees, and today—with a staff of four hundred and a comparable number of trade, college, and professional titles published each year—W. W. Norton & Company stands as the largest and oldest publishing house owned wholly by its employees.

Third Edition

Editor: Justin Hoffman
Editorial assistant: Grant Phelps
Managing editor, College: Marian Johnson
Associate project editor: Michael Fauver
Copyeditor: Elizabeth Bortka
Proofreader: Debra Nichols
Electronic media editor: Steve Hoge
Electronic media editorial assistant: Stephanie Eads
Production manager: Andy Ensor
Design director: Rubina Yeh
Music typesetting and page composition: David Botwinik; CodeMantra
Manufacturing: Quad Graphics-Taunton

ISBN 978-0-393-26405-0 (pbk.)

W. W. Norton & Company, Inc., 500 Fifth Avenue, New York, NY 10110
www.wwnorton.com
W. W. Norton & Company, Ltd., Castle House, 75/76 Wells Street, London WIT3QT

1 2 3 4 5 6 7 8 9 0

Contents

Preface   vii

Part I   Elements of Music

Chapter 1   2
Chapter 2   9
Chapter 3   23
Chapter 4   37
Chapter 5   48
Chapter 6   67
Chapter 7   82
Chapter 8   97
Chapter 9   110
Chapter 10   125

Part II   Diatonic Harmony and Tonicization

Chapter 11   140
Chapter 12   155
Chapter 13   171
Chapter 14   186
Chapter 15   198
Chapter 16   210
Chapter 17   225
Chapter 18   241
Chapter 19   255
Chapter 20   268
Chapter 21   283

Part III   Chromatic Harmony and Form

Chapter 22   300
Chapter 23   317
Chapter 24   333
Chapter 25   351
Chapter 26   365
Chapter 27   379
Chapter 28   397
Chapter 29   415
Chapter 30   425
Chapter 31   435
Chapter 32   446
Chapter 33   467

Part IV   The Twentieth Century and Beyond

Chapter 34   482
Chapter 35   497
Chapter 36   509
Chapter 37   520
Chapter 38   530
Chapter 39   545
Chapter 40   558

Keyboard Lessons

Part I   582
Part II   597
Part III   627
Part IV   645

Credits   C1

Preface

The Musician's Guide series is the most comprehensive set of materials available for learning music theory and aural skills. Consisting of a theory text, workbook, and anthology, along with a two-volume aural-skills text, the series features coordinated resources that can be mixed and matched for any theory curriculum.

The two volumes of *The Musician's Guide to Aural Skills* teach the practical skills students need as professional musicians—dictation, sight-singing, rhythm-reading, keyboard harmony, improvisation, ear-training, and composition—through real music. Though the two volumes of this book correspond to *The Musician's Guide to Theory and Analysis* in ordering and terminology, they are designed to be used together, individually, or in conjunction with other theory texts.

This Sight-Singing volume emphasizes the skills required for real-time performance, and also includes strategic, progressive training in rhythm-reading, improvisation, and keyboard skills. The companion Ear-Training volume helps students develop listening skills with two innovative types of dictation activities: short *Try It* dictations develop students' skills in recognizing tonal patters, while Contextual Listening exercises guide students through the process of taking dictation from the literature. Both volumes feature a wide range of real musical repertoire—including classical, popular, and folk selections—throughout. The Ear-Training volume emphasizes recordings of real musicians over synthesized performances.

The Musician's Guide to Aural Skills, 3rd Edition, Sight-Singing is distinctive in two significant ways. First, it integrates skills that students need in order to understand common musical patterns. These include the ability to imagine and perform the sounds of printed music; to recall music they hear by singing, playing, and writing it; and to demonstrate their grasp of a variety of musical styles in order to improvise music of their own. For example, in Chapter 4, as preparation for singing rhythms and melodies in compound meter, students are instructed how to conduct simple duple meter as part of a Point-and-Sing exercise in which they point to notated rhythmic patterns while singing and conducting them. They then improvise their own phrases using these same patterns in combinations of their own choosing. Finally, they are instructed to notate their improvisations and exchange them with others. Second, music for sight-singing, rhythm-reading, and improvisation includes many ensemble works—not only duets, but also music for three, four, and five parts. These range from the abundant two-part rhythms to be performed by a single person, in pairs, or in groups, to Thomas Morley's five-part motet "Now Is the Month of Maying" in Chapter 20.

Using This Volume

With this new edition, we've reorganized the Sight-Singing volume into 40 chapters to align with both the Ear-Training volume and *The Musician's Guide to Theory and Analysis*. Melodies, rhythms, and improvisation activities all appear together within each chapter. Keyboard activities—now enhanced and reorganized into 40 lessons—appear in the back of the volume. We hope that these changes will make it easier for instructors to plan for class and to coordinate aural skills with written theory.

As students move through the Sight-Singing volume, learning objectives at the beginning of each chapter identify the specific melodic and rhythmic skills to be addressed, and summarize what students will learn. The initial sight-singing melodies of Chapter 1 are études specifically composed to help students acclimate to singing and conducting, recognize patterns and interpret the visual elements of music notation, and develop a sense of scale degree and intonation by applying solfège syllables or scale-degree numbers. Students will want to return to these études throughout their study, using them for warm-ups, syllable mastery, and vocal development. Most of the remaining melodies are drawn from a wide range of styles and periods—from popular (Broadway musicals, movies and television, classic rock, jazz, and blues) to common-practice, as well as twentieth- and twenty-first century music literature.

Although the companion text, *The Musician's Guide to Theory and Analysis 3rd Edition* provides an overview of rhythmic concepts and terminology, this book emphasizes the practical application of reading and performing rhythms. The hundreds of exercises here are graduated so that students can learn to recognize patterns in a sequential, developmental fashion. We begin with the basics of beat and meter, incorporating divided, subdivided, and doubled beats, mapping these concepts onto different beat values. We provide explanations and études for understanding dotted and tied notes, managing interruptions of the tempo, coordinating super-subdivided beats in slow tempos, performing different types of syncopation, understanding swung rhythms, internalizing characteristic jazz and ragtime rhythms through actual literature, and singing rhythms of the spoken word. We conclude by presenting a great variety of techniques developed or revisited by composers of the twentieth and twenty-first centuries: ametric rhythms, serialized rhythms, "feathered" beams, added values, isorhythm, and non-retrogradable rhythms. With diagrams throughout, students receive guidance on conducting simple beat patterns while they perform rhythms.

Each chapter also presents one or more improvisation exercises to develop this important and creative aspect of making music. The lessons feature enough scaffolding so that even if students have never improvised before, they can succeed in this key skill and have fun in the process. These exercises, for both solo and group performance, are designed to reinforce key concepts in music theory and aural skills. Following most improvisations are Quick Composition exercises in which students are guided in notation of their improvisations so that they learn to capture their musical ideas for themselves and others to reproduce and retain.

Finally, we reinforce all musical concepts at the keyboard with a keyboard lesson corresponding to each chapter of the text. Our purpose here is not to develop pianists, but rather to teach students how to realize the sounds and ideas they study with this most fundamental musical tool. Although everyone should be able to play the easiest exercises, students should *try* to play all of them; it is important for students to learn to play as much as they can as soon as they can, and to develop these skills from the beginning. The keyboard exercises progress in a spiral fashion, often returning to earlier models to demonstrate and facilitate more-advanced aspects of keyboard harmony. For example, simple two-voice contrapuntal patterns return later as the soprano and bass of four-part exercises, and even later with chromatic alterations. Spiral learning demonstrates the simple origins of what might otherwise seem complex.

Planning Your Curriculum

The Musician's Guide covers concepts typically taught during the first two years of college instruction in music. For instructors who adopt both the *Theory and Analysis* and *Aural Skills* texts, we know you will appreciate the consistent pedagogical approach, terminology, and order of presentation that the two texts share. Nevertheless, you may find at times that students' aural and practical skills develop more slowly than their grasp of theoretical concepts. There is no harm done if aural/practical instruction trails slightly behind conceptual understanding. For this reason, we summarize the organization of the volumes and suggest strategies for using them. Typically deployed over four or five semesters, most college curricula might be addressed by one of the following two models.

Plan 1 (four semesters, including one semester dealing with musical rudiments)

	Sight-Singing	Ear-Training
Term 1	Chapters 1-10 including Keyboard Lessons	Chapters 1-10 and Compositions 1-4
Term 2	Chapters 11-21 including Keyboard Lessons	Chapters 11-21 and Compositions 5-11
Term 3	Chapters 22-33 including Keyboard Lessons	Chapters 22-33 and Compositions 12-13
Term 4	Chapters 34-40 including Keyboard Lessons	Chapters 34-40 and Compositions 14-17

Alternatively, the following organization is one suggestion for those curricula that offer a dedicated rudiments class in addition to a four-semester core sequence.

Plan 2 (a rudiments class followed by four semesters)

	Sight-Singing	Ear-Training
Rudiments	Chapters 1-8 omitting modal melodies in Chapter 5; Keyboard Lessons 1-8, omitting Lesson 5.2	Chapters 1-8 and Compositions 1-2
Term 1	Chapter 5 (modal melodies), and Chapters 9-14; Keyboard Lessons 5.2-14	Chapters 9-14 (with review of modes from Chapter 5) and Compositions 3-7

	Sight-Singing	Ear-Training
Term 2	Chapters 15-21 and Keyboard Lessons	Chapters 15-21 and Compositions 8-11
Term 3	Chapters 22-33 and Keyboard Lessons	Chapters 22-33 and Compositions 12-13
Term 4	Chapters 34-40 and Keyboard Lessons	Chapters 34-40 and Compositions 14-17

Applying Solfège Syllables and Scale-Degree Numbers

All singing systems have merit and choosing *some* system is far superior to using none. To reinforce musical patterns, we recommend singing with movable-*do* solfège syllables and/or scale-degree numbers, but we provide a summary explanation of both the movable- and fixed-*do* systems in Chapter 1 to help students get started. (A quick reference for diatonic and chromatic syllables also appears at the front of this volume.) For solfège in modal contexts, we present two systems in Chapter 5, one using syllables derived from major and minor, and one using relative (rotated) syllables.

Applying a Rhythm-Counting System

Many people use some counting system to learn and perform rhythms—in effect, "rhythmic solfège." For example, a rhythm in $\frac{2}{4}$ meter might be vocalized "du de, du ta de ta" (Edwin Gordon system), or "1 and, 2 e and a" (McHose/Tibbs system), or "Ta di Ta ka di mi" (Takadimi system). We leave it to the discretion of each instructor whether to use such a system and which to require.

Our Thanks to . . .

A work of this size and scope is helped along the way by many people. We are especially grateful for the support of our families and our students. Our work together as coauthors has been incredibly rewarding, a collaboration for which we are sincerely thankful.

For subvention of the recordings, we thank James Undercofler (director and dean of the Eastman School of Music), as well as Eastman's Professional Development Committee. For audio engineering, we are grateful to recording engineers John Ebert and John Baker. For audio production work, we thank Glenn West, Christina Lenti, and Lance

Peeler, who assisted in the recording sessions. We also thank our colleagues at both Westminster Choir College of Rider University and the Eastman School of Music who gave of their talents to help make the recordings. The joy of their music making contributed mightily to this project.

We are grateful for the thorough and detailed work of our prepublication reviewers, whose suggestions inspired many improvements, large and small: Michael Berry (University of Washington), David Castro (St. Olaf College), Melissa Cox (Emory University), Gary Don (University of Wisconsin-Eau Claire), Terry Eder (Plano Senior High School), Jeffrey Gillespie (Butler University), Melissa Hoag (Oakland University), Rebecca Jemian (University of Louisville), Charles Leinberger (University of Texas-El Paso), David Lockart (North Hunterdon High School), Robert Mills (Liberty University), Daniel Musselman (Union University), Kristen Nelson (Stephen F. Austin State University), Shaugn O'Donnell (City College, CUNY), Tim Pack (University of Oregon), Scott Perkins (DePauw University), and Sarah Sarver (Oklahoma City University). For previous editions, reviewers have included: Jeff Donovick (St. Petersburg College), Bruce Hammel (Virginia Commonwealth University), Ruth Rendleman (Montclair State University), Alexander Tutunov (Southern Oregon University), and Annie Yih (University of California at Santa Barbara).

We are indebted to the staff of W. W. Norton for their commitment to this project and their painstaking care in producing these volumes. Most notable among these are music theory editor Justin Hoffman, whose knowledge of music and detailed, thoughtful questions, and genuine support for this project made him a joy to work with, and Maribeth Anderson Payne, whose vision helped launch the series with great enthusiasm. Michael Fauver was project editor of the volume, with assistance from copyeditor Elizabeth Bortka and proofreader Debra Nichols. We appreciate the invaluable assistance of media experts Steve Hoge, Stephanie Eads, Meg Wilhoite, and Timothy Bausch. Grant Phelps was editorial assistant, David Botwinik was typesetter, and Andy Ensor was production manager.

Paul Murphy, Joel Phillips, Elizabeth West Marvin,
and Jane Piper Clendinning

THE MUSICIAN'S GUIDE
TO AURAL SKILLS

PART I

Elements of Music

CHAPTER 1

Melody:

- Stepwise melodic fragments in treble, bass, alto, and tenor clefs
- Applying a solfège system

In this chapter you'll learn to:

- Apply solfège syllables, scale-degree numbers, and letter names
- Improvise Point-and-Sing melodies
- Read treble, bass, alto, and tenor clefs
- Sing pitch-only melodies, both stepwise and with skips
- Check your pitch with Sing-Check

Applying Solfège Syllables, Scale-Degree Numbers, and Letter Names

When singing, solfège syllables help to orient yourself to the framework in which you are singing. Several systems are available, each of which is designed to reinforce a certain orientation. Two general categories of these systems are considered "movable" or "fixed":

Movable Systems:

- With **scale degrees**, you sing a number for each step of the scale; the numbers are the same for major and minor.
- With **movable *do***, each note of the scale is associated with a solfège syllable, some of which change between major and minor.
- The following table shows how scale degrees correlate with movable-*do* solfège syllables in major keys with the changes for minor shown in parentheses.

SCALE DEGREE	SOLFÈGE SYLLABLE
$\hat{1}$	*do*
$\hat{7}$ = "sev"	*ti (te)*
$\hat{6}$	*la (le)*
$\hat{5}$	*sol*
$\hat{4}$	*fa*
$\hat{3}$	*mi (me)*
$\hat{2}$	*re*
$\hat{1}$	*do*

Fixed Systems:

- With **letter names**, you sing the name of each note, dropping any accidentals. For example, C, C♯, and C♭ are all sung as "C."

- With **fixed-*do* solfège**, each solfège syllable is associated with a note name regardless of key.

- The following table shows how note names correlate with fixed-*do* solfège syllables.

LETTER NAME	SOLFÈGE SYLLABLE
C (C♯, C♭)	*do*
B (B♯, B♭)	*ti*
A (A♯, A♭)	*la*
G (G♯, G♭)	*sol*
F (F♯, F♭)	*fa*
E (E♯, E♭)	*mi*
D (D♯, D♭)	*re*
C (C♯, C♭)	*do*

Using Point-and-Sing Improvisations (P&S)

Point-and-Sing improvisations help you learn musical patterns. Practice them by yourself or with a partner.

Treble and Bass Clefs

Improvisation 1.1: Point-and-Sing with Treble and Bass Clefs

Play C, then sing it with solfège syllables, a scale-degree number, or letter name. Point to an adjacent pitch and sing it using the same system. Continue until you have made a satisfying melody. Use Sing-Check to ensure your pitch is correct.

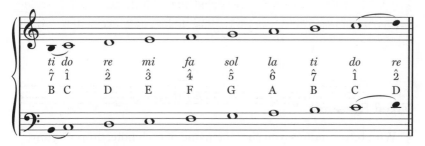

Using Sing-Check

Sing-Check can help you learn melodic pitches and their relationship to others. Play C then sing it. Sing pitch 2, then check it by playing it on the keyboard. Continue until you finish the melody, always singing the pitch first, then checking it by playing it.

Quick Composition Improvisation can be a rich source from which compositions can be written. Throughout the text you will be encouraged to build upon your improvisations and notate your favorite creations. This not only serves to record your ideas, but also helps you become skilled at transferring your ideas to written notation that you and others can read. Using Improvisation 1.1, for example, choose a clef and write with filled and hollow note heads; hollow notes are held longer than filled. Exchange with a peer and sing each other's melodies with solfège syllables, scale-degree numbers, or letter names.

Peer Evaluation of Quick Compositions

Share a notated Quick Composition with classmates. While one person sings it with solfège, others look at the music and listen for two items: correct pitches and solfège syllables (or scale-degree numbers or letter names). For each item, award 2 points for good to excellent; 1 for fair; and 0 for weak or omitted. For example, if someone sings with good pitch and fair solfège syllables, award 3 points out of 4.

Singing Melodies Notated in Treble, Bass, Alto, and Tenor Clefs

Play C, then sing these stepwise melodies with solfège syllables, scale-degree numbers, or letter names. Hold hollow note heads longer than filled ones.

Alto and Tenor Clefs

We use C clefs to accommodate the range of a particular instrument or voice so that the notes stay on the staff as much as possible. These clefs are *movable* in that they appear on different lines of the staff with center of the "B" shape always indicating C4. The alto clef is placed on the third line; the tenor clef on the fourth. When using these clefs it is quite helpful to think of steps, skips, and leaps in relation to specific reference notes, rather than memorizing the location of each letter name. For example if you start on C (*do* or $\hat{1}$) on the middle line you can determine that the note that is a skip up is E (*mi* or $\hat{3}$) just as the note that is a skip down is A (*la* or $\hat{6}$).

Improvisation 1.2: Point-and-Sing with Alto and Tenor Clefs

Play C, then sing it with a solfège syllable, scale-degree number, or letter name. Point to an adjacent pitch and sing it using the same system. Continue until you have made a satisfying melody.

With solfège sing pure vowels, as in Italian. Sing "sev" for scale-degree seven ($\hat{7}$). Use Sing-Check to ensure your pitch is correct.

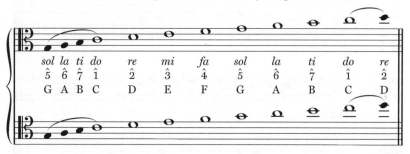

Quick Composition Notate your favorite improvisation. Choose a clef and write with filled or hollow note heads, holding hollow note heads longer than filled. Exchange with a peer and sing each other's melodies with solfège syllables, scale-degree numbers, or letter names.

9

10

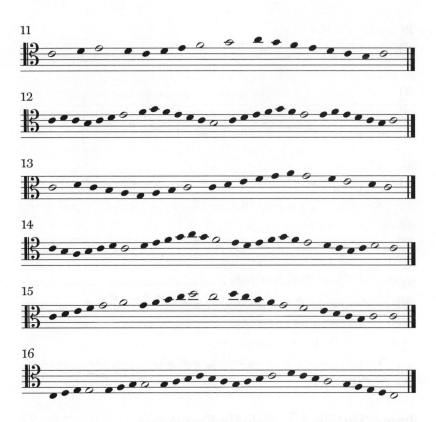

Singing Skips

Before singing each melody, locate the skips and practice them separately. To sing a skip from a given note, imagine the note that lies between that note and the one that is a skip away (line-to-line or space-to-space) and silently sing through the "missing" note.

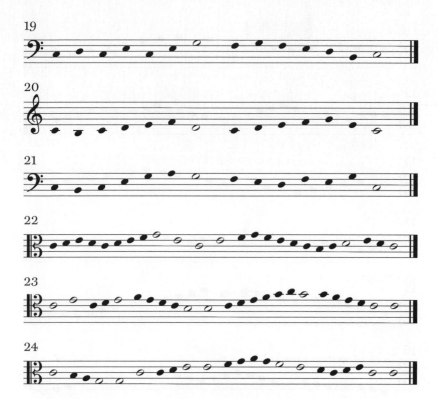

Improvisation 1.3: Melodic Fragments in Four Clefs

Improvise stepwise melodic fragments using the Point-and-Sing charts in each of the four clefs that you've learned thus far. Include at least two skips in each of your improvisations.

CHAPTER 2

Melody:

- Solfège syllables and scale-degree numbers in transposition

Rhythm:

- Simple meters
- Applying a rhythm-counting system

In this chapter you'll learn to:

- Conduct and perform simple duple, simple triple, and simple quadruple meters with the quarter-note beat unit
- Apply a rhythm-counting system
- Practice a melody and evaluate melodic performances
- Apply identical solfège syllables and scale-degree numbers to transpositions of a melody
- Improvise and notate rhythm patterns
- Perform an anacrusis

Conducting Duple Meter

To conduct in duple meter:

- Follow the pattern in the diagram, moving your hand, forearm, and elbow throughout each beat.
- Make a small bounce, called the *ictus*, on each beat number.
- Practice before a mirror until your gestures look natural and your arms move confidently and steadily.
- Conduct with both hands mirroring each other to improve the coordination of your nondominant hand.

Performing Simple Duple Rhythms

- Where a tempo indication is indicated, perform the rhythm at that tempo. Where one is not given, set a tempo *before* performing that you can maintain throughout.
- Conduct or tap lightly to maintain your tempo.
- Perform *musically*, giving attention to dynamics and the relative stress of stronger and weaker beats.
- Sing with counting syllables or on a neutral syllable like "da" or "ta," as your teacher directs.

Applying a Rhythm-Counting System

Many musicians use a counting system when performing rhythms—in effect, "rhythmic solfège." The most sophisticated of these is Takadimi, devised by Richard Hoffman, William Pelto, and John W. White. A downloadable guide is found on the Internet. Your teacher will tell you which system, if any, you are required to use.

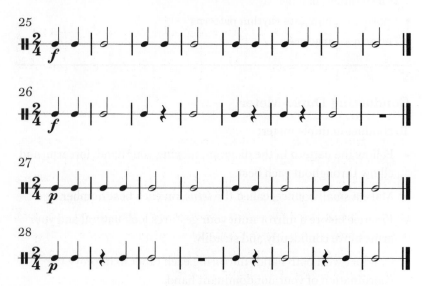

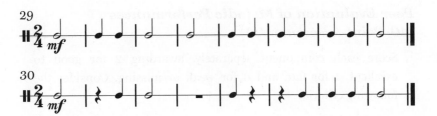

Rhythmic Duets

Perform with a partner, or conduct and perform one part aloud while tapping the other.

Variations

- Switch parts and perform again until each musician has performed both parts.
- Choose ensembles that feature more than one performer on each part.
- One performer can perform the rhythm of two parts simultaneously— tapping with each hand on a different surface or tapping one part while performing the other part vocally

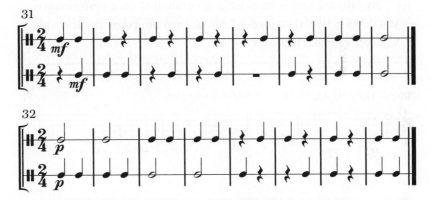

Practicing a Melody

A melodic performance includes five components—*conducting, rhythm, pitch, solfège/scale-degree numbers,* and *nuance and expressiveness.* Practice these separately then put them together. For example, conduct and perform the rhythm only. Then use Sing-Check to master the pitches. Speak aloud the solfège syllables/scale-degree numbers, then sing pitches with solfège syllables/scale-degree numbers. Finally, conduct and perform the melody musically with accurate pitch, rhythm, and solfège syllables/scale-degree numbers.

Peer Evaluation of Melodic Performances (10-Point Assessments)

Score each component separately, awarding 2 for good to excellent, 1 for fair, and 0 for weak or missing. Consider the following criteria:

- conducting
- rhythm
- pitch
- solfège syllables/scale-degree numbers
- nuance and expressiveness

For example, a musical performance with good pitch, excellent, rhythm, good conducting, weak solfège/scale-degree numbers, and weak nuance and expressiveness would receive 2 + 2 + 2 + 1 + 0 + 0 = 7 points. Your scores highlight components that need attention or have improved. For the sample performance, a reviewer might suggest: "Try Sing-Check to learn pitches and practice syllables separately. Your conducting has really improved!"

By offering and acknowledging comments on a performance you develop useful strategies for your own improvement through valuable external feedback.

Duet

Perform with a partner. Switch parts and perform again.

Applying Identical Solfège Syllables and Scale-Degree Numbers to Transpositions of a Melody

Exercises 37-42 pair an original melody with one of its transpositions. For each pair, play C and sing the first melody with solfège syllables or scale-degree numbers. Play the first pitch of the second melody and sing it with identical syllables or numbers. Accidental(s) that appear after a clef apply to all octaves of that pitch.

Conducting Quadruple Meter

Following the downbeat, beat 2 crosses the chest, beat 3 swings out to the side, and beat 4 is the upbeat. Again, to clarify the direction for beat 2, practice conducting with both hands mirroring each other.

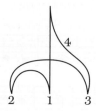

Improvisation 2.1: Point-and-Sing Rhythm Patterns: with Beat Divisions _____

Point to one of the following rhythm patterns and perform it. While keeping a steady beat, point to a new pattern and perform it. Continue in this way, changing the order of patterns until you have performed all patterns three times. Optional: Read each pattern with counting syllables recommended by your teacher.

Rhythm Patterns: ○ Duration

Improvisation 2.2: Point-and-Sing Rhythm Patterns: ○ with Ties, Dots, and Syncopations

1. Perform example (a), (b), and (c), to learn how to change patterns 4, 5, and 3 (from Improvisation 2.1) into new patterns. Point to one of the following rhythm patterns and perform it. While keeping a steady beat, point to a new pattern and perform it. Continue in this way, changing the order of patterns until you have performed all patterns three times. Optional: Read each pattern with counting syllables recommended by your teacher.

Rhythm Patterns

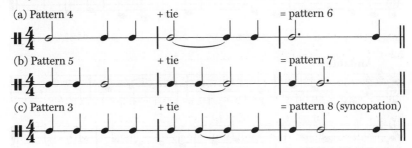

2. Improvise phrases drawn from all eight patterns. Variation: Have a classmate point to patterns, in any order, while you perform them. Switch roles.

Quick Composition Notate your favorite rhythmic improvisation on a single staff. Indicate the meter signature, bar lines, and a specific tempo. Exchange with a peer and sing each other's rhythm with a neutral syllable or with counting syllables.

Anacrusis

An anacrusis is a note or group of notes that move *toward* a downbeat. For this reason it is sometimes called an "upbeat." The anacrusis builds in energy and releases this energy on the following downbeat. To perform an anacrusis, conduct and count silently one full measure plus the "missing" beat(s). Then, perform aloud beginning with the anacrusis, moving *toward* the downbeat, and continue with a steady tempo until the end.

57

Allegretto

58

Slowly

59

Allegro

60

Moderato

61

Allegretto

Sing *do* ($\hat{1}$), the final pitch of each melody, and then sing up or down to find *sol* ($\hat{5}$), the anacrusis.

62 **Adagio**

63 **Allegretto**

64 **Allegro**

Duets

Conducting Triple Meter

Conduct the downbeat, then move your hand to the right for beat 2. Beat 3 returns inward and upward Again, to clarify the direction for beat 2, practice conducting with both hands mirroring each other.

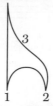

Improvisation 2.3: Point-and-Sing Rhythm Patterns: dotted half-note Beat Unit

Point to one of the following rhythm patterns and perform it. While keeping a steady beat, point to a new pattern and perform it. Continue in this way until you have performed four patterns.

Rhythm Patterns: dotted half-note Duration

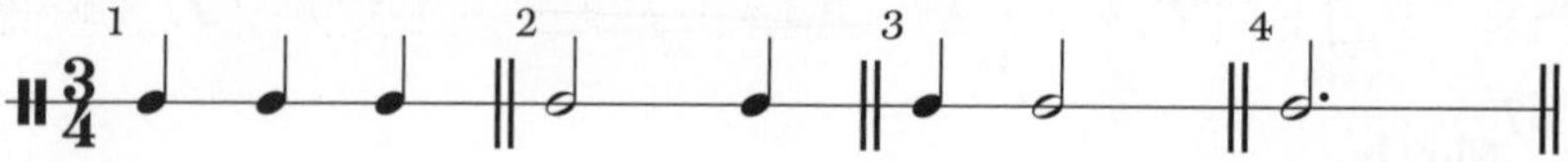

69
Slowly

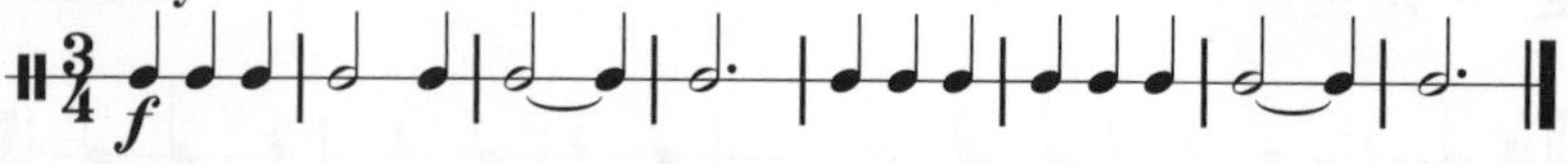

70
Allegretto

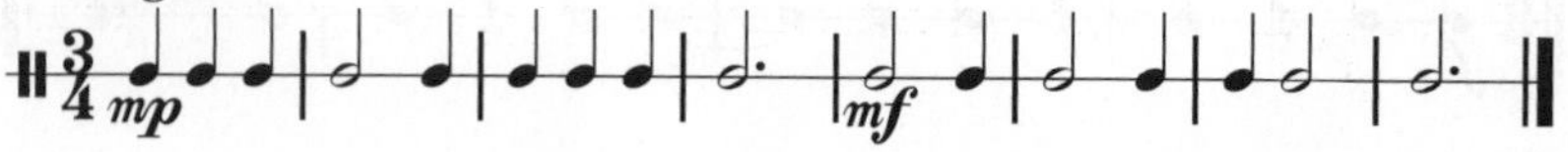

71
Moderato

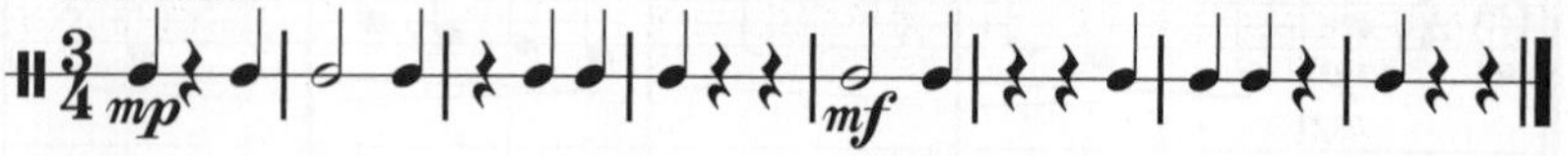

72
Allegro

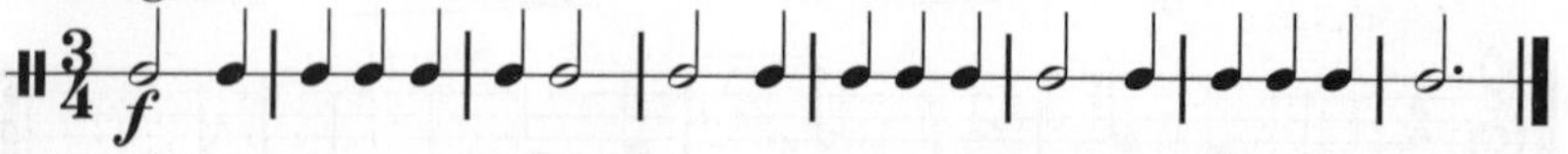

73
Fast

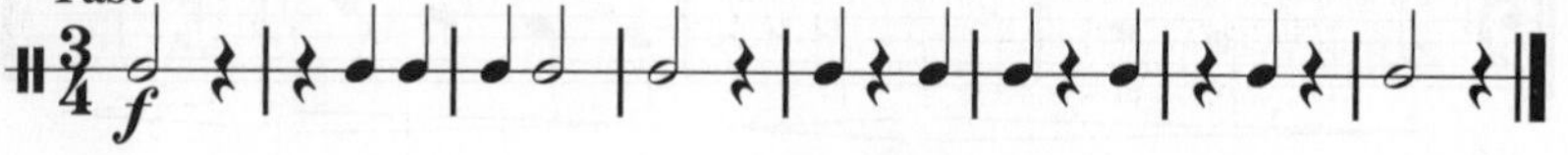

Always take note of the written range of the melody and choose a starting pitch that allows you to sing the melody comfortably within the range of your voice.

82 Bartók, *Mikrokosmos*, Vol. 1, No. 2a

83 "Yankee Doodle" (traditional)

84 "Hot Cross Buns" (traditional)

Round

In a round, performers follow a leader (the first performer). For this four-part round, the second performer begins when the leader reaches ②; the third begins when the leader reaches ③, and the fourth performer begins when the leader reaches ④.

85 "Frère Jacques" (French)

CHAPTER 3

Melody:

- The major pentachord
- Major scales
- Introduction to the major pentatonic scale

Rhythm:

- Divisions of the quarter-note beat unit

In this chapter you'll learn to:

- Perform melodies and rhythms with simple divisions and multiples of the quarter- and half-note beat
- Sing melodies using the major pentachord and major pentatonic scale
- Sing melodies based on the major scale
- Improvise rhythm patterns with simple divisions and multiples of the quarter- and half-note beat

---

Quarter-Note Beat Divisions

- Where a tempo indication is marked, perform the rhythm at that tempo. Where one is not given, set a tempo before performing that you can maintain throughout.
- Conduct or tap lightly to maintain your tempo.
- Perform *musically*, giving attention to dynamics and the relative stress of stronger and weaker beats.
- Sing with counting syllables, if required, or on a neutral syllable such as "da" or "ta."

- Perform duets with a partner, or conduct and perform one part aloud while tapping the other. In either case, switch parts and perform again.

Improvisation 3.1: Point-and-Sing Rhythm Patterns: ♩ Beat Unit

Point to one of the following patterns and perform it. While keeping a steady beat, point to a new pattern and perform it. Continue in this way, changing the order of patterns until you have performed all patterns three times. Optional: Read each pattern with counting syllables recommended by your teacher.

Rhythm Patterns: ♩ Duration

1. Basic patterns

2. Ties, dots, and syncopation

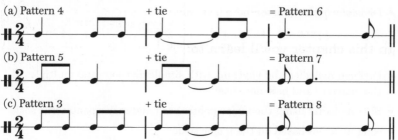

3. Complete patterns

Quick Composition Notate your favorite improvisation. Choose a clef and write note values for simple duple meter. Exchange with a peer and sing each other's melody with solfège syllables, scale-degree numbers, or letter names.

Rhythms with ♩ Divisions

Simple Duple

86

Simple Quadruple

94

Duets

95

Simple Triple

96

97

98

Duet

The Major Pentachord

Improvisation 3.2: Melodies Based on the Major Pentachord

Improvise short melodies from the embellished major pentachord. Play them and sing with solfège syllables, scale-degree numbers, or letter names. Before starting, conduct in silence until you establish a comfortable, steady tempo. Always sing dynamically, with inflection and expressiveness to make your performance musical and interesting.

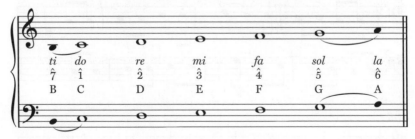

Example

Now organize the melodies into simple duple, simple triple, or simple quadruple meter. At first, limit your rhythm to full beats. As you improve, add beat divisions.

Example

101

102

103

104 Bartók, No. 16 from *44 Duets*, Vol. I (adapted)
Repeat this melody and sing it as a canon with a partner. When the first singer begins measure 2, the second begins measure 1.

105

Performing Rhythms in Cut Time

- In cut time or $\frac{2}{2}$ meter, because the half note gets one beat, remember to conduct each measure in two.

- Where a tempo indication is indicated, perform the rhythm at that tempo. Where one is not given, set a tempo before performing that you can maintain throughout.

- Conduct or tap lightly to maintain your tempo.

- Perform *musically*, giving attention to dynamics and the relative stress of stronger and weaker beats.

- Sing with counting syllables, if required, or on a neutral syllable such as "da" or "ta."

Improvisation 3.3: Point-and-Sing Rhythm Patterns: ♩ Beats and Beat Divisions

In cut time or $\frac{2}{2}$ meter, the half note is the beat unit; the two quarters are the beat division. Point to one of the following rhythm patterns and perform it. While keeping a steady beat, point to a new pattern and perform it. Continue in this way, changing the order of patterns until you have performed all patterns three times. Optional: Read each pattern with counting syllables recommended by your teacher.

Rhythm Patterns: ♩ Beat Unit

1. Patterns

2. Improvise phrases drawn from this new list of patterns. Variation: Have a classmate point to patterns, in any order, while you perform them. Switch roles.

Quick Composition Notate your favorite improvisation. Choose a clef and write with filled and hollow note heads; hollow notes are held longer than filled. Exchange with a peer and sing each other's melody with solfège syllables, scale-degree numbers, or letter names.

Cut-Time Rhythms

111

112

113

The following rhythm is performed exactly like the one just given.

114

Duet

Melodies in Cut Time

For cut-time melodies, because the half note gets one beat, remember to conduct each measure in two.

The Major Scale and Major Keys

127

128

129 Richard Rodgers, "Bye and Bye"

130

131 Mahler, Symphony No. 2, first movement (adapted)

132

133

134 John R. Cash, "I Walk the Line"
The anacrusis consists of three quarter notes.

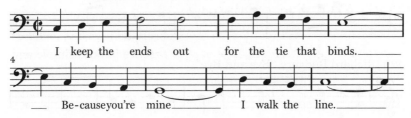

I keep the ends out for the tie that binds._____

Be-cause you're mine_____ I walk the line._____

135

The Major Pentatonic Scale

The major pentatonic scale can be considered a subset of the major scale in that it contains five of its seven pitches. Significantly, scale degrees $\hat{4}$ and $\hat{7}$ do not appear, such that there are no half steps. Although the *sol-do* ($\hat{5}$-$\hat{1}$) succession is still possible as a conclusion to major pentatonic melodies, many such melodies—especially those that form the basis of American folk songs—conclude with *la-do* ($\hat{6}$-$\hat{1}$) instead. We introduce the major pentatonic scale here and elaborate in greater detail in succeeding chapters.

C major pentatonic scale

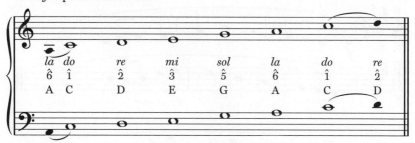

Improvisation 3.4: Melodies Based on the Major Pentatonic Scale

Follow the procedures for Improvisation 3.2 to improvise melodies in the major pentatonic scale. Be sure to practice in both simple and compound meters.

CHAPTER 4

Melody:

- The major pentachord and major scale in compound duple meter
- Plagal division of the octave

Rhythm:

- Compound duple meter

In this chapter you'll learn to:

- Perform melodies and rhythms in compound duple meter with the dotted-quarter note as the beat unit
- Sing melodies using the major pentachord and the major scale in compound duple meter
- Improvise rhythm patterns with compound divisions of the dotted-quarter-note beat

---

Dotted-Quarter-Note Beat Divisions

- Where a tempo indication is indicated, perform the rhythm at that tempo. Where one is not given, set a tempo before performing that you can maintain throughout.
- Conduct or tap lightly to maintain your tempo.
- Note that, except in slow tempos, the lower number of the compound meter signature indicates the *division* of the beat, not the beat itself. To determine the number of beats in each measure of compound meter, divide the top number of the meter signature by 3. For example, in ⁶₈ there are two beats per measure.
- Perform musically, giving attention to dynamics and the relative stress of stronger and weaker beats.

- Sing with counting syllables, if required, or on a neutral syllable such as "da" or "ta."

- Perform duets with a partner, or conduct and perform one part aloud while tapping the other. In either case, switch parts and perform again.

Improvisation 4.1: Point-and-Sing Rhythm Patterns: ♩. Duration

In compound meters, the dotted note gets one beat that divides into three parts. Point to one of the following rhythm patterns and perform it. While keeping a steady beat, point to a new pattern and perform it. Continue in this way, changing the order of patterns until you have performed all patterns three times. Optional: Read each pattern with counting syllables recommended by your teacher.

Rhythm Patterns: ♩. Beat Unit

Tying two dotted-quarter notes produces a dotted-half, which fills an entire measure in this compound duple meter.

Quick Composition Notate your favorite improvisation. Choose a clef and write with note values for compound duple meter. Exchange with a peer and sing each other's melody with solfège syllables, scale-degree numbers, or letter names.

Rhythms in Compound Duple Meter with ♩. Durations

These rhythms are to be conducted in a two-beat pattern.

142

143

144

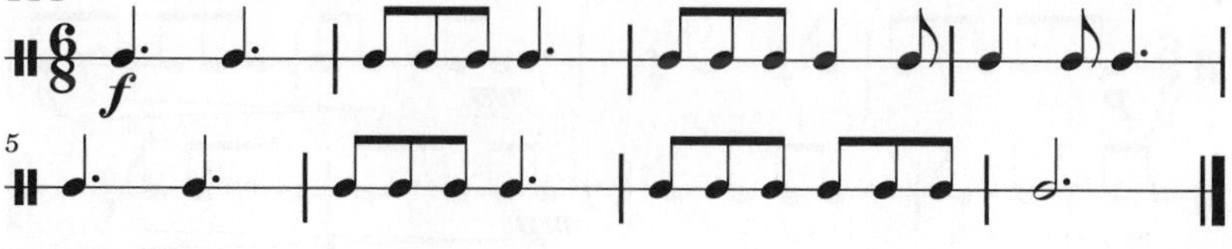

145

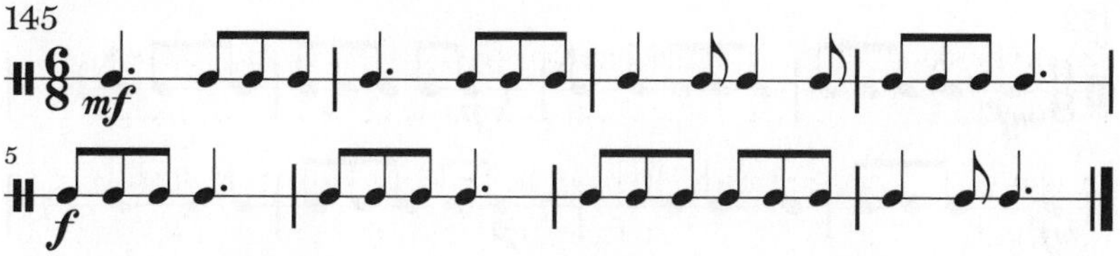

146

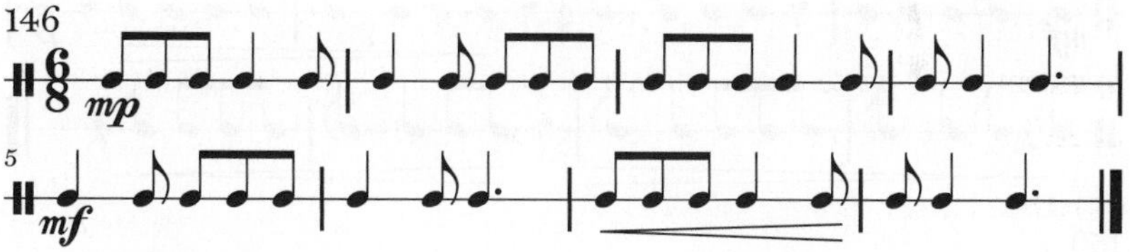

147

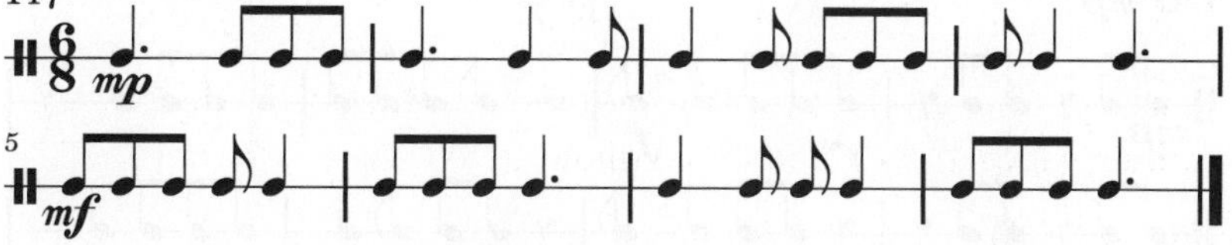

148

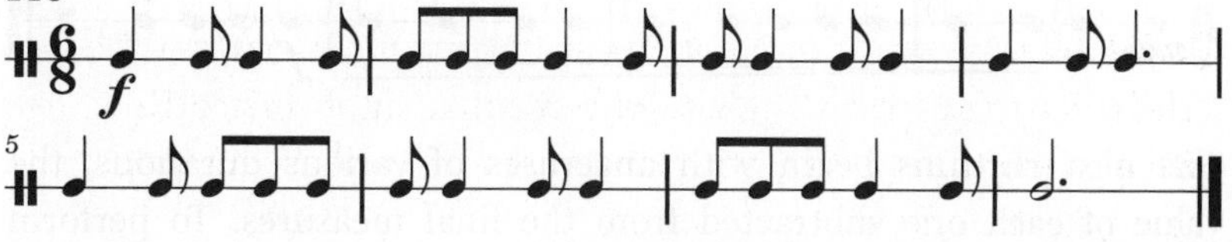

149

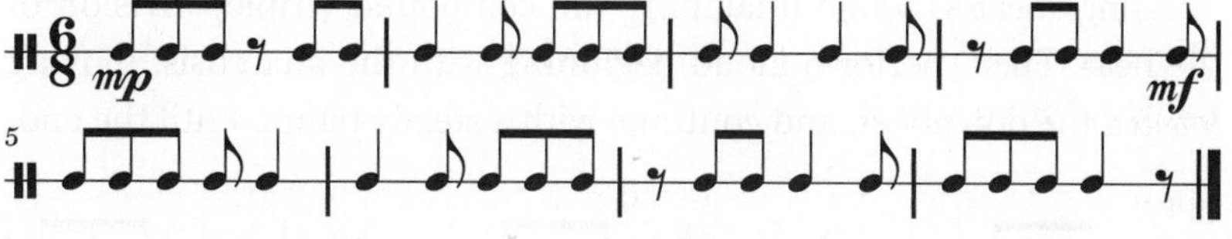

150

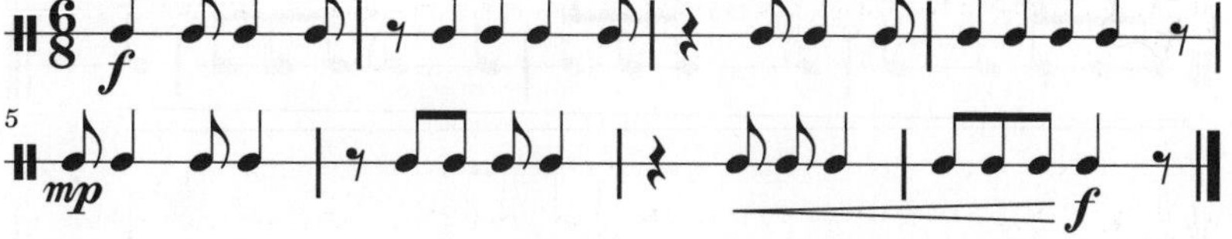

The next rhythms begin with anacruses of various durations, the value of each one subtracted from the final measures. To perform an anacrusis, conduct and count silently one full measure plus the "missing" beat(s) while imagining the compound (triple) division of the beat. Then, perform aloud beginning with the anacrusis, moving *toward* the downbeat, and continue with a steady tempo until the end.

Duets

The Major Pentachord in Compound Duple Meter

The following melodies present the embellished major pentachord in which the range is expanded above or below by one note.

The Major Scale and Major-Key Melodies
in Compound Duple Meter

176

177

178

179

180 Beethoven, Sonatina in G Major, second movement (Romanze)

181

The following melodies present a plagal division of the octave: *sol-sol* with *do* in the middle of the range.

182

183 "Auprès de ma Blonde" (France)

184

185

186 Schumann, *Album for the Young*, Op. 68, No. 18

187 Philip P. Bliss, "Wonderful Words of Life"

In the following melodies the range from *do-do* is expanded downward to *sol*.

188

Round

For instructions on performing rounds see page 22 in Chapter 2.

189 "Three Blind Mice" (England)

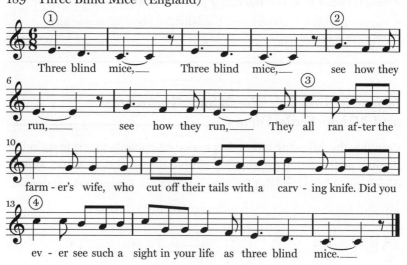

Three blind mice,— Three blind mice,— see how they run,— see how they run,— They all ran af-ter the farm-er's wife, who cut off their tails with a carv-ing knife. Did you ev-er see such a sight in your life as three blind mice.—

CHAPTER 5

Melody:

- The minor pentachord
- Minor scales
- Introduction to the minor pentatonic scale
- Introduction to the diatonic modes

Rhythm:

- Subdivided beats in simple and compound meters

In this chapter you'll learn to:

- Sing melodies using the minor pentachord
- Sing melodies using the minor scale
- Sing major-key and minor-key melodies in simple and compound meters with subdivided beats
- Sing melodies based on the minor pentatonic scale
- Improvise rhythm patterns with subdivided beats in simple and compound meter

---

Improvisation 5.1: The Minor Pentachord and Minor-Scale Forms

Combine the following minor-key melodic segments to create melodies in each of the following meters: simple duple, simple triple, simple quadruple; compound duple, compound triple, compound quadruple.

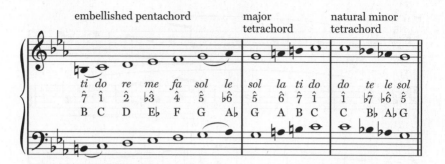

Strategies

1. In melodic minor, complete the upper tetrachord. When *sol* rises to *la*, continue upward through *ti* to *do* ($\hat{5}$-$\hat{6}$-$\hat{7}$-$\hat{1}$). When *do* descends to *te*, continue downward through *le* to *sol* ($\hat{1}$-♭$\hat{7}$-♭$\hat{6}$-$\hat{5}$).

2. In harmonic minor, use the pitches of the embellished pentachord. Fall from *le* to *sol* (♭$\hat{6}$-$\hat{5}$); rise from *ti* to *do* ($\hat{7}$-$\hat{1}$).

Examples

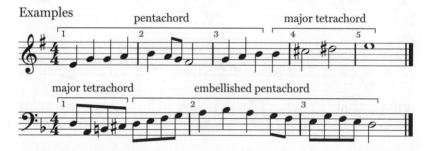

Quick Composition Notate your favorite improvisation. Choose a clef and indicate a key and meter. Notate the rhythm and solfège syllables of your improvisation above the staff, then convert this information to notation on the staff. Exchange with a peer and sing each other's melodies with solfège syllables, scale-degree numbers, or letter names.

The Minor Pentachord

Note that in the first two melodies each phrase presents the minor pentachord.

The Melodic Minor Scale and Minor Keys

Improvisation 5.2: Point-and-Sing Rhythm Patterns: ♩ Beat Unit

Point to one of the following rhythm patterns and perform it. While keeping a steady beat, point to a new pattern and perform it. Continue in this way, changing the order of patterns until you have performed all patterns three times. Optional: Read each pattern with counting syllables recommended by your teacher.

Rhythm Patterns: ♩ Beat Unit

1. Patterns

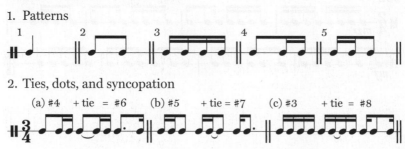

2. Ties, dots, and syncopation

3. Improvise phrases drawn from the new list of patterns just given. Variation: Have a classmate point to patterns, in any order, while you perform them. Switch roles.

Simple Duple

The next two rhythms show how a tie within the beat can be added to one pattern in order to create a new one.

Duet

Simple Quadruple

Simple Triple

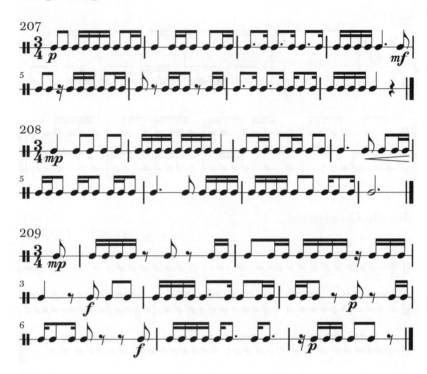

Duet

Melodies

211 Haydn, String Quartet in G Minor, Op. 74, No. 3, second movement

212 Telemann, Quartet in E Minor, third movement

213 Beethoven, Agnus Dei, from *Mass in C*, Op. 86

214 Brahms, Intermezzo in C♯ Minor, Op. 117, No. 3 (adapted)

215

216 Clara Schumann, *Le Ballet des Revenants* (adapted)

D. C. al Fine

Round

For instructions on performing rounds see page 22 in Chapter 2.

221 "Ah, Poor Bird" (traditional; round in three parts)

Improvisation 5.3: Point-and-Sing Rhythm Patterns: ♩. Beat Unit

Point to one of the following rhythm patterns and perform it. While keeping a steady beat, point to a new pattern and perform it. Continue in this way, changing the order of patterns until you have performed all patterns three times. Optional: Read each pattern with counting syllables recommended by your teacher.

Rhythm Patterns: ♩. Beat Unit

1. Patterns

2. Improvise phrases drawn from the list of patterns just given. Variation: Have a classmate point to patterns, in any order, while you perform them. Switch roles.

Compound Duple

222

Ties

Improvisation 5.4: Point-and-Sing Rhythm Patterns: ♩. Beat Unit _____

Point to one of the following rhythm patterns and perform it. While keeping a steady beat, point to a new pattern and perform it. Continue in this way, changing the order of patterns until you have performed all patterns three times. Optional: Read each pattern with counting syllables recommended by your teacher.

Rhythm Patterns: ♩· Beat Unit

1. Patterns

2. Ties, dots, and syncopation

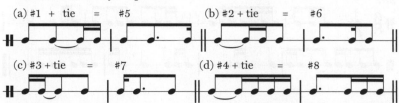

3. Improvise phrases drawn from the new list of patterns just given. Variation: Have a classmate point to patterns, in any order, while you perform them. Switch roles.

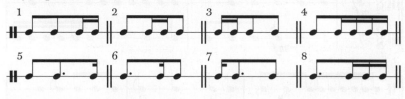

The next five rhythms reinforce how a tie within the beat can be added to one pattern in order to create a new one.

Duets

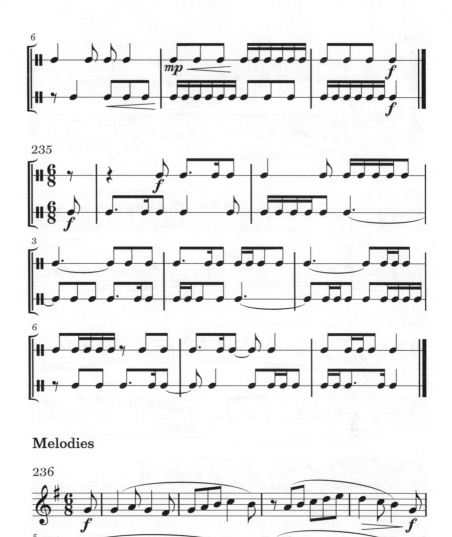

Melodies

The Minor Pentatonic Scale

Analogous to the major scale and the major pentatonic scale, the minor pentatonic scale can be considered a subset of the minor scale in that it contains five of its seven pitches. Significantly, scale degrees $\hat{2}$ and $\hat{6}$ do not appear, such that there are no half steps. Although the *sol-do* ($\hat{5}$-$\hat{1}$) succession is still possible as a conclusion to minor pentatonic melodies, many such melodies conclude with *te-do* ($\flat\hat{7}$-$\hat{1}$) or *me-do* ($\flat\hat{3}$-$\hat{1}$) instead. We introduce the minor pentatonic scale here, along with a selection of model melodies, and elaborate in great detail in succeeding chapters.

Improvisation 5.5: Melodies Based on the Minor Pentatonic Scale

C minor pentatonic scale

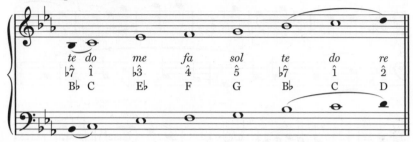

Follow the procedures for Improvisation 5.4 to improvise melodies in the minor pentatonic scale. Be sure to practice in both simple and compound meters.

Melodies

The Diatonic Modes

The diatonic collection of pitches from C to C may be rotated to begin with any pitch. Each rotation forms a diatonic mode. These are (in order, from C) Ionian, Dorian, Phrygian, Lydian, Mixolydian, and Aeolian. Such rotations of the diatonic collection have yielded a rich repertoire of music that will be explored throughout this text. Here we provide two introductory strategies for singing modal melodies and elaborate in detail in succeeding chapters with a variety of exercises and melodies from the literature.

READING WITH PARALLEL SYLLABLES	READING WITH RELATIVE SYLLABLES
Because our twenty-first-century ears are accustomed to the major and minor scales, we sometimes hear the diatonic modes as alterations of these more familiar scales. We can therefore group the modes into two families, according to whether their third scale degree comes from the major or minor pentachord. We thus apply "parallel" syllables, using chromatic syllables for those pitches that differ from major and minor scales. This method requires that we assign chromatic solfège syllables to pitches that often appear without a written sharp or flat.	To apply solfège syllables with the "relative" method, think of the major key associated with the melody's key signature and use major-key solfège syllables regardless of where the melody concludes. This method is often easier for *reading* modal melodies because there are no chromatic syllables to assign to notated pitches.

Dorian mode

Perform a natural minor scale and raise ♭6̂ a half step.

Call the first pitch *re* (2̂). Perform a major scale from *re* to *re* (2̂-2̂).

Phrygian mode

Perform a natural minor scale and lower $\hat{2}$ a half step (sung *ra*).

Call the first pitch *mi* ($\hat{3}$). Perform a major scale from *mi* to *mi* ($\hat{3}$-$\hat{3}$).

do	ra	me	fa	sol	le	te	do
$\hat{1}$	$\flat\hat{2}$	$\flat\hat{3}$	$\hat{4}$	$\hat{5}$	$\flat\hat{6}$	$\flat\hat{7}$	$\hat{1}$

mi	fa	sol	la	ti	do	re	mi
$\hat{3}$	$\hat{4}$	$\hat{5}$	$\hat{6}$	$\hat{7}$	$\hat{1}$	$\hat{2}$	$\hat{3}$

Lydian mode

Perform a major scale and raise $\hat{4}$ a half step (sung *fi*).

Call the first pitch *fa* ($\hat{4}$). Perform a major scale from *fa* to *fa* ($\hat{4}$-$\hat{4}$).

do	re	mi	fi	sol	la	ti	do
$\hat{1}$	$\hat{2}$	$\hat{3}$	$\sharp\hat{4}$	$\hat{5}$	$\hat{6}$	$\hat{7}$	$\hat{1}$

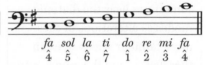

fa	sol	la	ti	do	re	mi	fa
$\hat{4}$	$\hat{5}$	$\hat{6}$	$\hat{7}$	$\hat{1}$	$\hat{2}$	$\hat{3}$	$\hat{4}$

Mixolydian mode

Perform a major scale and lower $\hat{7}$ a half step (sung *te*).

Call the first pitch *sol* ($\hat{5}$). Perform a major scale from *sol* to *sol* ($\hat{5}$-$\hat{5}$).

do	re	mi	fa	sol	la	te	do
$\hat{1}$	$\hat{2}$	$\hat{3}$	$\hat{4}$	$\hat{5}$	$\hat{6}$	$\flat\hat{7}$	$\hat{1}$

sol	la	ti	do	re	mi	fa	sol
$\hat{5}$	$\hat{6}$	$\hat{7}$	$\hat{1}$	$\hat{2}$	$\hat{3}$	$\hat{4}$	$\hat{5}$

Aeolean mode

Perform a major scale and lower $\hat{3}$, $\hat{6}$, and $\hat{7}$ a half step (sung *me, le,* and *te*).

Call the first pitch *la* ($\hat{6}$). Perform a major scale from *la* to *la* ($\hat{6}$-$\hat{6}$).

do	re	me	fa	sol	le	te	do
$\hat{1}$	$\hat{2}$	$\flat\hat{3}$	$\hat{4}$	$\hat{5}$	$\flat\hat{6}$	$\flat\hat{7}$	$\hat{1}$

la	ti	do	re	mi	fa	sol	la
$\hat{6}$	$\hat{7}$	$\hat{1}$	$\hat{2}$	$\hat{3}$	$\hat{4}$	$\hat{5}$	$\hat{6}$

CHAPTER 6

Melody:

- Intervals

Rhythm:

- Compound duple, quadruple, and triple meters

In this chapter you'll learn to:

- Perform études that isolate specific melodic intervals
- Perform melodies and rhythms in compound duple, quadruple, and triple meter with the dotted-quarter note as the beat unit
- Improvise rhythm patterns with compound divisions of the dotted-quarter-note beat

Rhythms in Compound Quadruple and Compound Triple Meter with ♩. Durations

Interval Études

The following études isolate specific intervals in predictable patterns. Each étude focuses on a particular concept and skill. For example, the first étude presents all of the diatonic intervals above and below the tonic in major keys; the second one reinforces the same but in the natural minor mode.

247 Intervals above and below the tonic in the major scale

248 Intervals above and below the tonic in the natural minor scale

249 Intervals above and below the tonic in the melodic minor scale

250 Major-key thirds

251 Minor-key thirds

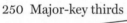

252 Major-key fourths

253 Minor-key fourths

254 Major-key fifths

255 Minor-key fifths

256 Major-key sixths

257 Minor-key sixths

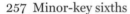

258 Major-key sevenths

259 Minor-key sevenths

Rounds

For instructions on performing rounds see page 22 in Chapter 2.

Notice in this round the common result of voices singing in parallel thirds.

260 "Oh, How Lovely Is the Evening" (traditional; round in three parts)

Compound Duple (Review)

To review more compound duple rhythms with beat divisions refer to Chapter 4.

Duet

Improvisation 6.1: Alternating Improvised Patterns in Simple and Compound Quadruple and Triple Meters

With a partner, clap, tap, or sing on a neutral syllable improvised two-measure patterns that alternate between simple and compound meter. Start with the following examples, which alternate between $\frac{4}{4}$ and $\frac{12}{8}$, and between $\frac{3}{4}$ and $\frac{9}{8}$. Challenge yourself to convert what the leader presents into the new meter type. Conduct the meter while your partner is performing.

- Start with simple/compound quadruple meter.
- Decide who will be the leader.
- Perform a total of four phrases.

- Switch leader/follower roles.
- Switch to simple/compound triple meter.

Examples

Simple/Compound Quadruple

Simple/Compound Triple

Quick Composition Notate your favorite improvisation on a single-line staff with changing time signatures. Exchange with a peer and sing each other's melodies with solfège syllables, scale-degree numbers, or letter names.

Compound Quadruple

Remember that, except in slow tempos, the lower number of the compound meter signature indicates the *division* of the beat, not the beat itself. To determine the number of beats in each measure of compound meter, divide the top number of the meter signature by 3. For example, $\frac{12}{8}$ should be conducted with four beats per measure ($12 \div 3 = 4$).

264

The next three rhythms begin with anacruses of various durations, the value of each one subtracted from the final measure. Count silently two or three beats, imagining the three-part division of each beat. Perform aloud beginning with the anacrusis, moving *toward* the downbeat, and continue with a steady tempo until the end.

269

270

271

Duets

272

Compound Triple

Remember that, except in slow tempos, the lower number of the compound meter signature indicates the *division* of the beat, not the beat itself. To determine the number of beats in each measure of compound meter, divide the top number of the meter signature by 3. For example, $\frac{9}{8}$ should be conducted with three beats per measure (9 ÷ 3 = 3).

The next four rhythms begin with anacruses of various durations, the value of each one subtracted from the final measure. Count silently two or three beats, imagining the three-part division of each beat. Perform aloud beginning with the anacrusis, moving *toward* the downbeat, and continue with a steady tempo until the end.

Duets

284

285

Melodies

286 "Hunting Call" (traditional)

287 Gounod, "Où voulez-vous aller?" ("Where Do You Want to Go?")
(adapted)

288 Hensel, "Schwanenlied" ("Swan Song") (adapted)

289 "The Haymaker's Jig" (traditional)

290 "The New-Married Couple" (traditional)

291 Alan Price, "The House of the Rising Sun"

There is ___ a house ___ in New Or-leans, ___ they call ___ the Ris - ing Sun, ___ and it's been ___ the ruin ___ of man-y a poor boy, ___ and God, ___ I know ___ I'm one. ___

292 Bach, Chorale: "Jesus bleibet meine Freude," from Cantata No. 147 (adapted)

293 Bach, Violin Concerto No. 1 in A Minor, third movement (adapted)

The next two melodies present subdivisions of the beat in rhythmic patterns that were explored in Chapter 4.

294 Handel, Harpsichord Suite in G Major, Gigue

295 "Beaux of London City" (English)

CHAPTER 7

Melody:

- Triads

Rhythm:

- Beat units of the eighth note and dotted-eighth note
- Disruptions of the pulse

In this chapter you'll learn to:

- Improvise major-key and minor-key triadic patterns in simple and compound meter
- Perform études that isolate diatonic triads in major and minor keys
- Perform melodies and rhythms in simple and compound meter with eighth-note and dotted-eighth-note beat units
- Conduct disruptions in tempo as you perform

Improvisation 7.1: Major and Minor Triads _____

In preparation for improvising your own melodies, clap, tap, or sing on a neutral syllable each rhythm while conducting.

(1)

Moderato

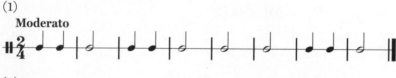

(2)

Waltz

(3)

March

(4)

Dolce

A. Choose a rhythm from (1) through (4) and improvise a melody with *do*, *mi*, and *sol* ($\hat{1}$-$\hat{3}$-$\hat{5}$).

Sample solution with rhythm (1)

| do | do | mi | | mi | mi | sol | | sol | | mi | | sol | mi | do |
| $\hat{1}$ | $\hat{1}$ | $\hat{3}$ | | $\hat{3}$ | $\hat{3}$ | $\hat{5}$ | | $\hat{5}$ | | $\hat{3}$ | | $\hat{5}$ | $\hat{3}$ | $\hat{1}$ |

B. Choose a rhythm from (1) through (4) and improvise a melody with *do*, *me*, and *sol* ($\hat{1}$-♭$\hat{3}$-$\hat{5}$).

Sample solution with rhythm (1)

C. Duet: Choose a rhythm from (1) through (4) and work with a partner to perform exercises A and B again. Face each other and sing alternate measures.

D. Duet: Perform exercise C again, but this time begin each measure with the same pitch and syllable with which your partner ended the previous measure.

Sample solution with rhythm (3)

E. Duet: Now alternate each measure between *do, mi,* or *sol* ($\hat{1}, \hat{3},$ or $\hat{5}$) and *sol, ti,* or *re* ($\hat{5}, \hat{7},$ or $\hat{2}$).

Sample solution with rhythm (3)

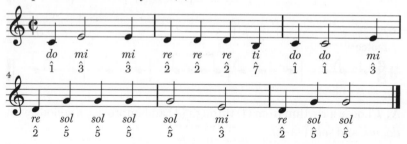

Quick Composition Notate your favorite improvisation. The rhythms are already given, so write the solfège syllables of your improvisation above the staff, and then choose an appropriate clef and convert to notation on the staff. Exchange with a peer and sing each other's melody with solfège syllables, scale-degree numbers, or letter names.

Triad Études

Major-key études

Minor-key études

Melodies

Many of these melodies review skills and concepts covered in previous chapters.

304 Bartók, No. 2 from *44 Duets*, Vol. I (adapted)

305 "Lil' Liza Jane" (traditional)

306 Donovan, "Brother Sun, Sister Moon"

307 A. Emmett Adams, "The Bells of St. Mary's"

308 Jerome Kern, "Look for the Silver Lining"

309 Gene Autry, "Back in the Saddle Again"

Note that the range of the next melody is a thirteenth. For such instrumental melodies it is often helpful to change octaves when the notes exceed your range. Here, for example, the last four notes can be sung an octave lower if they can't be sung where notated.

310 Mahler, Symphony No. 1, first movement

311 Bartók, No. 16 from *44 Duets*, Vol. I (adapted)

Repeat the melody and sing it as a canon with a partner. When the first singer begins measure 2, the second begins measure 1.

312 Bartók, No. 9 from *44 Duets*, Vol. I (adapted)

313 Kurt Weill and Maxwell Anderson, "September Song"

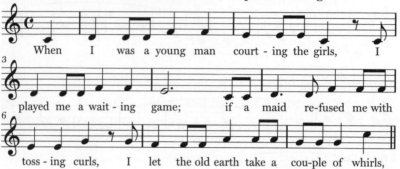

When I was a young man court - ing the girls, I
played me a wait - ing game; if a maid re - fused me with
toss - ing curls, I let the old earth take a cou - ple of whirls,

314 Ted Daffan, "Born to Lose"

mf

Improvisation 7.2: Point-and-Sing Rhythm Patterns: ♪ Beat Unit

1. Point to one of the following rhythm patterns and perform it. While keeping a steady beat, point to a new pattern and perform it. Continue this way until you have performed all five patterns. Optional: Read each pattern with counting syllables recommended by your teacher.

Rhythm Patterns of ♪ Beat Unit

2. Ties, dots, and syncopation: Perform the following examples to learn how to change rhythm patterns 4, 5, and 3 into three new patterns.

(a) #4   + tie = #6   (b) #5   + tie = #7   (c) #3   + tie = #8

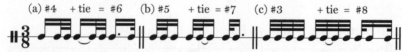

3. Create new rhythm compositions from the list of the following eight patterns. Variation: Have a classmate point to patterns, in any order, while you perform them. Switch roles.

Simple-Meter Rhythms with ♪ and ♪. Beat Unit

Remember that beams play a crucial role in rhythmic notation. By beaming together those notes that belong within a single beat the performer sees rhythmic groups that align with the beats of a particular meter. For the next rhythms, remember that the eighth note is the beat (not the beat division); the sixteenth note is the beat *division*, while the thirty-second note is the beat *subdivision*. For any confusion about the correct counting syllables simply imagine the notes with one fewer beams or flags, that is, as they would look in the familiar quarter-note beat units. The first rhythm is shown in both $\frac{2}{8}$ and $\frac{2}{4}$ for comparison; the counting syllables are the same.

315a

Here is the same rhythm "with one flag or beam removed."

315b

316

317

The next five rhythms indicate a disruption in pulse in different ways: a fermata (⌢), which indicates that a note or rest should be held for longer than its established duration; a breath mark (ʼ) or caesura (//); or a general pause (grand pause, GP). As you conduct, practice not only how you begin the disruption, but also how you return to the original tempo. Imagine "conducting yourself."

Melodies

Improvisation 7.3: Point-and-Sing Rhythm Patterns: ♪. Beat Unit

Choose from Patterns 1-5 and improvise a piece that is sixteen patterns long. Keep a steady beat as you perform.

Rhythm Patterns of the ♪. Beat Unit

Compound-Meter Rhythms with ♪. Beat Unit

Note that the next four rhythms are paired: (a) and (b), with the first in each sounding the same as the second. The first rhythm in each pair is notated with ties while the second is notated with combined- and dotted-note values.

337a

Allegro

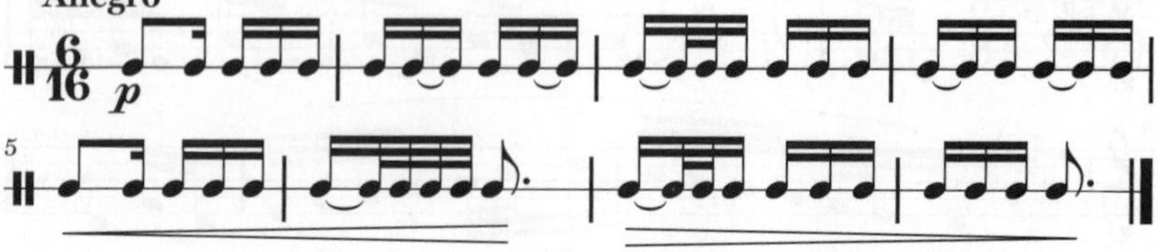

337b

Allegro

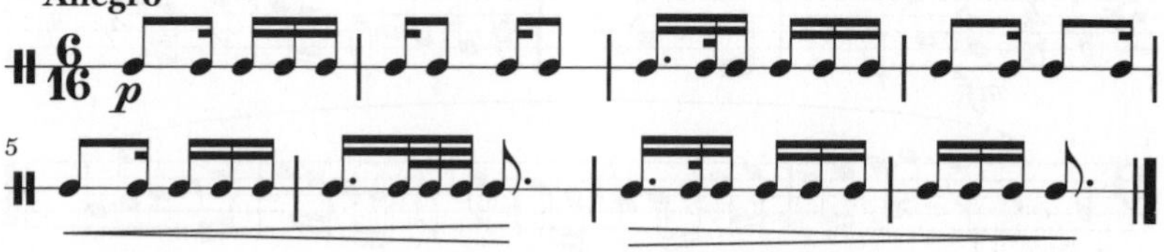

338a

Lento

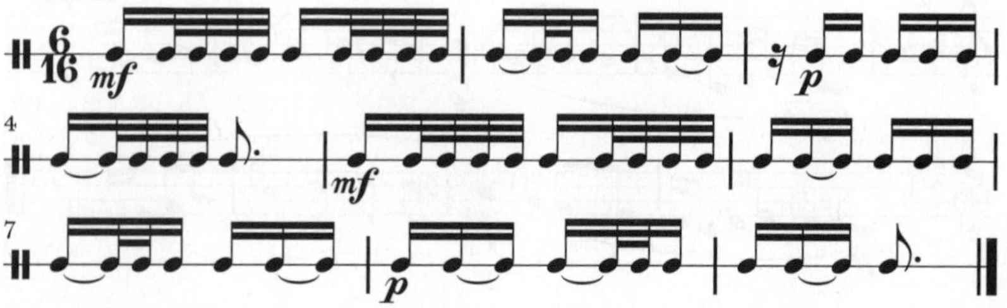

338b

Lento

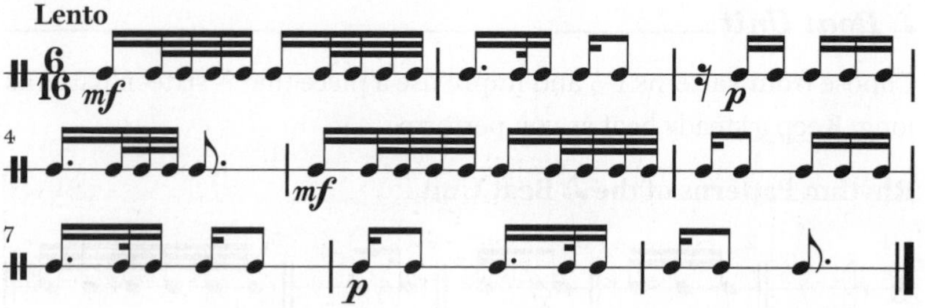

339

Andante

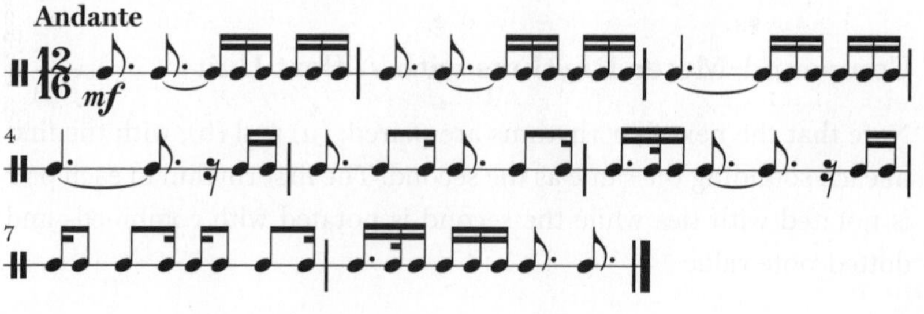

340

Vivo

341

Andantino

342

Duets

343

Allegretto

CHAPTER 8

Melody:

- Seventh chords

Rhythm:

- Beat units of the half note and dotted-half note

In this chapter you'll learn to:

- Improvise melodies outlining the Mm7, the MM7, and the mm7
- Perform études that isolate seventh chords in major and minor keys
- Perform melodies and rhythms in simple and compound meter with half-note and dotted-half-note beat units

---

Improvisation 8.1: The Mm7, MM7, and mm7

Review the following four rhythms, which serve as the basis for improvising seventh-chord melodies. In preparation for improvising your own melodies, clap, tap, or sing on a neutral syllable each rhythm while conducting.

(1)

Moderato

(2)

Waltz

(3)

March

(4)

Dolce

Choose a rhythm from (1) through (4) and improvise melodies that include the indicated seventh chord. Sing "sev" for $\hat{7}$ and end on *do* ($\hat{1}$).

A. Mm7 as *sol-ti-re-fa* ($\hat{5}$-$\hat{7}$-$\hat{2}$-$\hat{4}$)

Sample solution with rhythm (1)

sol	ti	re	fa	fa	re	fa	re	ti	re	do
$\hat{5}$	$\hat{7}$	$\hat{2}$	$\hat{4}$	$\hat{4}$	$\hat{2}$	$\hat{4}$	$\hat{2}$	$\hat{7}$	$\hat{2}$	$\hat{1}$

B. MM7 as *do-mi-sol-ti* ($\hat{1}$-$\hat{3}$-$\hat{5}$-$\hat{7}$)

Sample solution with rhythm (3)

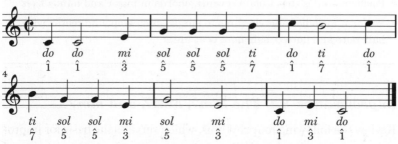

do	do	mi	sol	sol	sol	ti	do	ti	do
$\hat{1}$	$\hat{1}$	$\hat{3}$	$\hat{5}$	$\hat{5}$	$\hat{5}$	$\hat{7}$	$\hat{1}$	$\hat{7}$	$\hat{1}$

ti	sol	sol	mi	sol	mi	do	mi	do
$\hat{7}$	$\hat{5}$	$\hat{5}$	$\hat{3}$	$\hat{5}$	$\hat{3}$	$\hat{1}$	$\hat{3}$	$\hat{1}$

C. mm7 as *re-fa-la-do* ($\hat{2}$-$\hat{4}$-$\hat{6}$-$\hat{1}$)

Sample solution with rhythm (2)

re	fa	la	do	do	la	do	la	do	la	fa	la	fa	re	fa	re	do
$\hat{2}$	$\hat{4}$	$\hat{6}$	$\hat{1}$	$\hat{1}$	$\hat{6}$	$\hat{1}$	$\hat{6}$	$\hat{1}$	$\hat{6}$	$\hat{4}$	$\hat{6}$	$\hat{4}$	$\hat{2}$	$\hat{4}$	$\hat{2}$	$\hat{1}$

D. Duet. Choose a rhythm from (1) through (4) above, and one type of seventh chord—Mm7, MM7, or mm7. Facing a partner, each person sings one measure in turn.

Quick Composition Using rhythms (1) through (4), notate your favorite improvisation. Write the solfège syllables of your improvisation above the staff then choose an appropriate clef and convert to notation on the staff. Exchange with a peer and sing each other's melody with solfège syllables, scale-degree numbers, or letter names.

Seventh-Chord Études

346 Major-key seventh chords

347 Minor-key seventh chords

348 Major-key seventh chords

349 Minor-key seventh chords

For review of common cut-time rhythm patterns, refer to Improvisation 3.3 (p. 30) in relation to cut time.

When the half note or the dotted-half note is the beat unit, divisions of the beat cannot be shown with beams. For this reason, such rhythms can, at first, be challenging to read accurately. One way to improve reading fluency is to associate rhythmic patterns notated in these larger beat values with their equivalent patterns notated in the familiar quarter-note and dotted-quarter-note beat units. The same process can clarify any confusion about the correct counting syllables. The first rhythm is shown in both $\frac{2}{2}$ and $\frac{2}{4}$ for comparison; the counting syllables are the same.

Rhythms with ♩ Beat Unit

350a

350b

Here is the same rhythm notated with quarter-note beat units.

Simple Duple (Review)

For more cut-time rhythms, refer to Chapter 2.

Duet

353

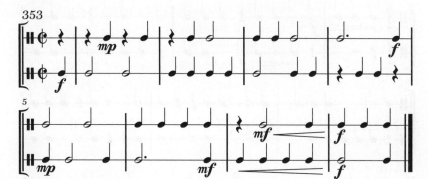

Simple Quadruple

354

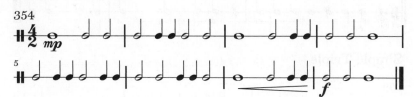

355

356

Duets

357

358

Simple Triple

359

360

361

Duets

362

Melodies

367 Ted Daffan, "Born to Lose"

368 William Byrd, Galliarde to the Firste Pavian (adapted), from *My Lady Nevell's Book*

369 Allegro

Improvisation 8.2: Point-and-Sing Rhythm Patterns: ♩. *Beat Unit*

Choose from the following patterns, and improvise a piece that is sixteen patterns long. Keep a steady beat as you perform.

Rhythms with the ♩. Beat Unit

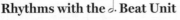

These rhythms are to be conducted in a two-beat pattern.

370a

370b

Here is the same rhythm notated with quarter-note beat units.

Compound Duple

371

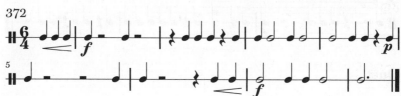

372

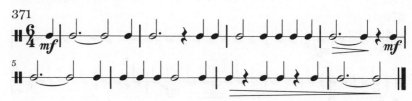

Duet

373

Compound Quadruple

These rhythms are to be conducted in a four-beat pattern.

374

375

376

Duet

377

Compound Triple

These rhythms are to be conducted in a three-beat pattern.

378

379

380

Duet

381

Melodies

382

383

384

385

386

CHAPTER 9

Melody:

- Note-to-note counterpoint
- Modal melodies

Rhythm:

- Borrowed beat divisions (triplets)

In this chapter you'll learn to:

- Perform solo cantus firmi
- Improvise note-to-note contrapuntal phrases to a given cantus firmus
- Perform two-part note-to-note contrapuntal exercises with a partner
- Perform rhythms with borrowed beat divisions (triplets) in simple meters

Cantus Firmi

The following cantus firmi (CFs) are notated exclusively in whole notes, with neither meter signatures nor bar lines. The reason for this is to concentrate focus on melodic line. However, this does not suggest you should sing these CFs in a dry, lifeless, metronomic manner. Rather, perform them dynamically, managing tempo and volume to create a musical statement that begins, moves toward the focal point (climax) somewhere near the middle, then moves away from this point for a satisfying ending.

   Note that the first two CFs are the same but notated in two different clefs.

391 Fux

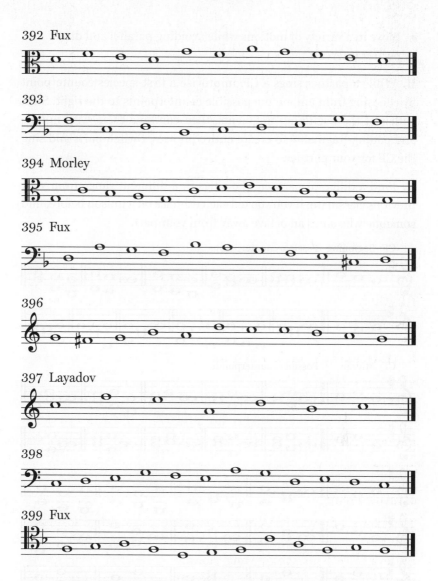

392 Fux

393

394 Morley

395 Fux

396

397 Layadov

398

399 Fux

Improvisation 9.1: First-Species Counterpoint _____

A. At the keyboard, play one of the given cantus firmus (CF) fragments with all of the possible counterpoints to the right. Next, play just the counterpoint while singing one of its possible counterpoints. Create a complete phrase by combining beginning, middle, and ending CF fragments while singing a corresponding contrapuntal line.

Strategies

- Play each of the CFs and memorize the counterpoints to train your ear to favor consonances (PU, 3, P5, 6, and P8).

- Move in a variety of motions while avoiding parallel and direct perfect intervals.

B. While a partner sings a CF, improvise a first-species counterpoint by choosing from among the possible counterpoints to the right. Start with just the beginning fragments, then combine them with middle and ending fragments to create entire phrases. Switch parts and sing the CF for your partner.

C. Find a different partner who sings in a different range from your previous classmate; if you started each exercise on a unison before, find someone who sings an octave away from your part.

Quick Composition Notate your favorite improvisation. Write the solfège syllables of your improvisation above a single staff, then choose an appropriate clef and convert to notation in whole notes on the staff. Exchange with a peer and sing each other's melody with solfège syllables, scale-degree numbers, or letter names.

First-Species Counterpoint

The cantus firmi appearing at the beginning of the chapter now appear with note-to-note counterpoints above and below. Sing the following exercises with a partner, in two groups, or alone, playing one part while singing the other.

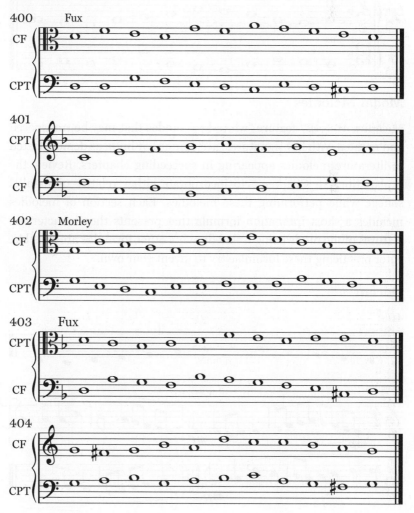

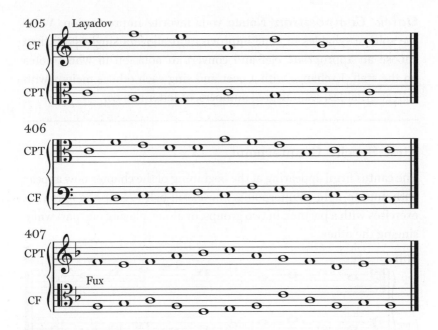

Modal Melodies

Melodies 408-427 feature "white-key" modes that may be transposed and notated with key signatures, accidentals, or both, as demonstrated in literature melodies appearing in succeeding chapters. Review the explanations in Chapter 5 to incorporate either relative or parallel solfège while performing these melodies. Each section of melodies includes a short intonation formula that presents the characteristic features of the mode being isolated; many other formulae are possible. After practicing these formulae try to invent your own.

Dorian

Phrygian

415

Lydian

416

417

418

419

Mixolydian

420

Aeolian

Ensemble Melodies

You have already performed rounds, rhythmic duets, and two-part counterpoint. We now expand such interactive performance with ensemble melodies for two, three, and four parts. Prepare each part separately, as for a single-line melody. Practice musically either with parts separately or in combination with the rhythm, conducting, pitch, solfège syllables, or scale-degree numbers. If a part is too high or too low for your voice range, transpose it down or up an octave so it will be in a more comfortable register.

Suggestions for Class Performance

- Choose an ensemble—one performer for each part, for example.
- Choose a conductor, who will provide the tonic pitch and establish the tempo. Then every performer should conduct, following the conductor's lead.
- Stand while singing in order to produce the best sound.
- Maintain eye contact with each performer.
- Balance your part with the others.

Variations

- Exchange parts and perform again until each musician has sung every part.
- Choose ensembles that feature more than one performer on each part.

- One musician can play one part while singing another.
- One performer can perform the rhythm of two parts simultaneously—tapping with each hand on a different surface or tapping one part while performing the other part vocally

428 Couperin, *Les Moissonneurs* (adapted)

429 Türk, "The Hunters" (adapted)

430 "Who Stole My Chickens?" (traditional)

Rhythms with Borrowed Beat Divisions: Triplets in Simple Meters

The counting syllables for triplets are the same as those used for compound-meter beat divisions. Unless indicated otherwise, the beat durations remain constant.

♩ **Beat Unit**

Duets

♩ Beat Unit

Duets

CHAPTER 10

Melody:

- Melodic/rhythmic embellishments in two-part counterpoint
- Plainchant melodies

Rhythm:

- Borrowed beat divisions (duplets and quadruplets)

In this chapter you'll learn to:

- Improvise embellishments in two-part counterpoint
- Perform two-part second-species contrapuntal exercises with a partner
- Perform rhythms with borrowed beat divisions (duplets) in compound meters

Improvisation 10.1: Second-Species Counterpoint

Analyze the contrapuntal implications of the following outline by writing interval numbers between the staves. Then, with a partner, perform the outline as notated. For the first time through, embellish the higher part with consonant skips, passing tones, suspensions, and/or neighbor tones. For the repetition, embellish the lower part. Note that suspensions can usually be created where the melodic line descends stepwise. What suspensions can be created in measures 4, 6, and 8?

Other members of the class can critique the counterpoint by taking dictation, notating both the harmonic intervals and the melodic lines.

Quick Composition Notate your favorite improvisation. Write the solfège syllables of your improvisation above and below a grand staff with a straight brace. Below each line of solfège, notate the rhythm of your improvisation. Indicate the key signature and meter, then convert the solfège syllables and rhythmic notation to notes on the staff. Exchange with a peer and sing each other's melodies with solfège syllables, scale-degree numbers, or letter names.

Melodic/Rhythmic Embellishments in Two-Part Counterpoint

The two-part contrapuntal exercises from Chapter 9 now appear with melodic and rhythmic embellishments along with two new examples from the literature.

Example

459

460 Layadov

461

462 Fux

463 Zarlino, from *The Art of Counterpoint* (adapted)

464 Zarlino, from *The Art of Counterpoint* (adapted)

Plainsong (Plainchant) Melodies

Medieval Roman Catholic liturgical music, called plainsong or plainchant, or simply chant, was monophonic and modal. Because the original form of chant notation is now archaic, the music is transcribed so that contemporary musicians may perform it more easily. Melismas (two or more pitches sung to a single syllable of text) are indicated with a slur between notes or by beaming notes together. Text phrase endings are marked with a short line through the top staff line or with a bar line. Syllabic emphasis is indicated by placing an acute accent symbol (´) over a vowel. The melodies are sung somewhat freely in rhythm, with modern rhythmic values indicating "short" or "long" more than precise rhythms.

Before singing these melodies, refer to the explanation of relative and parallel solfège syllables on page 65 of Chapter 5.

465 *Veni creator Spiritus* (anonymous plainsong)

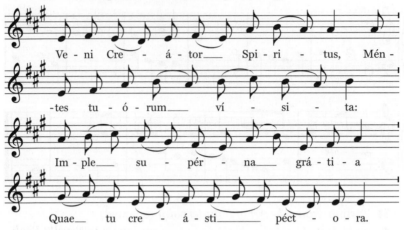

Ve - ni Cre - á - tor___ Spi - ri - tus, Mén -
-tes tu - ó - rum___ ví - si - ta:
Im - ple___ su - pér - na___ grá - ti - a
Quae___ tu cre - á - sti___ péct - o - ra.

466 *Pange lingua* (anonymous plainsong)

Pan-ge lin-gua___ glo-ri - ó - si Cór - po-ris my-sté-ri-um,___
San-gui-nis-que pre - ti - ó - si, Quam in mun di pré ti um
Fru-ctus ven-tris ge - ne - ró - si Rex ef-fú-dit___ gén - ti-um.

467 *Salve Regina* (anonymous plainsong)

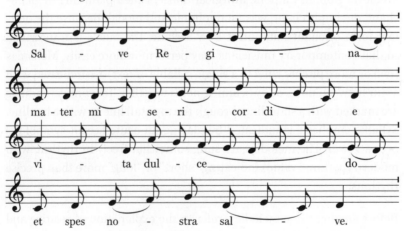

Sal - ve Re - gi - na___
ma - ter mi - se - ri - cor - di - e
vi - ta dul - ce___ do___
et spes no - stra sal - ve.

468 Antiphon for Vespers (anonymous plainsong), from *Liber usualis*

Mon-tes et óm - nes cól - les hu - mi - li - a - bún - tur:
et é-runt prá-va in di-réc-ta, et á-spe-ra in ví-as plá-nas:
vé-ni Dó - mi-ne, et nó-li tar-dá-re, al-le - lú - ia.

Ensemble Melodies

469 Byrd, Galliarde to the Sixte Pavian, from *My Lady Nevell's Book*

470 de Lassus, *Oculus non vidit*

O - cu - lus non vi - dit
O - cu - lus non
nec - au - ris au -
vi - dit nec - au -

471 Dowland, "Now, O Now I Needs Mus Part"

472 Weelkes, "Lady, Your Eye My Love Enforced"

473 de Lassus, *Expectatio justorum laetitia*

Rhythms with Borrowed Beat Divisions: Duplets and Quadruplets in Compound Meters

The counting syllables for duplets and quadruplets are the same as those used for simple-meter beat divisions and subdivisions. Unless indicated otherwise, the beat units remain constant.

♩. Beat Unit

♩. **Beat Unit**

487

488

489

490

491

Duets

492

PART II

Diatonic Harmony
and Tonicization

CHAPTER 11

Melody:

- Review of melodic/rhythmic embellishments in two-part counterpoint (late-sixteenth-century style)
- Soprano and bass lines in eighteenth-century style
- Conclusive and inconclusive cadences

Rhythm:

- More-advanced simple-meter rhythms with beat subdivisions

In this chapter you'll learn to:

- Improvise embellished melodic outlines
- Perform two-part soprano-bass duets in eighteenth-century style
- Recognize conclusive and inconclusive cadences in melodies
- Perform simple-meter rhythms with a variety of beat subdivisions

---

Improvisation 11.1: Embellishing Melodic Outlines ____

Improvise an embellished melody based on the following outline. Add consonant skips (CS) and neighbor tones (N), and expand upon the simple rhythm. Perform your improvisations in class. As you listen to the melodies of others, analyze the means by which the outline has been embellished—that is, where are the CS, P, and N?

Strategies

- Begin by singing each part as written, then sing the melody while playing the bass line.
- Create études consisting of a single type of embellishment. For example, sing a variation that consists of nothing but skips within the chords. Sing another that features only upper neighbors, one that features lower neighbors, and so on.

- Improvise melodies that combine ideas from your études into new, original music.

(Compare with Haydn, Piano Sonata No. 15 in C Major, Minuet.)

Variations

- Improvise in the parallel minor keys, and include the leading tone.
- Transpose the outline to major and minor keys from three flats to three sharps.
- Perform the improvisation as a duet with one person per staff.
- The class sustains the pitches of the outline while one or two performers improvise.

Quick Composition Notate your favorite improvisation on a grand staff showing the correct key and meter signature. Exchage with a peer and sing each other's part with solfège syllables, scale degrees, or letter names.

Rhythms with Subdivided ♪ Beat Unit

For a review of time signatures with the eighth-note beat, see Chapter 7, page 89.

496

Vivo

497

Moderato

498

Alla marcia

499

Allegro

500

Allegretto

Ensemble Rhythms

501

Andante

502

Moderato

Rhythms with Subdivided ♩ Beat Unit

508

Ensemble Rhythms

509

510

511

Rhythms with Subdivided ♩ Beat Unit

512

515

516

Ensemble Rhythms

517

Fast

518

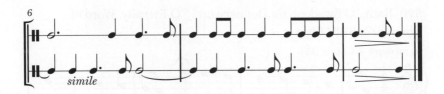

Duet

This duet appeared in Chapter 10 and provides a valuable comparison between late-sixteenth-century contrapuntal styles and those of the eighteenth century, which follow. Sing one part while playing the other, then switch. Perform this melody in class as a duet or ensemble.

519 Byrd, Galliarde to the Sixte Pavian, from *My Lady Nevell's Book*

Soprano and Bass Lines in Eighteenth-Century Style

How does the counterpoint in these excerpts differ from the previous duet? To help you understand the counterpoint of these soprano-bass frameworks, write interval numbers between the staves. You'll notice that, here, dissonant intervals are controlled differently, occasionally appearing on the beat and moving directly to consonant intervals. Sing one part while playing the other, then switch. Perform these melodies in class as duets or ensembles.

520 Bach, "O Ewigkeit, du Donnerwort" ("O Eternity, Word of Thunder"), BWV 60

In measure 4, C♯ is *si* (♯5̂).

521 Bach, "Was Gott tut, das ist wohlgetan" ("What God Does Is Well Done"), BWV 99

522 Bach, "Jesu, der du meine Seele" ("Jesus, Who Saved My Soul"), BWV 78

523 Bach, "Nun komm, der Heiden Heiland" (Now Come, Savior of the Gentiles"), BWV 61

In measure 5, hear *ti* (7̂, A♯), in relation to *do* (1̂).

524 Bach, "Wer nur den lieben Gott lässt walten" ("He Lets Only Beloved God Rule"), BWV 93

In measure 3, tune *te* ($\flat\hat{7}$) by imagining *do* ($\hat{1}$) during the quarter rest.

525 Bach, "Erhalt uns, Herr, bei deinem Wort" ("Preserve Us, God, by Your Word"), BWV 126

526 Bach, "Ich freue mich in dir" ("I Rejoice in You"), BWV 133

527 Haydn, String Quartet in E♭ Major, Op. 33, No. 2 (*The Joke*), third movement (adapted)

528 Haydn, String Quartet in F Major, Op. 20, No. 5, third movement (adapted)

529 Leonarda, Credo, from *Messa Prima*

This excerpt is actually two-part music. Because the upper parts have the same rhythm and contour, they act as a single part that counterpoints the bass. To analyze the intervals, first compare the highest part with the bass, then the middle part with the bass.

Conclusive and Inconclusive Cadences

For conclusive cadences: Listen for and identify the cadential melodic pitch as *do* (1̂). For inconclusive cadences: Listen for and identify pitches such as *re* (2̂), *ti* (7̂), or *sol* (5̂); less conclusive cadences might end with *mi* (3̂).

530 Liszt, *Hungarian Rhapsody* No. 14

531 James Horner and Will Jennings, "My Heart Will Go On," from *Titanic* (adapted)

532 Mahler, Symphony No. 2, first movement (adapted)

533 Grieg, *Norwegian Melodies*, Op. 63, first movement

(This melody is in a minor key.)

534 Gale Garnett, "We'll Sing in the Sunshine"

535 Chopin, Cello Sonata in G Minor, Op. 65, first movement

536 Al Kasha and Joel Hirschborn, "Candle on the Water"

I'll be your can-dle on the wa - ter,

My love for you will al - ways burn. I know you're

lost and drift-ing, but the clouds are lift - ing,

don't give up, you have some-where to turn.

537 John Denver, Bill Danoff, and Taffy Nivert, "Take Me Home, Country Roads"

Al-most heav - en__ West Vir-gin - ia____

Blue Ridge Moun - tains,__ Shen - an - do - ah

Riv - er.____

538 Redd Stewart and Pee Wee King, "Tennessee Waltz"

I was waltz-ing__ with my darlin'__ to the Ten-nes - see__

Waltz__ when an old friend I hap-pened to see.____

539 Haydn, String Quartet in G Minor, Op. 74, No. 3, second movment

Ensemble Melodies

540 Clementi, Sonatina in C Major, Op. 36, No. 1, third movement (adapted)

Play one part and sing the other, or perform as a duet.

541 Telemann, *Fantaisie* in E Minor (adapted)

542 Bach, Badinerie, from Orchestral Suite No. 2 for Orchestra, BWV 1067

CHAPTER 12

Melody:

- Phrases
- Melodic T-D-T progressions
- Authentic and half cadences

Rhythm:

- More-advanced compound-meter rhythms with beat subdivisions

In this chapter you'll learn to:

- Improvise phrases in pairs
- Perform and recognize melodic T-D-T progressions
- Recognize authentic and half cadences in melodies
- Perform compound meter rhythms with a variety of beat subdivisions

---

Improvisation 12.1: Melodies in Phrase Pairs

Improvise a melody that may be accompanied by the following progression. Sing the melody while accompanying yourself at the keyboard. Direct the melody of each phrase toward the cadence, ideally descending to *re* (2̂) at the first cadence (m. 4) and *do* (1̂) at the second cadence. For extra guidance, refer to the strategies presented in Improvisation 11.1.

Duet

While one person plays an embellished version of the progression, the partner improvises a melody by singing or playing an instrument. Switch roles and perform again.

Rhythms with Subdivided ♪. Beat Unit

543

Andantino

544

Grave

545

Moderato

546

Andante

Duets

Rhythms with Subdivided ♩. Beat Unit

555

556

557

Ensemble Rhythms

558

559

Allegretto

Rhythms with Subdivided ♩. Beat Unit

565

Largo

566

Larghetto

Ensemble Rhythms

567

568

Lively

Harmonic Progressions

Sing these études to learn the common sound of progressions that start in the tonic area, move to the dominant, then return to tonic (T-D-T). Stems-down pitches represent the bass lines; listen especially to these notes or have a partner sustain them while you sing the melody. Sing the melodies in their parallel keys, too.

569 I-V⁶-I

570 I-V⁶₅-I-V⁶₅-I

571 I-V⁴₃-I⁶-V⁴₃-I

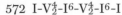

572 I-V$_2^4$-I^6-V$_2^4$-I^6-I

573 I-V7-I-V7-I

Getting the most out of this étude

- Play the bass line while singing the melody with solfège syllables and scale-degree numbers.
- Have a partner sing the bass line while you sing the treble part.
- Realize the progression in block chords at the keyboard by holding the three highest treble pitches while playing the bass line.
- Play the four-part progression in block chords while singing the melody as notated.

574

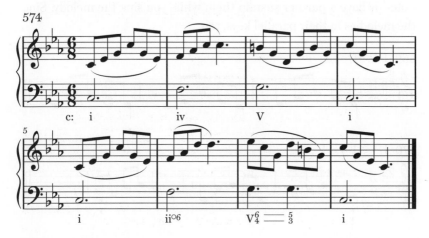

Authentic and Half Cadences

As you perform these melodies, listen carefully to the phrase endings and try to identify authentic cadences ending on *do* ($\hat{1}$), *mi* ($\hat{3}$), or *sol* ($\hat{5}$), and half cadences ending on *re* ($\hat{2}$), *sol* ($\hat{5}$), or *ti* ($\hat{7}$).

575 "Jingle Bells" (traditional)

576 Bach, No. 48, from *St. John Passion*

577 Caccini, "Maria, dolce Maria" (adapted)

578 Bruce Johnston, "I Write the Songs"

I write the songs— that make the whole world sing;

I write the songs— of love and spe - cial things.—

I write the songs— that make the young girls cry;—

I write the songs,— I write the songs.—

579 Martini, Gavotte in F

580 Bach, Violin Concerto No. 1 in A Minor, first movement

581 Johnny Marks, "Silver and Gold" (adapted)

Sil - ver and gold, sil - ver and gold,

ev' - ry-one wish - es for sil - ver and gold.

582 Mahler, Symphony No. 2, second movement

583 Hank Cochran, "Make the World Go Away"

Do you re-mem-ber when you loved me

be-fore the world took me a - stray? If you do, then for-

- give me, and make the world___ go a - way.

584 "Dubinushka" ("Hammer Song") (traditional)

585 Schubert, "Das Wandern" ("Wandering"), from *Die schöne Müllerin*

586 Mahler, Symphony No. 1, third movement

587 Bach, Burlesca, from Partita No. 3 in A Minor, BWV 827

Ensemble Melodies

As you perform these ensemble melodies, listen carefully to the soprano-bass phrase endings and try to identify cadences: perfect authentic (PAC), imperfect authentic (IAC), or half (HC).

588 Byrd, "The Carman's Whistle," *My Lady Nevell's Book*

589 Foster, "Better Times Are Coming"

Play the piano part and sing the melody, or perform as a quintet.

There are voic - es of hope that are borne on the air, and our

land will be freed from its clouds of des-pair, for brave men and true men to

bat-tle have gone, and good times, good times are now com-ing on.

590 Haydn, String Quartet in D Major, Op. 50, No. 6, first movement
Sing the tonic pitch, then find *re* (2̂), the starting pitch.

591 Haydn, String Quartet in G Minor, Op. 20, No. 3, first movement

A passing V$^4_3$ is implied in measure 1, but because the viola doubles violin 1, the *do-ti-do* ($\hat{1}$-$\hat{7}$-$\hat{1}$) line is not present.

592 Strozzi, "Dessistete omni, pensiere," from *Ariette a voce solo*, Op. 6

CHAPTER 13

Melody:

- The dominant seventh chord
- Predominant harmony and the predominant area
- Harmonizing melodies

Rhythm:

- Syncopation 1: beats and beat divisions

In this chapter you'll learn to:

- Improvise phrases that alternate between tonic and dominant harmonies, and that explore the predominant area
- Perform melodies that outline the dominant and dominant seventh chord as well as subdominant harmony and the subdominant area
- Harmonize a melody
- Perform syncopated rhythms in which accents occur on weak beats or on the division of the beat

---

Improvisation 13.1: More Phrases in Pairs _____

Improvise a melody that may be accompanied by the following progression paying particular attention to where the dominant and dominant seventh chords appear. Sing the melody while accompanying yourself at the keyboard. Direct the melody of each phrase toward the cadence, ideally descending to *re* ($\hat{2}$) at the first cadence (m. 4) and *do* ($\hat{1}$) at the second cadence. For extra guidance, refer to the strategies presented in Improvisation 11.1.

Duet

While one person plays an embellished version of the progression, the partner improvises a melody by singing or playing an instrument. Switch roles and perform again.

Intervals of the Dominant and Dominant Seventh

In each of the following melodies, isolate the dominant *sol-ti-re* ($\hat{5}$-$\hat{7}$-$\hat{2}$) and dominant seventh chords *sol-ti-re-fa* ($\hat{5}$-$\hat{7}$-$\hat{2}$-$\hat{4}$), and observe the resolution of tendency tones. For additional practice refer to the seventh-chord études presented in Chapter 8.

593 L. Mozart, *Minuet* (adapted)

594 Mozart, Piano Sonata in G Major, K. 283, third movement (adapted)

595 Schubert, *Ecossaise*, D. 299, No. 8 (adapted)

596 Verdi, *Rigoletto*, Act 1, No. 2

Questa o quel - la_____ per me pa - ri so - no a quan-

-t'al - tre d'in - tor - no,_____ d'in - tor-no mi ve - do

del mio co - re_____ l'im-pe-ro non ce - do_____

_____ me-glio ad u - na_____ che ad al-tra bel - tà.

597 Mozart, Symphony No. 39, K. 543, Movement 3, Trio, (adapted)

598 Schumann, "Curiose Geschichte" ("Curious Story"),
Op. 15, No. 2

599 Schubert, "Frühlingstraum" ("Dream of Spring"), from *Winterreise*

600 Schumann, "Silvesterlied" ("New Year's Eve Song"), Op. 68, No. 43 (adapted)

601 Diabelli, Sonatina, Op. 168, first movement (adapted)

Ensemble Melodies

602 Couperin, *Les Moissonneurs* (adapted)

603 Haydn, String Quartet in G Major, Op. 3, No. 3, first movement

Improvisation 13.2: Predominant Harmony _____

Improvise a melody that may be accompanied by the following progression paying particular attention to where the predominant harmonies appear. Sing the melody while accompanying yourself at the keyboard. Direct the melody of each phrase toward the cadence, ideally descending to *re* ($\hat{2}$) at the first cadence (m. 4) and *do* ($\hat{1}$) at the second cadence. For extra guidance, refer to the strategies presented in Improvisation 11.1.

$$\text{B}\flat: \quad \text{I} \qquad \text{IV} \quad \text{ii}^6 \quad \text{V}^6_4 - ^5_3 \qquad \text{I} \qquad \text{IV} \quad \text{ii}^6 \quad \text{V}^6_4 - ^5_3 \quad \text{I}$$

Variations

- Begin with four-measure solos. Later, extend them to eight or sixteen measures or shorten them to two measures.

- "Trade fours." One person improvises four bars, and then a second responds to the first improvisation.

- Try a variety of styles (art song, pop song, jazz, etc.). Create rhythmic embellishments to the accompaniment that are characteristic of the chosen style. Change the tempo, mood, and character to reflect your choice.

- Perform each example in its parallel minor mode.

- Transpose the examples to keys ranging from three flats to three sharps.

- Change the meters to compound meters.

- Create a "groove" by adding one or more percussionists who play on objects available in class (books, desktops, pencils, etc.).

Quick Composition Notate your favorite improvisation (melody only) on a single staff showing the correct key and meter signature. Exchange with a peer and sing each other's improvisation with solfège syllables, scale-degree numbers, or letter names.

Intervals of Predominant Harmony and the Predominant Area

In the following melodies, observe—both by ear and by sight—predominant harmonies and the predominant area. Notice that when predominant harmony moves to dominant harmony, the following melodic motions often occur: *fa-sol* ($\hat{4}$-$\hat{5}$); *re-re* ($\hat{2}$-$\hat{2}$); *la-sol* ($\hat{6}$-$\hat{5}$) or *la-ti* ($\hat{6}$-$\hat{7}$). Label the appropriate notes or measures with "PD" and a bracket below the staff.

604 Schubert, *Zwanzig Walzer* (Twenty Waltzes), D. 146, No. 13 (adapted)

605 Schumann, "Frölicher Landmann" ("The Happy Farmer"), Op. 68, No. 10

606 Bartók, *For Children*, Sz. 42, No. 1

607 Telemann, Gigue à l'Angloise, TWV 32:1

608 "The Banks of Sacramento" (folksong)

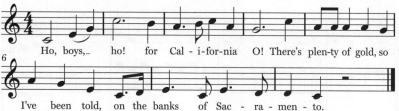

Ho, boys,_ ho! for Cal - i-for-nia O! There's plen-ty of gold, so I've been told, on the banks of Sac - ra - men - to.

609 Brahms, Waltz, Op. 39, No. 3 (adapted)

610 Burgmüller, L'Arabesque, Op. 100, No. 2

Because of the large range of this melody, perform measure 4 transposed down one octave.

611 "The Lane County Bachelor" (traditional)

My_ name is Frank Bale an old bach-'lor I am,_ I'm keep-'in old batch on an el - e-gant plan._ You'll find me out West in the coun-ty of Lane, Starv-ing to death on a gov-ern-ment claim.

Ensemble Melodies

612 Haydn, String Quartet in F Major, Op. 3, No. 5, second movement (adapted)

613 J. C. Bach, Sonata in C Minor, Op. 17, No. 2

Harmonizing Melodies

As an introduction to harmonizing melodies, follow these steps to develop a routine as you harmonize this melody and those that appear throughout the book.

- Harmonize melodies in keyboard style (three voices in the right hand, the bass voice in the left).

- Sing the melodies while you play your harmonization, or accompany a classmate's instrumental performance of the melody.
- Employ I(⁶), V(⁶), and all inversions of the dominant seventh chord, as well as ii⁶, IV, and V_{4-3}^{6-5}. For the latter, follow the path of the figures: $\hat{6}$ moves downward to $\hat{5}$ as $\hat{4}$ moves downward to $\hat{3}$.
- Look for common two- and three-pitch melodic patterns that may be harmonized with the progressions you have learned. Model your voice-leading on these progressions.
- Experiment with the harmonic rhythm, changing chords once per bar, once per beat, or each time you change the pitch.
- Play slowly, but with the correct time and rhythm, until you create a satisfying phrase. Doing so will allow the ear time to engage in, process, and predict what is occurring.
- Direct the motion of each phrase to its cadence through the use of expressive devices, including dynamic nuance.

For example, the first time you harmonize a melody try an easy possibility, such as that shown in the first line beneath the staff. When you have mastered the easy version, try the more challenging harmonizations, as in the second line.

614

Syncopation 1: Beats and Beat Divisions

Syncopation occurs when an expected accent is displaced or moved to another beat or part of a beat. The following rhythms present two kinds of syncopation, the first of which involves an accent on a metrically weak beat. Note the many ways in which this can occur as you perform these rhythms while conducting. Perform these rhythms and balance the regularity of the strong first beats with the irregularity of the accented beats occurring in the rest of the measure.

621

Duets

622

623

In the following rhythms, syncopation occurs when the weak part of the beat is accented. Observe the common feature of a divided beat value positioned at both the beginning and end of a syncopated pattern. In such cases, the same divided beat value "pushes" the notes off of the beat, then later back on to the beat. Perform these rhythms while conducting in strict time, and balance the regularity of the strong first beats with the irregularity of the accented off beats.

624

Moderato

625

Molto allegro

626

Allegro

627

Moderato

628

Slowly

629
Allegro

630
Gracefully

631
Vivace

632
Andante

Duets

633
Allegro

634

635

CHAPTER 14

Melody:

- $^6_4$ chord études
- Harmonizing melodies
- Swung melodies

Rhythm:

- Swung rhythms

In this chapter you'll learn to:

- Sing and recognize $^6_4$ chords in melodic contexts
- Embellish phrases with mixed beat divisions and motivic use of neighbor tones
- Perform rhythms and melodies in a swung style
- Harmonize melodies

$^6_4$ Chord Études

The following short études highlight different types of the $^6_4$ chord. Listen for the $^6_4$ chord in each melody and identify it by type: cadential, neighboring (pedal), arpeggiated, or passing. Stems-down pitches represent the bass lines; listen especially to these notes or have a partner sustain them while you sing the melody.

636

643

Improvisation 14.1: Predominant Chords _____

While one person plays the following accompaniment, everyone in turn should improvise a melody. Choose a part and embellish it, following the given strategies. Before anyone sings aloud, have someone play the progression several times while the class silently improvises. Each person should accompany as well as perform a melody.

Strategies

- Start by improvising a melody using a rhythm that matches the phrase's harmonic rhythm, and add nonchord tones once this framework has been created.

- Sing each part as written, then sing the melody while playing the bass line.

- Create études consisting of a single type of embellishment. For example, sing a variation that consists of nothing but skips within the chords. Sing another that features only upper neighbors, one that features lower neighbors, and so on.

- Improvise melodies that combine ideas from your études into new, original music.

B♭:   I   IV   ii⁶   V$^6_4$ — $^5_3$ I   IV   ii⁶   V$^6_4$ — $^5_3$ I

Variations

- Begin with four-measure solos. Later, extend them to eight or sixteen measures, or shorten them to two measures.

- "Trade fours." One person improvises four bars, then a second person responds to the first improvisation.

- Try a variety of styles (art song, pop song, jazz, etc.). Create rhythmic embellishments in the accompaniment that are characteristic of the chosen style. Change the tempo, mood, and character to reflect your choice.
- Perform each example in its parallel minor mode.
- Transpose the examples to keys ranging from three flats to three sharps.
- Change the meter to compound meter.
- Transcribe the examples for instruments available in class, and play the accompaniment on those instruments. Each player should improvise on his or her chosen part.
- Create a "groove" by adding one or more percussionists who play on objects available in class (books, desktops, pencils, etc.).

Quick Composition Notate your favorite improvisation on a grand staff showing the correct key and meter signature. Exchange with a peer and sing each other's part with solfège syllables, scale-degree numbers, or letter names.

Harmonizing Melodies

Refer to Chapter 13 for instructions on harmonizing melodies, then accompany yourself at the piano as you and your classmates sing the following melodies.

644 Mozart, Serenade in G, *Eine kleine Nachmusik*, K. 525, first movemt

645 Beethoven, Symphony No. 9 in D Minor, fourth movement (adapted)

646 Schubert, "Wiegenlied" ("Lullaby"), Op. 98

647 Haydn, Symphony No. 13, Hob. I:13, first movement

Allegro Molto

648 Handel, *Water Music*, Suite No. 2, No. 12, HWV 349 (adapted)

Alla Hornpipe

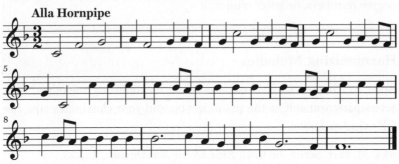

Swung Rhythms

The following rhythms are similar to those encountered earlier in Chapter 3 and do not present any new rhythmic complexities. Here, however, the rhythms are to be "swung"—that is, the beat should be divided in an unequal, long-short manner, similar to (♩-♪) rhythm of compound meter. Swung rhythms are often performed with a slight stress on the shorter notes. Although swung, these rhythms should be conducted in a steady tempo. For comparison, try performing each rhythm in both a swung and strict-time manner. Compare the first two rhythms (649a and 649b), the second of which approximates the swung sound of the first.

649a

649b

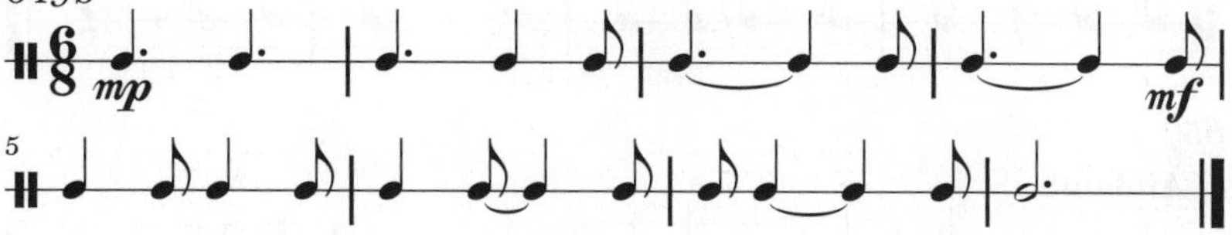

650

651

652

653

Sometimes dotted notation was used in mid-twentieth-century melodies to indicate that the rhythm should be swung.

654

Moderato

Cut Time

These melodies should also be swung.

655

Andante

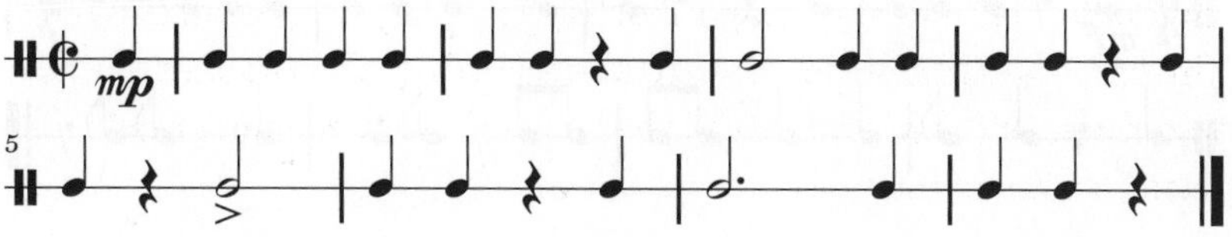

662

Allegretto

663

Duets

664

665

Moderato

cresc. poco a poco

cresc. poco a poco

669

Swung Melodies

The next melodies should be swung.

670

671

672

673

674

675 Horace Silver, "The Preacher"

He would stand up there in the pul - pit, horn in his hand,___ and let that mel - o - dy take___ you to the Prom - ised Land.___

676 Frank Perkins, "Stars Fell on Alabama"

We lived our lit - tle dram - a. We kissed in a field of white and stars fell on A - la - ba - ma last night.___

Remember that dotted notation was often used in mid-twentieth-century melodies to indicate that the rhythm should be swung.

677 Jule Styne and Sammy Cahn, "It's Been a Long, Long Time"

Just kiss me once, then kiss me twice, then kiss me once again, it's been a
long, long time. Have-n't felt like this, my dear, since
can't re-mem-ber when, it's been a long, long time.

Some slow jazz pieces are notated in cut time because there is a two-beat feel in the accompaniment. You may perform this melody as if it were notated in common time, with a ♩ beat c. 60.

678 Ted Koehle and Harold Arlen, "Stormy Weather"

Don't know why_____ there's no sun up in the sky, Storm-y
Weath-er,_____ Since my man and I____ ain't to-geth-er,_____
keeps rain-in' all__ the time._____

CHAPTER 15

Melody:

- Diatonic root progressions
- Modal melodies from the literature
- Harmonizing melodies with other cadence types

Rhythm:

- Syncopation 2: Subdivisions

In this chapter you'll learn to:

- Sing and recognize diatonic root progressions in melodic contexts
- Perform melodies with mixed beat divisions
- Sing modal melodies from the literature
- Perform syncopations in which subdivisions of the beat are accented

---

Diatonic Root-Progression Études

The following short études include common root progression. Listen for these progressions in each melody and identify it by type: fifth, third, second. Stems-down pitches represent the bass lines; listen especially to these notes or have a partner sustain them while you sing the melody.

679

Harmonizing Melodies with Other Cadence Types

Refer to Chapter 13 for instructions on harmonizing melodies, then accompany yourself at the piano as you and your classmates sing the following melodies.

685 "We Three Kings" (traditional), adapted

Harmonize phrase 1 in E minor and phrase 2 in G major, as indicated. Remember to raise scale-degree $\hat{7}$ in the dominant chord. At the end, try a plagal resolution.

686 "On the Erie Canal" (traditional); D Aeolian (or natural minor)

Try a Phrygian resolution in measure 2 and a deceptive cadence in measure 4.

687 Brahms, Symphony No. 3 in F Major, fourth movement (adapted)

Look closely at the key signature; end with a Phrygian cadence.

688 Beach, "Barcarolle"

Each phrase may be harmonized with a plagal cadence.

689 Beach, "Forgotten"

Conclude with a Phrygian cadence.

Improvisation 15.1: Diatonic Root Progressions ____

The following progression presents three different root progressions. While one person plays the accompaniment, everyone in turn should improvise a melody. Choose a part and embellish it, following the strategies given in Improvisation 14.1. Before anyone sings aloud, have someone play the progression several times while the class silently improvises. Each person should accompany as well as perform a melody. Vary the improvisations with the suggestions given for Improvisation 14.1.

B♭:   I   vi   IV   V   I   ii⁶   V⁷   I

Quick Composition   Notate your favorite improvisation on a single staff showing the correct key and meter signature. Exchange with a peer and sing each other's part with solfège syllables, scale-degree numbers, or letter names.

Syncopation 2: Subdivisions

In the following rhythms, syncopation occurs when a subdivision of the beat is stressed. In these cases, consider the syncopated notes as immediately anticipating or following the beat, that is, as moving either directly *toward* or *from* the beat or division of the beat. Observe the many ways in which this can occur as you perform these rhythms while conducting.

690

Andante

691

Spirited

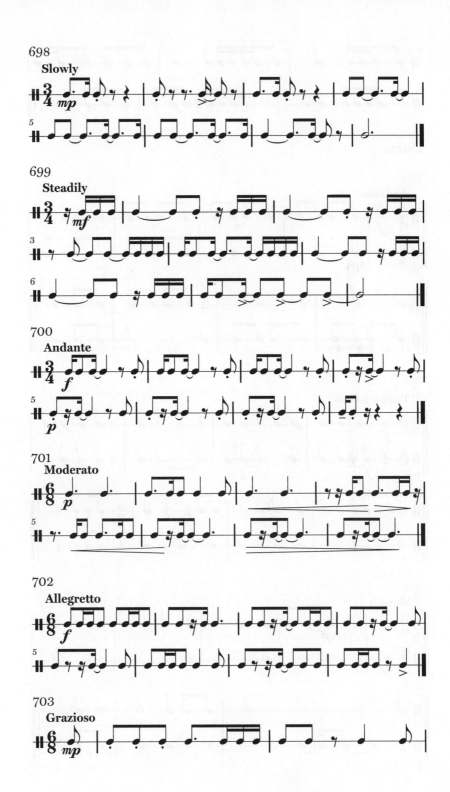

Duets

704

Andante

705

Tempo guisto

706

Slowly

Modal Melodies from the Literature

The diatonic modes were introduced in Chapter 5 along with strate-gies for reading with parallel and relative solfège syllables. More modal melodies, including plainchant and short intonation formulae, were presented in Chapters 9 and 10. A selection of modal melodies from the literature appears next. Before performing each melody, first deter-mine the mode by comparing its centric pitch (often called simply the "final" because it is usually the last note of the melody) to both the key signature and any accidentals that appear, then sing an intonation formula—one from Chapter 9 or your own—to orient yourself to the particular mode of the melody.

709 "Old Joe Clark" (traditional)

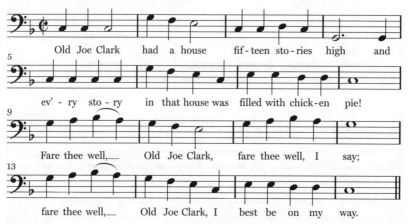

Old Joe Clark had a house fif-teen sto-ries high and
ev' - ry sto - ry in that house was filled with chick-en pie!
Fare thee well,— Old Joe Clark, fare thee well, I say;
fare thee well,— Old Joe Clark, I best be on my way.

710 Bartók, No. 18 from *44 Duets*, Vol. I (adapted)

711 Bartók, No. 37 from *44 Duets*, Vol. II (adapted)

712 "Cumberland Nelly" (traditional)

The melody concludes on its final, E.

713 John Logan, "Consolation," from *Sixteen Tune Settings* (1812)

714 "Dance of Youth" (traditional)

The final of this mode is D.

715 Bartók, No. 6 from *44 Duets*, Vol. I (adapted)

The final of this mode is E.

716 "Land of the Silver Birch" (traditional)

Land of the sil-ver birch, home of the beav-er, where still the

might-y moose wan-ders at will. Blue lake and rock-y shore

I will re-turn once more. Boom did-dy boom boom boom did-dy boom boom boom did-dy boom boom boom!

717 "The Bird Song" (traditional)

Hi say the black - bird, sit - ting on a chair,
Once I court - ed a la - dy fair; She proved fick - le and
turned her back, and ev - er since then I've dressed in black.

Rounds

718 "Hey, Ho, Anybody Home?" (traditional; round in three parts)

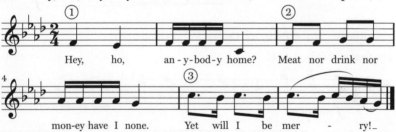

Hey, ho, an - y - bod - y home? Meat nor drink nor
mon - ey have I none. Yet will I be mer - ry!_

719 "Shalom, Chaverim" ("Peace, Friends") (traditional; round in three parts)

Duet

720 Bartók, No. 39 from *44 Duets*, Vol. II (adapted)

CHAPTER 16

Melody:

- Embellished melodies
- Harmonizing modal melodies

Rhythm:

- Compound (super) triplets

In this chapter you'll learn to:

- Embellish a given melody with a variety of nonchord tones
- Recognize and perform melodies with melodic embellishments
- Harmonize melodies

Improvisation 16.1: Embellishment of Melodic Outlines

Improvise an embellished melody based on the given outline following the strategies given in Improvisation 14.1. Add consonant skips (CS), passing tones (P), and neighbor tones (N), and expand upon the simple rhythm. Perform your improvisations in class. As you listen to the melodies of others, analyze the means by which the outline has been embellished—that is, where are the CS, P, and N?

Chord symbols are included as a guide. (Compare with the traditional song "Good Night Ladies.")

Variations

- Improvise in the parallel minor key, and include the leading tone.
- Transpose the outline to major and minor keys from three flats to three sharps.
- Perform the improvisation as a duet with one person per staff.
- The class sustains the pitches of the outline while one or two performers improvise.

Quick Composition Notate your favorite improvisation on a grand staff showing the correct key and meter signature. Exchange with a peer and sing each other's part with solfège syllables, scale-degree numbers, or letter names.

Embellished Melodies

The next group of melodies emphasizes the motivic use of nonchord tones. Look and listen for them, and try to identify them by specific type: diatonic or chromatic passing tones; and diatonic, chromatic, incomplete or complete neighbor tones.

721 Jerome Kern, "The Song Is You"

722 Irving Berlin, "White Christmas"

723 John Hill Hewitt, "All Quiet Along the Potomac Tonight"

Tune *fi* (♯$\hat{4}$) in measure 14 by hearing its resolution to *sol* ($\hat{5}$) in measure 15 as part of a double neighbor figure.

"All qui - et a - long the Po - to - mac," to - night, Ex - cept now and
then a stray pick - et_____ Is shot as he walks on his
beat to and fro By a ri - fle - man hid in_____ the
thick - et._____ 'Tis noth - ing. A pri - vate or
two now and then Will not count in the news of the
bat - tle;_____ Not an of - fi - cer lost! On - ly one of the
men Moan-ing out all a - lone the death rat - tle._____

724 Bert Kaempfert, "Strangers in the Night"

725 Mendelssohn, *Song Without Words*, Op. 62, No. 4 (adapted)

726 Gene Lees and Amando Manzanero, "Yesterday I Heard the Rain"

727 Rodgers and Hart, "Bewitched"

728 Ned Washington and Leigh Harline, "When You Wish Upon a Star"

729 Andrew Lloyd Webber, Charles Hart, and Richard Stilgoe, "All I Ask of You" (adapted)

All I ask for is one love, one life-time; say the word and I will fol-low you.__ Share each day with me, each night, each morn-ing. Love me, that's all I ask of you.

Improve your proficiency with solfège syllables or scale-degree numbers by practicing these melodies slowly, then increasing your speed.

730 Mozart, String Quartet No. 2 in D Major, K. 155, first movement (adapted)

731 Mozart, Piano Sonata in D Major, K. 311, third movement (adapted)

732 Haydn, Piano Sonata No. 40 in G Major, third movement (adapted)

Ensemble Melodies

733 Haydn, Piano Sonata No. 5 in C Major, Menuetto

734 Beethoven, *Ecossaise* in G (adapted)

735 Bartók, No. 39 from *44 Duets*, Vol. II

Compound (Super) Triplets

The following rhythms include compound triplets, also called super triplets, three notes that occur in the space of two beats. To prepare, perform rhythm 736 while conducting in two. In measures 4-5, perform only the notes with stems up, while imagining the triplet division (stems down).

736

Now compare measures 3, 5, and 7 in rhythm 737a with those in rhythm 737b. Rhythm 737a features true compound (super) triplets, which are always evenly spaced. Rhythm 737b includes an unequal pattern of sixteenth notes (3 + 3 + 2) that is often mistaken for compound triplets; these false triplets are sometimes called "Broadway" or "rumba" triplets.

737a

737b

♩ Beat Unit

738

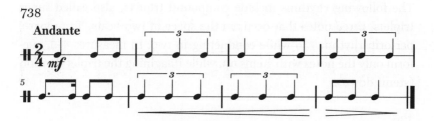

739

740

741

742

Duets and Trios

747

Andantino

748

Allegro con moto

♩ **Beat Unit**

749

Prestissimo

750

Largo

751

Alla marcia

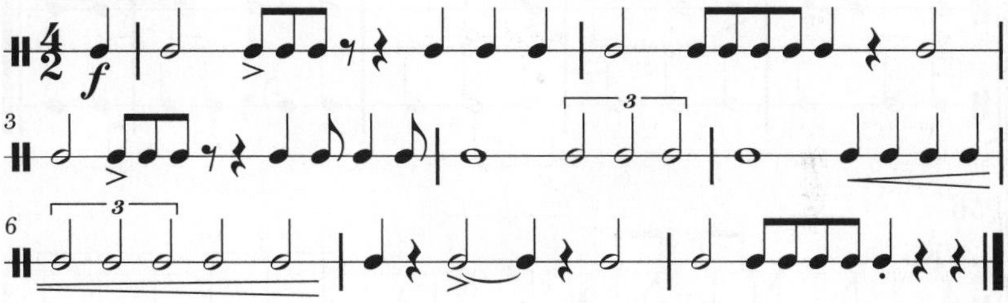

752

Lento

753

Waltz

754

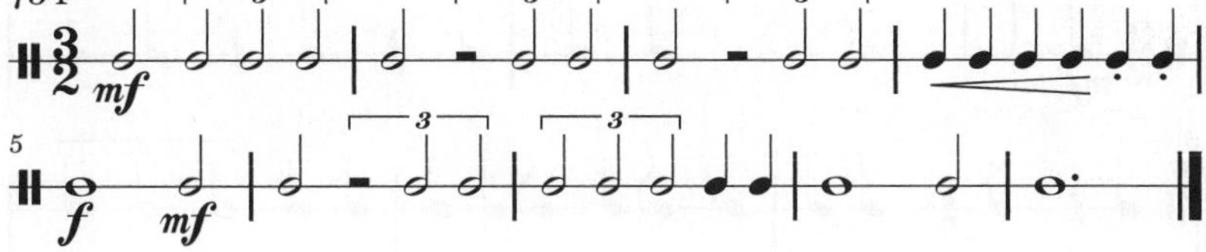

Duets

755

756

757

Harmonizing Modal Melodies

Refer to Chapter 13 for instructions on harmonizing melodies, then accompany yourself at the piano as you and your classmates sing the following melodies.

758 "Canoeing Song" (traditional)

759 "Scarborough Fair" (traditional)

760 Bartók, *Hungarian Folk Song*

761 George Gershwin and Ira Gershwin, "Oh, Lord, I'm on My Way," from *Porgy and Bess*

O,   Lord,_____ I'm on my   way._____   I'm on my

way_____   to   a heav'n - ly   land._____

762 "Morrison's Jig" (traditional)

Modes can have conclusive and inconclusive cadences, too.

CHAPTER 17

Melody:

- Mixed beat divisions
- Singing diminished triads and seventh chords
- Harmonizing melodies

Rhythm:

- Compound (super) duplets

In this chapter you'll learn to:

- Perform melodies with both simple and compound beat divisions
- Recognize and perform arpeggiations of the vii°7 chord in different inversions
- Harmonize melodies
- Improvise melodies based on diminished triads and seventh chords
- Perform compound (super) duplets by yourself and with others

---

Improvisation 17.1: Diminished Triads and Seventh Chords

A. The following four rhythms serve as the basis for improvising melodies. Clap, tap, or sing on a neutral syllable each rhythm while conducting in preparation for improvising your own melodies.

(1)

Moderato

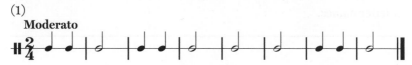

(2)

Waltz

(3)

March

(4)

Sweetly

B. Choose one of the rhythms (1-4), and improvise melodies using the notes of the vii° chord, the vii°7 chord and the vii⌀7 chord. End on *do* (1̂). Perform the following examples, and then create your own melodies.

vii°

| *ti* | *re* | *fa* | | *fa* | *re* | *ti* | *fa* | | *re* | | *ti* | *re* | *do* |
| 7̂ | 2̂ | 4̂ | | 4̂ | 2̂ | 7̂ | 4̂ | | 2̂ | | 7̂ | 2̂ | 1̂ |

vii°7

| *ti* | *re* | *fa* | *le* | *fa* | *re* | *fa* | *le* | *fa* | *re* | *fa* | *re* | *ti* | *re* | *fa* | *re* | *ti* | *re* | *do* |
| 7̂ | 2̂ | 4̂ | ♭6̂ | 4̂ | 2̂ | 4̂ | ♭6̂ | 4̂ | | 2̂ | 4̂ | 2̂ | 7̂ | 2̂ | 4̂ | 2̂ | 7̂ | 2̂ | 1̂ |

vii⌀7

| *ti* | *re* | *fa* | *la* | *la* | *fa* | *la* | *fa* | *la* | *fa* | *la* | *fa* | *re* | *fa* | *re* | *ti* | *do* |
| 7̂ | 2̂ | 4̂ | 6̂ | 6̂ | 4̂ | 6̂ | 4̂ | 6̂ | 4̂ | 6̂ | 4̂ | 2̂ | 4̂ | 2̂ | 7̂ | 1̂ |

C. With a partner, perform exercise B. While facing each other, alternate measures.

Quick Composition Notate your favorite improvisation on a single staff showing the correct key and meter signature. Exchange with a peer and sing each other's part with solfège syllables, scale-degree numbers, or letter names.

Mixed Beat Divisions

Before singing the next group of melodies, prepare by establishing the meter's simple beat division, then alternate between simple and compound divisions as notated. Associate the notated pitches that end the phrases with their sound and decide if a cadence is conclusive, less conclusive, or inconclusive.

763 Liszt, *Hungarian Rhapsody* No. 15

764 Mahler, Symphony No. 2, fifth movement

765 Chausson, "Les Papillons," Op. 2, No. 3

poco rit.

766 Chopin, Nocturne in G Minor, Op. 37, No. 1

767 Beach, "Chanson d'Amour" ("Song of Love")

768 Bach, Fugue in E Minor, from *The Well-Tempered Clavier*, Book II, BWV 879

Observe the subtle relationship between the descending-line portion of the compound melody (beginning in measure 2, beat 4, with the equivalent durations of half notes: C-B-A-G-F♯s) and the same series of pitches in diminution (beginning in measure 5, beat 3: C-B-A-G-F♯s).

For the next five melodies, perform first with solfège syllables or scale-degree numbers, and then with the text.

769 "Aine, dé, trois, Caroline" (Creole folk song)

Aine, dé, trois, Ca-ro-line Ça, ça, yé comme ça, ma chère!

Aine, dé, trois, Ca-ro-line Ça, ça, yé comme ça, ma chère!

Pa-pa di "Non," Ma-man di "Oui," C'est li m'ou-lé, c'est li ma pren.

Ya pas lar-zan, poùa-che-té ca-banne, C'est li m'ou-le, c'est li ma pren.

770 "Belle Layotte" (Creole folk song)

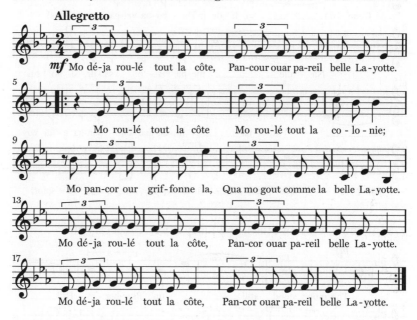

Mo dé-ja rou-lé tout la côte, Pan-cour ouar pa-reil belle La-yotte.

Mo rou-lé tout la côte Mo rou-lé tout la co-lo-nie;

Mo pan-cor our grif-fonne la, Qua mo gout comme la belle La-yotte.

Mo dé-ja rou-lé tout la côte, Pan-cor ouar pa-reil belle La-yotte.

Mo dé-ja rou-lé tout la côte, Pan-cor ouar pa-reil belle La-yotte.

771 Brahms, "Guter Rat," Op. 75, No. 2, from *Four Ballades and Romances* (adapted)

Lebhaft und lustig

Ach Mut - ter, lie - be Mut - ter, ach gebt mir ei - nen Rat! Es rei - tet mir al - le früh - mor - gen ein hur - ti - ger Reu - ter nach, ein hur - ti - ger Reu - ter nach.

772 Yradier, "*La Paloma*," (adapted)

Cuan - do sa - lí de la Ha - ba - na val - ga - me Dios! Na - die me ha vis - to sa - lir, si no fui yo. Yu - na lin - da gau - chi - nan - ga a - llá voy yo! que se vi - no tras de mí que sí se - gñor.

773 Al Lewis, Vincent Stock, and Larry Rose, "Blueberry Hill"

mf

The moon stood still on Blue - ber - ry Hill and lin - gered un - til my dreams came true.

Ensemble Melodies

774 Haydn, Piano Sonata No. 18 in B♭ Major, second movement (adapted)

775 Radziwill, *Polonaise* (adapted)

Tapping the eighth notes will help you perform the triplet correctly. Sing the melody while playing the bass, or perform as a trio.

776 Haydn, String Quartet in F Major, Op. 3, No. 5, second movement, Trio (adapted).

Singing vii°7

The following étude (777) features the common progressions i-vii°7-i, i-vii°6-i6, and i-vii°$^4_3$-i6. The accompaniment is provided as a guide. The vii°7 chord is often suggested by the outline of intervals d7 and A2, which are created by *ti* ($\hat{7}$) and *le* ($\flat\hat{6}$) in the harmonic minor scale.

- Sing with the accompaniment to help tune the chord, then without.

- Follow the melodic tendencies of vii°7's chord tones: *ti* ($\hat{7}$) leads to *do* ($\hat{1}$); *le* ($\flat\hat{6}$) falls to *sol* ($\hat{5}$); *fa* ($\hat{4}$) falls to *me* ($\flat\hat{3}$).

- Sing in the parallel major. Recall that the leading-tone seventh chord's quality is half-diminished (vii°7).

777

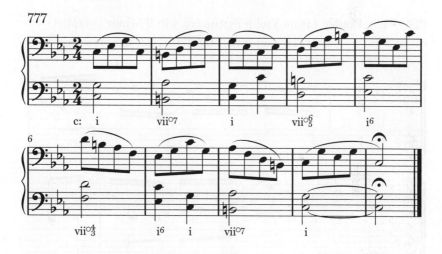

778 Bach, Fugue in C Minor, BWV 546

Measure 3 outlines a vii°7.

779 Bach, Invention No. 4 in D Minor, BWV 775

Measure 2 outlines a vii°7, which has been filled in with passing tones.

780 Beethoven, String Quartet in F Major, Op. 18, No. 1, second movement (adapted)

The arrows show a vii°7, which is filled in with passing tones and embellished with a chromatic lower neighbor.

781 Bach, Double I from Violin Partita No. 1 in B Minor (adapted)

In measure 1 *ti* ($\hat{7}$) and *le* ($\flat\hat{6}$) suggest vii°7. Follow the guide tones in the lower staff to help you perform this compound melody.

Harmonizing Melodies

Refer to Chapter 13 for instructions on harmonizing melodies, then accompany yourself at the piano as you and your classmates sing the following melodies.

782 Wolf, "Das verlassene Mägdlein" ("The Abandoned Maiden")

783 Handel, Fugue from Suite in F Major (G. 178)

Try hamonizing the last two measures using ii6-V7-I. Could IV-V7-I work, too?

Compound (Super) Duplets

The following rhythms include compound duplets, also called super duplets, two notes that occur in the space of three beats. To prepare, perform rhythm 784 while conducting in three. In measures 3-4 perform only the notes with stems up, while imagining the duplet division (stems down).

784
Andante

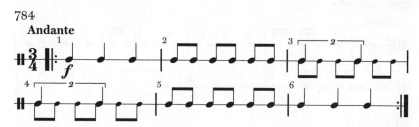

Simple Meter

Rhythm 785 is a *palindrome*; measures 5-8 are the exact reverse (retrograde) of measures 1-4. In measures 3 and 6, imagine the duplet division of the beat, but articulate only the first note of the measure and the second note of the second beat.

785
Moderato

786
Allegretto

Duets

793

794

Lively

Compound Meter

For compound (super) duplets in compound meter we can use simple (sub) duplets to precisely place the compound (super) duplets. To prepare, first compare rhythm 795 to rhythm 784, and then perform the latter while conducting in three. In measures 4-5 perform only the notes with stems up, while imagining the duplet division (stems down).

795

Rhythm 796 omits the measures with articulated simple (sub) duplets. In measures 3-4 perform only the notes with stems up, while imagining the duplet division (stems down).

796

797

Allegro

798

Moderato

799

Vivo

800

Sustained

801

Andantino

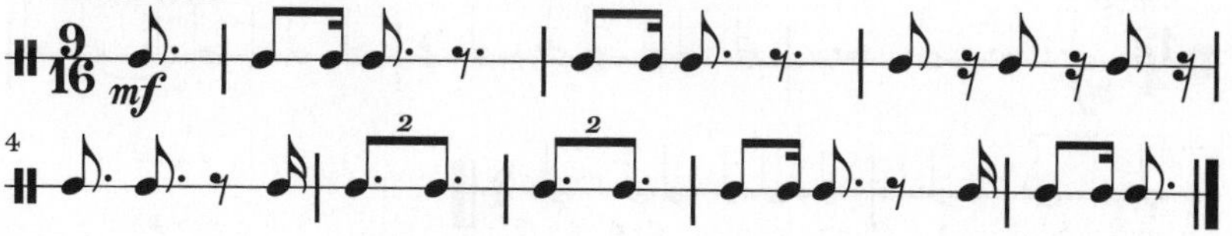

802

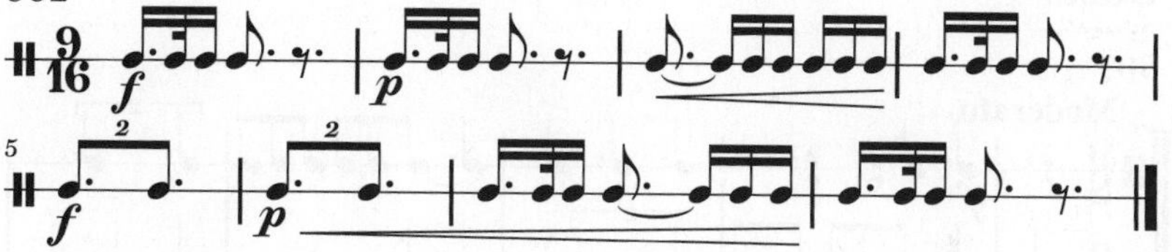

803

Allegro

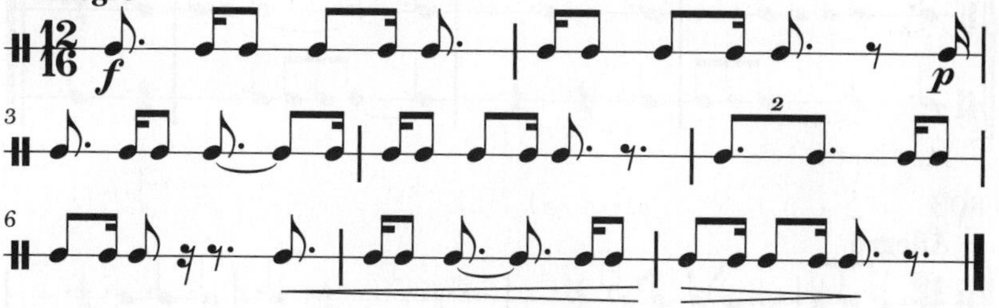

804

Allegro

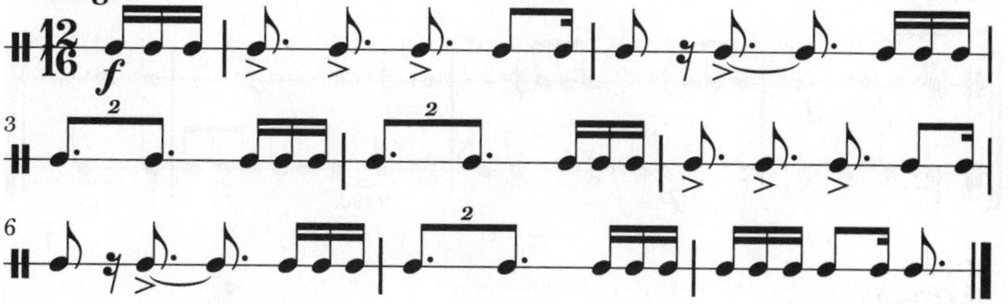

805

Andante

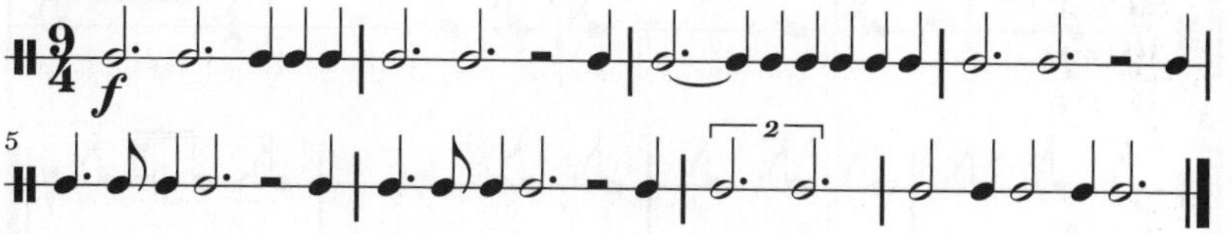

806

Allegro

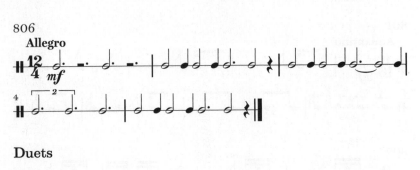

Duets

807

Moderato

808

Allegro

809

Calmly

Melody:

- Phrase structure
- Harmonizing melodies

Rhythm:

- Syncopation 3: Triplets and Duplets

In this chapter you'll learn to:

- Sing and recognize a variety of phrase structures
- Improvise periods by yourself and with a partner
- Harmonize melodies
- Perform syncopations that incorporate duplets and triplets

Sentences

A sentence is a phrase comprised of three segments, often in the proportion 1:1:2. In a four-measure phrase, the sentence might be 1 + 1 + 2 measures. In longer phrases, the sentence may still follow the same proportion (e.g., 2 + 2 + 4). Segment 1 states an idea, which is repeated or varied in segment 2; segment 3, which may or may not be related to the original idea, leads to a cadence. (Recall the first phrase of Beethoven's Fifth Symphony.)

810 Schubert, String Quartet in E♭ Major, Op. 125, No. 1, second movement (adapted)

811 Bach, Fugue in C Minor, from *The Well-Tempered Clavier*, Book I, BWV 847

812 Handel, Sonatina, HWV 585 (adapted)

813 George Gershwin and Ira Gershwin, "'S Wonderful"

'S won - der - ful!_____   'S mar - vel-ous!_____

You should care_____   for   me!_____

814 Foster, "Camptown Ladies"

Gwine to run all   night!   Gwine to run all   day!   I'll__

bet my mo-ney on de bob-tail nag.   Some-bo-dy bet on de bay.

Periods

A period is typically a two-phrase harmonic structure: an inconclusive tonal motion followed by a conclusive one. The first phrase, the antecedent, initiates a harmonic motion that resolves in the second, the consequent. The antecedent usually cadences on V; the consequent phrase always reaches a perfect authentic cadence (PAC). Some theorists define the antecedent-consequent relationship strictly, reserving the term "period" for only those structures of HC-PAC. Others permit different weak-strong phrases (e.g., IAC-PAC).

815 Based on Mozart's Piano Sonata in D Major, K. 576, first movement (adapted)

816 Based on the traditional Shaker melody "Simple Gifts" (adapted)

817 Based on Mendelssohn's "Spring Song," from *Songs Without Words*, Op. 62, No. 6 (adapted)

818 "El Coqui" ("Little Frog") (traditional)

819 Beethoven, Symphony No. 8, first movement (adapted)

820 Tony Velona and Remo Capra, "O Bambino"

821 Elton John and Tim Rice, "Can You Feel the Love Tonight?"

And can you feel_ the love____ to-night,____

how it's laid_ to rest?____ It's e-nough_ to make

kings_ and_ vag-a-bonds_ be-lieve the ver - y best._____

822 Tom Blackburn and George Bruns, "Ballad of Davy Crockett"

Born on a moun-tain top in Ten - nes - see, Green-est state in the

land of the free, Raised in the woods so's he knew ev-'ry tree,

kilt him a b'ar when he was on - ly three.

823 Lionel Richie, "Three Times a Lady"

Thanks for the times that you've giv - en me._ The

mem-'ries_ are all_ in my mind._

824 Based on Schubert's "Des Müllers Blumen" ("The Miller's Flowers"), from *Die schöne Müllerin* (adapted)

Note that in the following excerpts periods can also be constructed from two or more sentences!

825 Petzold, Minuet, from the *Anna Magdalena Bach Notebook*

826 Mozart, Piano Sonata, K. 331, first movement

Ensemble Melodies

827 Haydn, String Quartet in G Major, Op. 3, No. 3, third movement (adapted)

828 Beethoven, German Dance No. 3

Sing *le* (♭6̂) for D♭ and *fi* (♯4̂) for B♮.

829 Clementi, Sonatina in G Major, Op. 36, No. 5, Rondo

Play the left hand and sing the melody, or perform as a trio.

830 Morley, "Sing We and Chant It"

Improvisation 18.1: Periods _____

This étude will help you learn to improvise a parallel period. First sing line 1 to learn the melodic outline of each tune in lines 2–5. Sing parts 2–5 as individual melodic lines, or improvise a new variant of the melody by jumping from line to line on each measure or half measure.

Variations

- Sing with a partner, alternating phrases, then alternating measures or half measures.

- Choose a theme and invent a text to fit with the first phrase. Have your partner respond in the second phrase with a text that fits your theme.

Quick Composition Notate your favorite improvisation on a grand staff showing the correct key and meter signature. Exchange with a peer and sing each other's part with solfège syllables, scale-degree numbers, or letter names.

Harmonizing Melodies

Refer to Chapter 13 for instructions on harmonizing melodies, then accompany yourself at the piano as you and your classmates sing the following melody.

831 "Amazing Grace" (traditional)

832 Haydn, String Quartet in D Major, Op. 33, No. 6, first movement

Try using a neighboring $^6_4$ in your hamonization of measure 1, and I⁶-V$^4_3$-I-V in measure 2.

Syncopation 3: Duplets and Triplets

In the following rhythms, syncopation occurs when a borrowed division of the beat is stressed. In these cases, consider the syncopated notes as falling directly between beats (duplets) or moving either directly *toward* or *from* the beat (triplets). Observe the many ways in which this can occur as you perform these rhythms while conducting.

833

840
Moderato

841
Andante

842
Moderato

843
Calmy

844
Allegro

Fine

subito *p*

Duet

850

Tempo guisto

CHAPTER 19

Melody:

- Sequences
- Harmonizing melodies

Rhythm:

- Hemiola

In this chapter you'll learn to:

- Recognize and perform melodic sequences by yourself and with others
- Improvise melodic sequences over a given harmonic progression
- Harmonize melodies
- Perform hemiolas in two- and three-part rhythms

Sequences

A sequence is a musical pattern stated at different pitch levels. Discover the sequence type by determining the harmonic progression implied at its beginning. Here, focus on the implied root movement beginning in measure 5, which falls by fifths.

851 "Music Alone Shall Live" (traditional; canon in three parts)

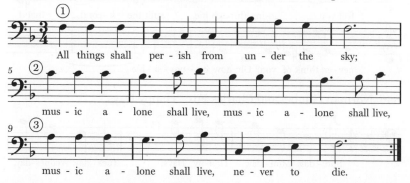

852 Jacquet de la Guerre, Chaconne, from *Pièces de Clavecin*

853 Jackie Rae and James Last, "Happy Heart" (adapted)

Mus - ic fills my soul___ now, I've lost all con-trol___ now,

I'm not half, I'm whole___ now with your love.___

854 Manos Hadjidakis, "Never on a Sunday" (adapted)

Come an - y day_____ and you'll be my guest,___

___ an-y day you say,___ but my day of rest.___

855 Amdando Manzanero and Sid Wayne, "It's Impossible"

Can I hold you___ clos - er to me,___ and not

feel you___ go-ing through me,___ split the se-cond___ that I

nev-er think of you? Oh, how im - pos - si - ble.___

856 Norman Gimbel and Charles Fox, "Happy Days"

Sun - day, Mon - day, Hap-py Days;___ Tues - day, Wednes-day,

857 Haydn, String Quartet in E♭ Major, Op. 50, No. 3, first movement (adapted)

858 Schubert, Piano Sonata in G Major, Op. 147, third movement

859 Jay Livingson and Ray Evans, "Mona Lisa"

Mo-na Li-sa, Mo-na Li-sa men have named you. You're so like the la-dy with the mys-tic smile. Is it on-ly 'cause you're lone-ly___ they have blamed you for that Mo-na Li-sa strange-ness___ in your smile?

860 Beethoven, Kyrie, from *Mass in C*, Op. 86

Ensemble Melodies

861 Hensel, *Notturno* in G Minor

862 Bach, Sonata II, from *Six Trio Sonatas*, BWV 526

863 Haydn, String Quartet in E♭ Major, Op. 50, No. 3, second movement (adapted)

Discover the sequence type by determining the harmonic progression implied at the beginning of each phrase.

864 C. P. E. Bach, Sonata in F Major, W. 62/9 (adapted)

865 Haydn, Piano Sonata No. 33 in D Major, third movement (adapted)

866 Bach, Versus V, from Cantata No. 4, *Christ lag in Todesbanden* (*Christ Lay in Death's Bonds*), BWV 4 (adapted)

867 Haydn, String Quartet in C Major, Op. 20, No. 2, third movement (adapted)

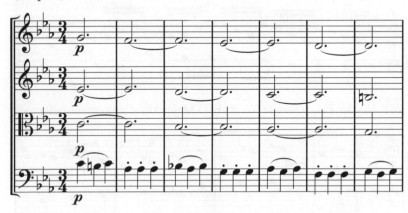

868 Haydn, String Quartet in E♭ Major, Op. 50, No. 3, fourth movement (adapted)

Improvisation 19.1: Singing and Playing Diatonic Sequences

Use each of the following sequences as the basis for improvisation. Play the outline at the keyboard while singing an improvised melody, or improvise on your instrument while someone improvises a keyboard accompaniment.

Strategies

- Because the patterns are sequential, think of a motive that you can perform over a two-chord segment. Then transpose this pattern down to the next segment.

- Compound melodies work beautifully over these sequences. Create motives that imply two melodic strands.

- Follow the strategies from Improvisation 14.1.

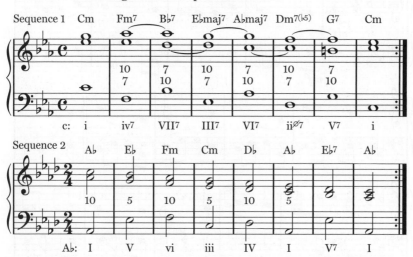

Variations

- Change to triple meter.

- Change to compound meter.

- Perform each sequence in its parallel minor key.

- Add melodic embellishments, such as suspensions (e.g., in sequence 2: I–V$^{4-3}$–vi$^{9-8}$–iii$^{4-3}$, etc.).

- Chromaticize sequence 1 with secondary dominants.

- Assign the given soprano voice to a different part to create a different linear intervallic pattern (LIP).

- Change the inversions of the chords (e.g., in sequence 1: i–iv^6–VII–III^6, etc.).

Quick Composition Notate your favorite improvisation on a single staff showing the correct key and meter signature. Exchange with a peer and sing each other's part with solfège syllables, scale-degree numbers, or letter names.

Harmonizing Melodies

Refer to Chapter 13 for instructions on harmonizing melodies, then accompany yourself at the piano as you and your classmates sing the following melody.

869 Dottie West, Bill Davis, and Dianne Whiles, "Country Sunshine"

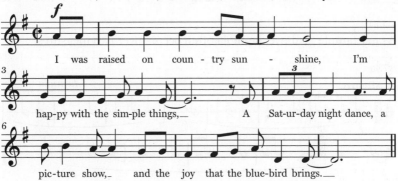

870 Haydn, String Quartet in E♭ Major, Op. 20, No. 1, second movement (adapted)

871 Roger Miller, "Oo-De-Lally"

Hemiola

Six equal note values may be divided into two groups of three or three groups of two. When one of these divisions is prevalent, a temporary change to the other creates *hemiola*. One common example of hemiola occurs when two dotted-half notes are replaced by three half notes (examples 1 and 2), but any values in the ratio of 3:2 create hemiola.

Perform examples 1 and 2 first by tapping both parts, then sing one part while tapping the other.

872

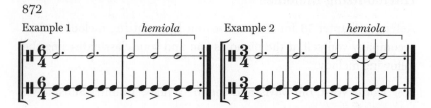

As in example 2, above, hemiola often occurs over two measures.

873a

873b

Conduct rhythms 874a and 874b as the meter signature indicates (in two for $\frac{6}{8}$ and in three for $\frac{3}{4}$.

874a

Andante

874b

Andante

Compound Meter

875

Allegretto

876

Moderato

877

Andante

Duets

Simple Meter

881

CHAPTER 20

Melody:

- Tonicization of V

Rhythm:

- Combined beat divisions (3:2 and 2:3) in simple meters

In this chapter you'll learn to:

- Perform melodies that outline secondary dominants and leading-tone chords to V
- Harmonize melodies with secondary-dominant-function chords
- Perform rhythms in which triple and duple divisions of the beat occur simultaneously in simple meter
- Improvise musical periods that include a secondary dominant to V

Improvisation 20.1: Tonicizing the Dominant (V) in Musical Periods

While one person plays the following accompaniment, everyone in turn should improvise a melody that includes a secondary dominant seventh of V to conclude the first phrase. Note the crucial alteration of *fa* ($\hat{4}$) to *fi* ($\sharp\hat{4}$) in both major and minor. Follow the strategies from Improvisation 14.1. Before anyone sings aloud, have someone play the progression several times while the class silently improvises. Each person should accompany as well as perform a melody.

$$B\flat:\ I \quad ii^6 \quad V^7/V \quad V \quad I \quad ii^6 \quad V \quad I$$

Variations

- "Trade fours." One person improvises the first four bars, and then a second responds with a conclusion to the phrase.

- Try a variety of styles (art song, pop song, jazz, etc.). Create rhythmic embellishments in the accompaniment that are characteristic of the chosen style. Change the tempo, mood, and character to reflect your choice.

- Perform each example in its parallel minor mode.

- Transpose the examples to keys ranging from three flats to three sharps.

- Change the meter to compound meter.

- Transcribe the examples for instruments available in class, and play the accompaniment on those instruments. Each player should improvise on his or her chosen part.

- Create a "groove" by adding one or more percussionists who play on objects available in class (books, desktops, pencils, etc.).

Quick Composition Notate your favorite improvisation on a single staff showing the correct key and meter signature. Exchange with a peer and sing each other's part with solfège syllables, scale-degree numbers, or letter names.

Harmonizing Melodies With Secondary-Dominant-Function Chords

Sing each of the following melodies, and then harmonize them. Sing again and accompany yourself with your harmonization. At places indicated with an arrow, use a secondary dominant or leading-tone chord to V.

885 Haydn, String Quartet in G Major, Op. 64, No. 4, third movement (violin 1 part)

886 Richard Rodgers, "People Will Say We're in Love," from *Oklahoma!*

Treat the chromatic pitches in measures 5-6 as neighbor tones.

887 Peter Yarrow, "Puff, the Magic Dragon"

Here is a rare chance (in m. 2) to play the mediant triad, which is used when the melody falls through *ti* ($\hat{7}$).

888 "The Ash Grove" (traditional Welsh folk song)

889 Rodgers and Hammerstein, "Climb Ev'ry Mountain," from *The Sound of Music*

Climb Ev'-ry Moun-tain, search high and low,

Fol - low ev' - ry by - way, ev' - ry path you know.

890 Türk, Gavotte (adapted)

891 Schubert, "Mit dem grünen Lautenband" ("With the Lute's Green Ribbon"), from *Die schöne Müllerin*

More Melodies that Tonicize V

In the following melodies, observe how scale degree $\sharp\hat{4}$ signals a tonicization of V.

892 Mendelssohn, "Volkslied" ("Folk Song"), Op. 47, No. 4

893 Mendelssohn, "Lieblingsplätzchen" ("Favorite Place"), Op. 99, No. 3

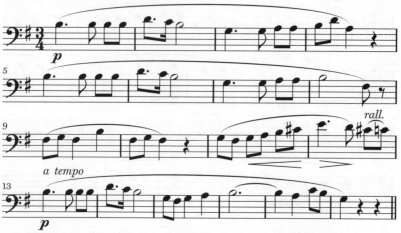

894 R. Strauss, "Für fünfzehn Pfennige" ("For Fifteen Pennies")

895 Mendelssohn, "Frühlingslied" ("Spring Song"), Op. 79, No. 2

896 Reinecke, Polka

In the following melodies, V is tonicized, but scale degree ♯4̂ is either implied or appears in another voice.

897 Beach, "Chanson d'Amour" ("Song of Love")
Note the duplets in compound meter. When harmonizing, tonicize V at the end.

898 Brahms, String Sextet No. 1 in B♭ Major, Rondo (cello part)
When harmonizing, try a deceptive resolution in measure 4 and V7/V at the cadence.

899 Mendelssohn, "Wartend" ("Waiting"), Op. 9, No. 3 (adapted)

Ensemble Melodies

900 Brahms, *Liebeslieder Waltzer*, Op. 52, No. 11

901 Beethoven, Piano Sonata in G Major, Op. 79, third movement

902 Pescetti, *Presto* (adapted)

903 Beethoven, *German Dance* No. 6, Trio

904 Thomas Morley, "Now Is the Month of Maying"

905 Bach, "Herr Jesu Christ, dich zu uns wend" ("Lord Jesus Christ, Turn to Us"), from *Eighteen Chorale Preludes for Organ*, BWV 655 (adapted)

Combined Beat Divisions in Simple Meters

To internalize the feeling of 2:3 and 3:2, practice rhythms 906a and 906b by tapping the upward stems with your right hand and the downward stems with your left hand.

906a

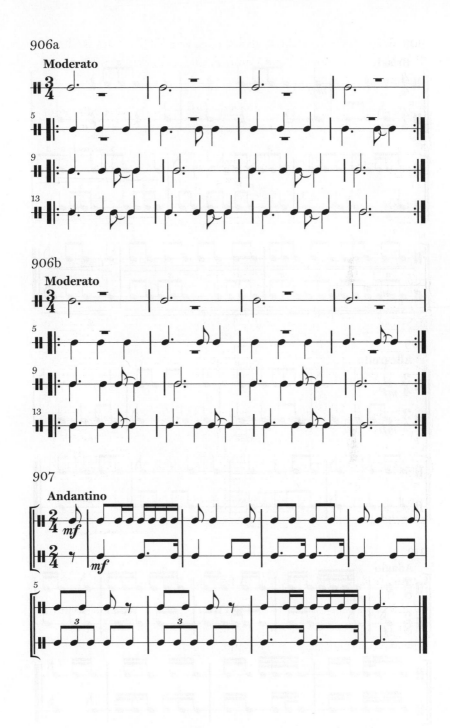

906b

907

914

Allegretto

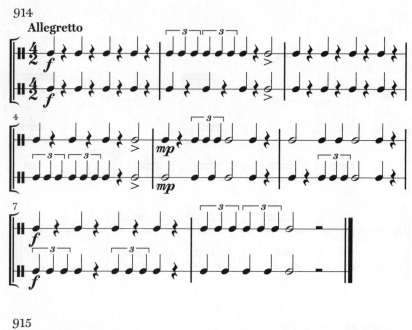

915

Tempo di valzer

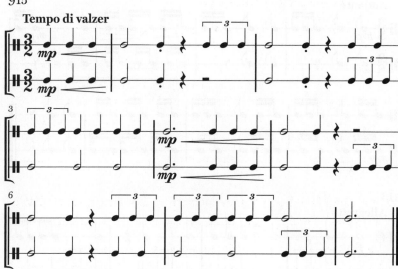

CHAPTER 21

Melody:

- Tonicization of scale degrees other than V

Rhythm:

- Combined beat divisions (3:2 and 2:3) in compound meters

In this chapter you'll learn to:

- Perform melodies that outline secondary dominants and leading-tone chords to scale degrees other than $\hat{5}$
- Harmonize melodies with secondary-dominant-function chords
- Perform rhythms in which triple and duple divisions of the beat occur simultaneously in compound meter
- Improvise musical periods that include secondary dominants to a variety of scale degrees

Improvisation 21.1: Tonicizing the Subdominant (IV) in Musical Periods

While one person plays the following accompaniment, everyone in turn should improvise a melody that includes a secondary dominant seventh of IV in the first phrase. Note the crucial alteration of *ti* ($\hat{7}$) to *te* ($\flat\hat{7}$) in major, and both *ti* ($\hat{7}$) to *te* ($\flat\hat{7}$) and *me* ($\flat\hat{3}$) to *mi* ($\hat{3}$) in minor. Follow the strategies from Improvisation 14.1. Before anyone sings aloud, have someone play the progression several times while the class silently improvises. Each person should accompany as well as perform a melody.

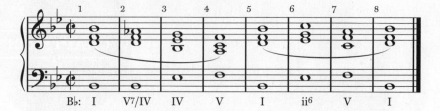

Variations

- "Trade fours." One person improvises the first four bars, and then a second responds with a conclusion to the phrase.

- Try a variety of styles (art song, pop song, jazz, etc.). Create rhythmic embellishments in the accompaniment that are characteristic of the chosen style. Change the tempo, mood, and character accordingly.

- Perform each example in its parallel minor mode.

- Transpose the examples to keys ranging from three flats to three sharps.

- Change the meter to compound meter.

- Transcribe the examples for instruments available in class. Play the accompaniment on those instruments. Let each player improvise within his or her part.

- Create a "groove" by adding one or more percussionists who play objects available in class (books, desktops, pencils, etc.).

Quick Composition Notate your favorite improvisation on a single staff showing the correct key and meter signature. Exchange with a peer and sing each other's part with solfège syllables, scale-degree numbers, or letter names.

Harmonizing Melodies with Secondary-Dominant-Function Chords

Sing each of the three melodies that follow, and then harmonize them. Sing again and accompany yourself with your harmonization. At places indicated with an arrow, use a secondary dominant or leading-tone chord.

916 Jacquet de la Guerre, "Air," from *Semelé*

917 Brahms, *Liebeslieder Waltzer*, Op. 39, No. 15

Observe measure 6 to determine the harmony that is being tonicized in measure 7!

918 Rodgers and Hammerstein, "Climb Ev'ry Mountain," from *The Sound of Music*

Melodies that Tonicize Scale Degrees Other than V

In the following melodies, observe how raised scale degrees often suggest a tonicization of the scale degree a half step higher.

919 Fred Ebb and John Kander, "Willkommen," from *Cabaret*

920 Mendelssohn, "Gruß" ("Greeting"), Op. 19, No. 5

921 James Rado, Gerome Ragni, and Galt MacDermot, "Where Do I Go?"

Here the raised notes function as chromatic neighbor tones. In measure 3, experiment with a tonicization of ii.

922 Bart Howard, "Fly Me to the Moon"

923 Mendelssohn, "Auf Flügeln des Gesanges" ("On the Wings of Song"), Op. 34, No. 2

924 Hensel, Song No. 3, from *Songs for Pianoforte*

The next three melodies feature the common alteration of *ti* ($\hat{7}$) to *te* ($\flat\hat{7}$) for tonicizations of the subdominant (IV).

925 Dorothy Fields and Cy Coleman, "Sweet Charity"

Here was a man__ with no dream and no plan__ and one lone-ly night I found__ Sweet Char-i-ty.__ You make life fun__ for me, oh, what it's done__ for me, hav-ing you a-round.__

926 Schubert, "Dankgesang an den Bach" ("Song of Thanks to the Brook"), from *Die schöne Müllerin*

927 Rodgers and Hammerstein, "It Might as Well Be Spring," from *State Fair*

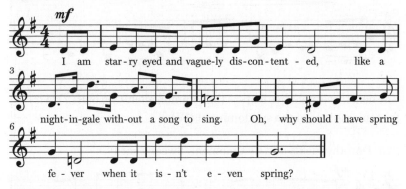

I am star-ry eyed and vague-ly dis-con-tent - ed, like a

night-in-gale with-out a song to sing. Oh, why should I have spring

fe - ver when it is - n't e - ven spring?

Ensemble Melodies

928 Bach, "Ich liebe Jesum alle Stund" ("I Love Jesus in Every Hour")

929 Beethoven, *German Dance* No. 6, Minuet (adapted)

Tempo di menuetto

930 Bach, "Nun lob', mein' Seel', den Herren" ("Now Praise, My Soul, the Lord"), BWV 390

From the anacrusis to measure 5 to beat 1 of measure 6, switch solfège syllables or scale-degree numbers to reflect the tonicization of vi.

931 Bach, Bourrée II, from Suite No. 2 for Orchestra, (adapted)

932 Purcell, "Air" (adapted)

933 Bach, "Herr, wie du willst, so schicks mit mir" ("Lord, Deal with Me as You Wish"), BWV 73

Look for raised pitches to act as leading tones to the scale degree they tonicize.

934 Bach, Duet 2, from *Clavierübung III*

935 Bach, "Jesus Christus, unser Heiland" ("Jesus Christ, Our Savior"), from *Eighteen Chorale Preludes for Organ*, BWV 666 (adapted)

Sing the chorale (first line), then the prelude that follows to discover how Bach derives and develops his motive.

936 Bach, Duet 3, from *Clavierübung III* (adapted)

Combined Beat Divisions in Compound Meters

To internalize the feeling of 2:3 and 3:2, practice rhythm 939 by tapping the upward stems with your right hand and the downward stems with your left hand.

937

Moderato

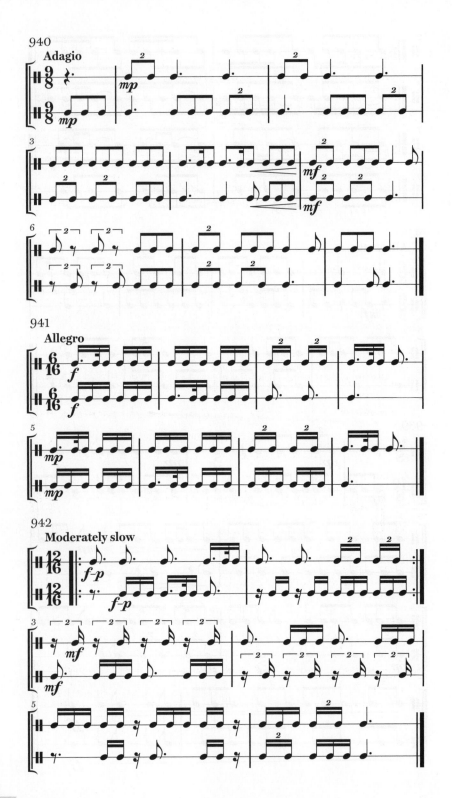

943

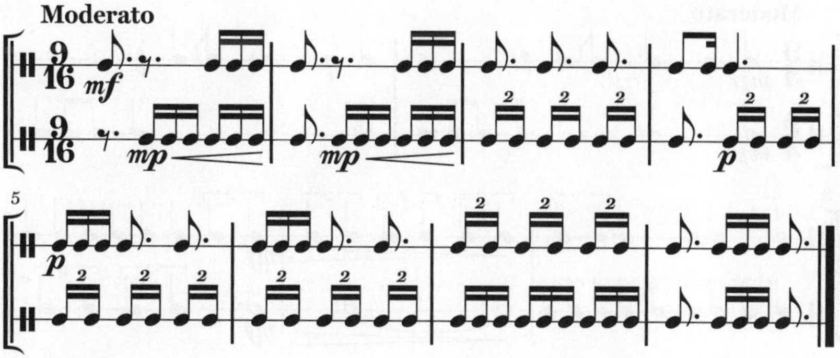

944

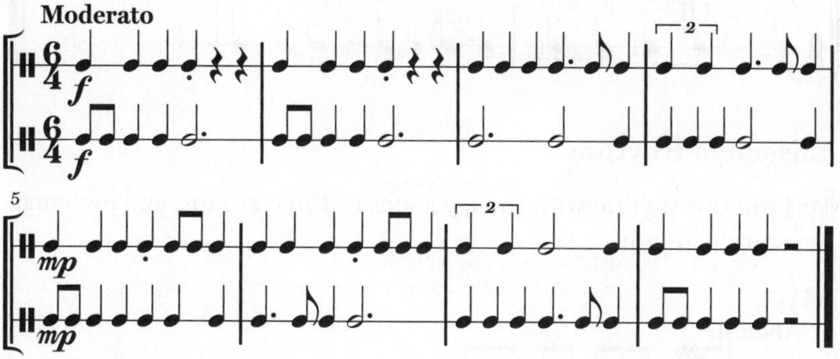

945

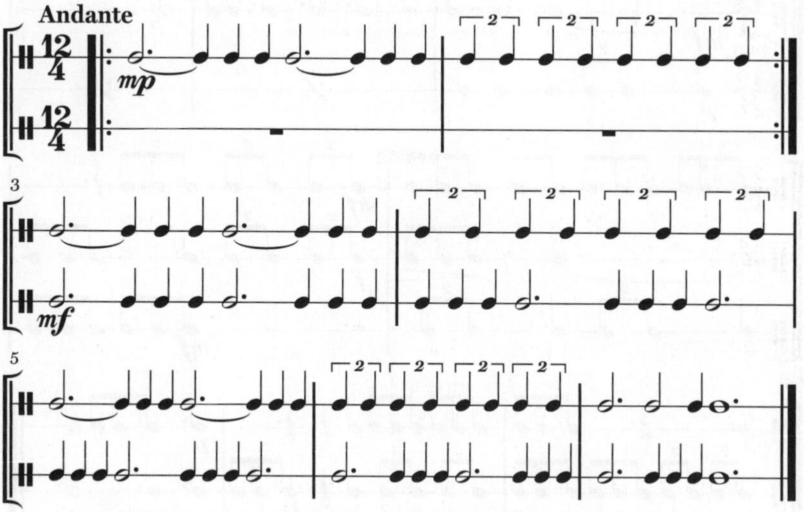

946

Moderato

Ensemble Rhythm

Perform this rhythm with three persons or three groups, and exchange parts at the repeat.

947

Andante

PART III

Chromatic Harmony and Form

CHAPTER 22

Melody:

- Tonicizations (review)
- Modulations to closely related keys (V, III, and v)

Rhythm:

- Changing meters 1: note-value constant (note-value equivalence)

In this chapter you'll learn to:

- Improvise musical periods that modulate to the dominant (V)
- Perform melodies that tonicize other keys
- Perform melodies that modulate to other keys
- Perform rhythms that change meters while keeping a note value constant

Improvisation 22.1: Major-Key Musical Phrases that Modulate To The Dominant (V)

At the keyboard, improvise modulatory phrases in major keys following the plan demonstrated in Keyboard Lesson 22a.

- Start with the bass line alone.
- Add your own soprano melody with the right hand.
- Play the progression as written while singing an improvised melody.

Variations

- Create an interesting texture by playing arpeggios, a "boom-chick" rhythm, and so on.

- Embellish your improvisation with passing tones, neighbor tones, suspensions, and consonant skips.
- Play your own accompaniment while improvising a melody.
- Improvise an accompaniment while a classmate improvises a melody, and then switch roles.
- Create your own key-defining progression.

Quick Composition Notate your favorite improvisation on a grand staff showing the correct key and meter signature. Exchange with a peer and sing each other's part with solfège syllables, scale-degree numbers, or letter names.

Tonicizations (Review)

948 Mendelssohn, "Jagdlied" ("Hunting Song"), Op. 84, No. 3

949 Brahms, String Quartet No. 3 in B♭ Major, second movement

950 Mendelssohn, "Der Mond" ("The Moon"), Op. 86, No. 5

951 Mendelssohn, "Nachtlied" ("Night Song"), Op. 71, No. 6

Ensemble Melody

952 Beethoven, Piano Sonata in A♭ Major, Op. 110, first movement (adapted)

Modulations to V, III, and v

For the following melodies, first identify the starting key. Next, scan the melody for chromatic pitches that suggest a new key, and make a mental note of the syllables applied to them. Finally, identify a point in the melody where you will switch to the new key.

The next four melodies include modulations to V.

953 Bach, No. 13, from *St. John Passion* (adapted)

954 Mendelssohn, "Das erste Veilchen" ("The First Violets"), Op. 19, No. 2

955 Brahms, String Sextet No. 1 in B♭ Major, Rondo

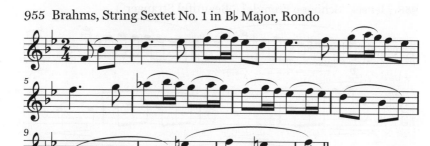

956 Bach, Cello Suite No. 1 in G Major, Courante

The next four melodies demonstrate the common feature of starting in minor and modulating to the relative major (III).

957 Handel, Suite in D Minor, Gigue

958 Hensel, "Schöone Fremde" ("Beautiful Stranger")

959 Purcell, "Or if more influencing to be brisk," from *From Rosy Bow'rs*

Recall that in minor keys, the key of the dominant is minor as well. The next five melodies include modulations to v.

960 Mendelssohn, "Erntelied" ("Harvest Song"), Op. 8, No. 4

961 Hensel, "Schwanenlied" ("Swan Song"), from *Six Songs*, Op. 1, No. 1

962 Mendelssohn, String Quartet in E♭ Major, Op. 12, fourth movement

963 Mendelssohn, "Pagenlied" ("The Page's Song") (adapted)

964 Mendelssohn, "Suleika," Op. 34, No. 4 (adapted)

Ensemble Melodies

The ensemble melodies emphasize modulations from I to V, i to III, and i to v.

965 Purcell, "A Farewell" (adapted)

966 Hensel, "Schilflied" ("Reed Song")

967 Hensel, Suite in F♯ Minor (G. 207), Gigue (adapted)

968 Haydn, String Quartet in C Major, Op. 20, No. 2, first movement (adapted)

969 Beethoven, Piano Sonata in F Minor, Op. 2, No. 1, third movement (adapted)

Changing Meters 1: Note-Value Constant
(Note-Value Equivalence)

Sometimes changes of meter include an indication to show that the *note values* of the outgoing meter remain the same in the new one; ♪ = ♪ or ♩. = ♩., for example. When no such indication is present, this note-value equivalence is assumed.

Conduct the meter changes indicated, paying particular attention to how you show the changes with your conducting gestures.

970

Each of the following melodies demonstrates note-value equivalence. Here, the tempo and beat durations will stay the same, but the number of beats in each bar changes. As you sing, adjust your conducting for these changes.

971

973

974

Notice in the next rhythms that the note representing the beat *division* remains constant. In the following rhythm the eighth note remains constant, but because there are two eighth notes in the simple beats of $\frac{2}{4}$ and three eighth notes in the compound beats of $\frac{6}{8}$ meter, the latter beats will be longer. Your conducting will reflect this with a slower tempo in measures 5-6, and a return to the original tempo in measures 7-8.

975

976

977

Etwas langsam

978

Leicht

979

Animé

980

Schnell

CHAPTER 23

Melody:

- Binary and ternary forms
- Changing meters 1: note-value constant (review)

Rhythm:

- Changing meters 2: beat-unit constant (beat-unit equivalence)

In this chapter you'll learn to:

- Perform solo and ensemble melodies that present complete binary and ternary forms
- Improvise musical phrases that begin in a minor key and modulate to the relative major (III)
- Perform melodies that change meters in which the number of beats per measure changes
- Perform rhythms in which the beat remains constant but the division of the beat changes

---

Improvisation 23.1: Minor-Key Musical Phrases that Modulate from Minor to the Relative Major (III) _____

At the keyboard, improvise modulatory phrases in minor keys following the plan demonstrated in Keyboard Lesson 22a.

- Start with the bass line alone.
- Add your own soprano melody with the right hand.
- Play the progression as written while singing an improvised melody.

Variations

- Create an interesting texture by playing arpeggios, a "boom-chick" rhythm, and so on.
- Embellish your improvisation with passing tones, neighbor tones, suspensions, and consonant skips.
- Play your own accompaniment while improvising a melody.
- Improvise an accompaniment while a classmate improvises a melody, and then switch roles.
- Create your own key-defining progression.

Quick Composition Notate your favorite improvisation on a grand staff showing the correct key and meter signature. Exchange with a peer and sing each other's part with solfège syllables, scale-degree numbers, or letter names.

Binary and Ternary Forms

981 Mozart, String Quartet in B♭ Major, K. 458, Menuetto (adapted)

982 Grieg, String Quartet in G Minor, Op. 27, third movement
(adapted)

Ensemble Melodies

983 Purcell, Minuet (adapted)

984 Purcell, "Me Judah's daughters once caress'd," from *Harmonia Sacra*, Vol. II (adapted)

985 Beethoven, *German Dance* No. 2 (adapted)

986 Jacquet de la Guerre, Suite in D Minor, second Rigadoun
(adapted)

987 Mozart, Allegro in B♭ Major, K. 3

988 Türk, "Evening Song"

989 Mozart, Clarinet Quintet, K. 581, fourth movement (adapted)

990 Purcell, "Or say, ye pow'rs," from *From Rosy Bow'rs*

Changing Meters 1: Note-Value Constant (Review)

Each of the following melodies demonstrates note-value equivalence. Here, the tempo and beat durations will stay the same, but the number of beats in each bar changes. As you sing, adjust your conducting for these changes.

991 Brahms, *Variations on a Hungarian Song*, Op. 21, No. 2

992 Jim Webb, "Galveston"

Gal - ves-ton,__ oh, Gal - ves - ton,

I still hear__ your sea_____ winds__ blow-ing,__

993 Mahler, Symphony No. 2, fifth movement (adapted)

994 Tchaikovsky, String Quartet in F Major, Op. 22, Scherzo (adapted)

Changing Meters 2: Beat-Unit Constant (Beat-Unit Equivalence)

For this type of meter change, two different note values are made equivalent in duration; ♪ = ♪. or ♩ = ♩., for example. Consequently, the duration of the beats will stay the same but the beat division will change.

Rhythms 995a and 995b sound identical. Conduct them in duple meter throughout while keeping the same duration for each beat.

995a

995b

996

997

Andante

998

Lustig

999

Allegretto ($\quarternote = \dottedquarternote$)

1000

Lourd

1005

CHAPTER 24

Melody:

- Counterpoint and contrapuntal practices

Rhythm:

- Recurring meter changes and dual time signatures

In this chapter you'll learn to:

- Perform imitative and nonimitative counterpoint in pairs and groups
- Perform rhythms in which two meters operate simultaneously, by yourself and with others

---

Improvisation 24.1: Figured Basses and Roman Numeral Progressions

Practice realizing the short preparatory exercises that follow (A [1] and B [1]), then incorporate them into the progression that follows (A [2] and B [2]). Use voice-leading identical to that of Keyboard Lessons 12 and 13. Play the realized progression, and sing a melodic variation of an upper part. Perform again, and base your improvisation on a different part.

Strategies

- Sing each part as written, then sing the melody while playing the bass line.
- Create études consisting of a single type of embellishment. For example, sing a variation that consists of nothing but skips within the chords. Sing another that features only upper neighbors, one that features lower neighbors, and so on.
- Improvise melodies that combine ideas from your études into new, original music.

A. (1) Major-key preparation

(2) Figured-bass progression 1

B. (1) Minor-key preparation

(2) Figured-bass progression 2

Quick Composition Notate your favorite improvisation on a grand staff showing the correct key and meter signature. Exchange with a peer and sing each other's part with solfège syllables, scale-degree numbers, or letter names.

Ensemble Melodies

Rounds

The vertical alignment of the vocal entrances reveals the counterpoint in the following round.

1006 Billings, "Babylon" (round in three parts)

Perform the following song as a four-part round. First listen to the melody and try to find logical places for other voices to enter. Write the numbers 1, 2, 3, and 4 above the staff to indicate the points at which each part begins. Sing through the melody twice, sustaining the final note until all performers have concluded.

1007 "Are You Sleeping?" (traditional)

Two-Part Chorale Frameworks

While singing these chorale frameworks notice how the outer parts relate to species counterpoint.

1008 Bach, "Brunnquell aller Güter" ("Fountain of All Good Things")

1009 Bach, "Auf, auf! die rechte Zeit ist hier" ("Up! Up! The Right Time Is Here!")

1010 Bach, "Jesu, deine Liebeswunden" ("Jesus, Your Dear Wounds")

1011 Bach, "Dir, dir, Jehovah, will ich singen ("To You, Jehovah, Will I Sing")

Four-Part Chorale Textures

1012 Bach, "Jesu, meine Fruede" ("Jesus, My Joy"), BWV 227 (adapted)

1013 di Lasso, *Matona mia cara* (*My Dear Lady*)

Melodies with Contrapuntal Accompaniment

1014 Bach, Recitativo, from Cantata No. 51, *Jauchzet Gott in allen Landen* (*Praise God in All Lands*), BWV 51 (adapted)

Translation: Yet feeble praise can still please Him.

1015 Bach, Agnus Dei, from *Mass in B Minor*

1016 Bach, "Et Spiritum Sanctum Dominum" ("And in the Holy
Spirit"), from *Mass in B Minor*

1017 Bach, Violin Partita No. 1 in B Minor, Courante

Play the accompaniment of the grand staff while singing the melodic framework in the top staff. Have the class sing the accompaniment while one person sings the melodic framework and another plays Bach's melody on an instrument.

Imitative Counterpoint

1018 Bach, Invention 6 in E Major, BWV 777 (adapted)

1019 Beethoven, Piano Sonata in A♭ Major, Op. 110, Fugue (adapted)

1020 Handel, Suite in B♭ (G. 33), Gigue

When a part exceeds your range, change octaves as inconspicuously as possible.

1021 Palestrina, *Alleluia tulerunt Dominum*, first three entrances

Even though this piece looks as if it is in C major, use G as the tonic. Sing *te* (♭7̂)
for the F-naturals in the middle part.

1022 Beethoven, Gloria, from *Mass in C*, Op. 86

1023 Bach, No. 8, from *Mass in B Minor*

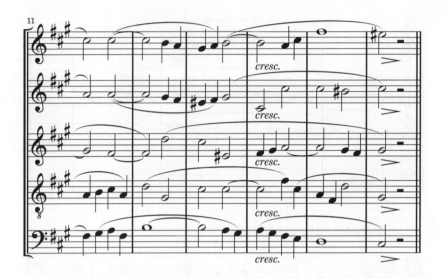

Rhythms: Dual Meter Signatures

When meter changes recur consistently, dual meter signatures are often indicated.

1024

Tempo di Huapango

1025

Allegro

1026

Modéré

1032

1033 Rodrigo, *Concierto de Aranjuez*, first movement (adapted)

1034

1035

CHAPTER 25

Melody:

- Continuous variations
- Sectional variations

Rhythm:

- Super-subdivided beats in slow tempos 1: simple meters

In this chapter you'll learn to:

- Improvise alone and in duets and trios over a ground bass
- Perform a theme and sectional variations of that theme
- Perform slow simple-meter rhythms in which the beat is subdivided then divided again

---

Improvisation 25.1: Continuous Variations

Improvise a series of continuous variations based on the following "Lament." Listen to this accompaniment and practice singing your improvisation.

- *Solos*: Play the outer voices at the keyboard, and improvise the melody. Sing with solfège syllables or scale-degree numbers.

- *Duets*: One person improvises a keyboard accompaniment from the outline while the other improvises a melody. Switch parts and perform again.

- *Trios*: Three instrumentalists improvise a line based on one of the parts. On each repetition, switch parts until each performer has improvised on each part.

Very slow and expressive

e: i   10-10 LIP ———————————— V   VI ii°6 V   i

Perform the bass line by itself. Then on the first repetition, sing a simple melody in counterpoint. On each successive repetition, make your melody more elaborate. After your most elaborate embellishment, recapitulate the simple (first) melody as the last variation.

Quick Composition Notate your favorite improvisation and create a score that includes all parts. Make sure to align the parts so all players can both see and hear each other's part. Use the appropriate clef, key signature, and meter signature. Exchange with a peer and sing each other's part with solfège syllables, scale-degree numbers, or letter names.

Melodies

For the next four melodies, one person performs the ground bass repeatedly while the other person improvises melodic variations.

1036 Bach, *Passacaglia* in C Minor for Organ

1037 Bach, *Art of the Fugue*, Contrapunctus I

1038 Purcell, ground bass from "A New Ground," from *Musick's Hand-Maid* (adapted)

1039 Purcell, ground bass from "Ground in Gamut," from *Musick's Hand-Maid*

The next two melodies are well-known examples of chromatically descending ground basses.

1040 Purcell, "Dido's Lament," from *Dido and Aeneas* (adapted)

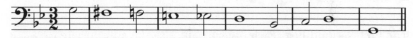

1041 Bach, Crucifixus, from *Mass in B Minor* (adapted)

The next excerpt can be divided into two sections: measures 1-10 and measures 10-18. As you sing, notice the circle-of-fifths progression that departs from A minor and returns there in measure 10.

1042 Bach, Aria, from Cantata No. 51, *Jauchzet Gott in allen Landen* (*Praise God in All Lands*), BWV 51

Translation: Highest One, renew your goodness with every new morning.

Melodies 1043b and 1043c present the conclusion of the composer's original theme and two variations on that theme. Notice the common feature in sectional variations of presenting the original theme in the parallel key.

1043a Clara Schumann, Theme, from *Variations on a Theme by Robert Schumann*

1043b Clara Schumann, Variation 3, from *Variations on a Theme by Robert Schumann*

1043c Clara Schumann, Variation 6, from *Variations on a Theme by Robert Schumann*

Melodies 1044 and 1045 feature a complete theme followed by sectional variations.

1044a Brahms, Theme, from *Variations on an Original Theme for Piano*, Op. 21, No. 1

1044b Brahms, Variation 2, from *Variations on an Original Theme for Piano*, Op. 21, No. 1

1044c Brahms, Variation 3, from *Variations on an Original Theme for Piano*, Op. 21, No. 1

1044d Brahms, Variation 4, from *Variations on an Original Theme for Piano*, Op. 21, No. 1

1045a Beethoven, Theme, from *Variations for Piano*, Op. 76
(adapted)

1045b Beethoven, Variation 1, from *Variations for Piano*, Op. 76
(adapted)

1045c Beethoven, Variation 3, from *Variations for Piano*, Op. 76 (adapted)

Rhythms: Super-Subdivided Beats in Slow Tempos 1: Simple Meters

Super-subdivided beats occur when a beat is divided, divided again, and then divided a third (or further) time, for example, a quarter-note beat divided into thirty-second notes. In slow tempos, super-subdivided beats may be indicated with multiple beams. To maintain accurate counting, conduct the beat divisions.

- Conduct the beat division as separate beats: in $\frac{2}{4}$, for example, conduct in four.

- Conduct the normal beat pattern, but articulate each beat division with an additional rebound on each beat to indicate the division.

Simple Duple Meter

1046

1047

1048

1049

1050

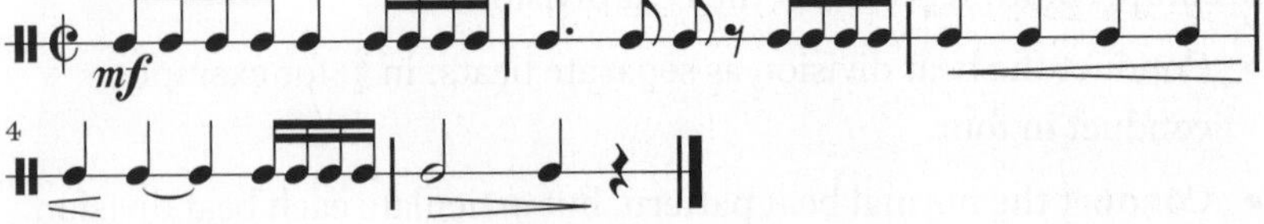

1051

1052

Simple Triple Meter

1053

1054

1055

1056

CHAPTER 26

Melody:

- Modal mixture

Rhythm:

- Super-subdivided beats in slow tempos 2: compound meters

In this chapter you'll learn to:

- Perform melodies that borrow pitches from the parallel mode
- Perform slow compound-meter rhythms in which the beat is subdivided then divided again
- Improvise phrases with pitches borrowed from the parallel minor key

---

Improvisation 26.1: Predominant Chords with Modal Mixture

While one person plays the following accompaniment, everyone in turn should improvise a melody in major, then borrow ♭6 from the minor for the repeat. The upper and lower lines of Roman numerals identify the differences in harmony. Choose a part and embellish it, following the given strategies. Before anyone sings aloud, have someone play the progression several times while the class silently improvises. Each person should accompany as well as perform a melody.

Strategies

- Begin by singing each part as written, then sing the melody while playing the bass line.

- Create études consisting of a single type of embellishment. For example, sing a variation that consists of nothing but skips within the chords. Sing another that features only upper neighbors, one that features lower neighbors, and so on.

Improvise melodies that combine different ideas from your études to create new, original phrases.

$$\text{I} \quad \text{IV} \quad \text{ii}^6 \quad \text{V}^6_4 \text{—} \,^5_3 \qquad \text{I} \quad \text{IV} \quad \text{ii}^6 \quad \text{V}^6_4 \text{—} \,^5_3 \quad \text{I}$$
$$\text{I} \quad \text{iv} \quad \text{ii}^{\circ 6} \quad \text{V}^6_4 \text{—} \,^5_3 \qquad \text{I} \quad \text{iv} \quad \text{ii}^{\circ 6} \quad \text{V}^6_4 \text{—} \,^5_3 \quad \text{I}$$

Variations:

- Begin with four-measure solos. Later, extend them to eight or sixteen measures, or shorten them to two measures.
- "Trade fours." One person improvises four bars, and then a second responds to the first improvisation.
- Try a variety of styles (art song, pop song, jazz, etc.). Create rhythmic embellishments in the accompaniment that are characteristic of the chosen style. Change the tempo, mood, and character to reflect the chosen style.
- Perform each example in its parallel minor mode.
- Transpose the examples to keys ranging from three flats to three sharps.
- Change the meter to compound meter.
- Transcribe the examples for instruments available in class. Play the accompaniment on those instruments. Let each player improvise within his or her part.
- Create a "groove" by adding one or more percussionists who play on objects available in class (books, desktops, pencils, etc.).

Quick Composition Notate your favorite improvisation and create a four-part choral score to show all parts. Make sure to align the parts so all players can both see and hear each other's part. Include the correct key and meter signature. Exchange with a peer and sing each other's part with solfège syllables, scale-degree numbers, or letter names.

Modal Mixture

1057 Brahms, String Sextet No. 2 in G Major, first movement (adapted)

1058 Dan Fogelberg, "Longer"

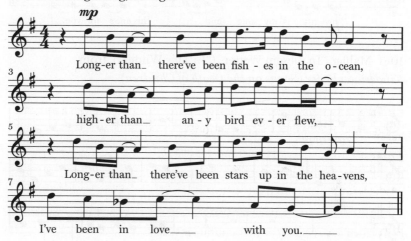

Long-er than there've been fish - es in the o - cean,

high-er than an - y bird ev - er flew,

Long-er than there've been stars up in the hea - vens,

I've been in love with you.

1059 Verdi, "Un dì, felice, eterea," from *La Traviata* (adapted)

1060 Elton John and Bernie Taupin, "Your Song"

If I were a sculp-tor— but then a-gain no,— or a
man who makes po - tions in a trav-el - in' show,— I
know— it's not much but it's— the best I can do,—
my gift— is my song and— this one's for you.—

1061 Mahler, "In diesem Wetter" ("In This Winter"), from
Kindertotenlieder (Songs on the Death of Children)

pp sempre

1062 Beethoven, Piano Sonata in C Major, Op. 53 (*Waldstein*), first movement (adapted)

1063 Brahms, *Liebeslieder Waltzer*, Op. 52, No. 3 (adapted)

1064 Mahler, "Die zwei blauen Augen von meinem Schatz" ("The Two Blue Eyes of My Sweetheart"), from *Lieder eines fahrenden Gesellen* (*Songs of a Wayfarer*) (adapted)

1065 Brahms, *Intermezzo* in E♭ Major, Op. 117, No. 1

1066 Brahms, Piano Sonata No. 1 in C Major, first movement (adapted)

1067 Mendelssohn, "Neue Liebe" ("New Love"), Op. 19, No. 4

1068 Beethoven, "Lustig, traurig" ("Funny, Sad"), WoO 43 (adapted)

Ensemble Melodies

1069 Brahms, *Liebeslieder Walzer*, Op. 65, No. 14 (adapted)

Pitches notated in treble clef with an "8" beneath it sound one octave lower than written.

1070 Mahler, Symphony No. 2, fourth movement (arranged by David Geary)

Rhythms: Super-Subdivided Beats in Slow Tempos 2: Compound Meters

Compound Duple

Remember that even in slow tempos $\frac{6}{8}$ meter should retain the feel of a compound duple meter rather than converting to a simple triple meter ($\frac{3}{4}$). For that reason, we often conduct each eighth note and divide our gestures between the right and left side of our body. For the following exercises, conduct in six as indicated, or according to your teacher's instructions.

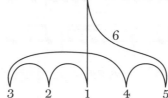

1071

Adagio (♪ = **72**)

1072

Einfach

1073

Langsam

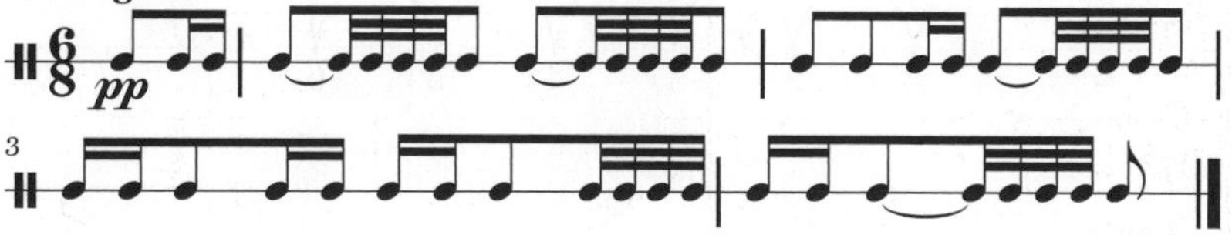

1074

Adagio

1075

1076

1077

Compound Triple

For the next melodies, conduct in nine as indicated, or according to your teacher's instructions.

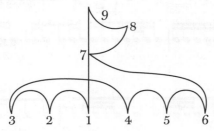

1078

1079

1080

Ensemble Rhythms

1081

CHAPTER 27

Melody:

- Lowered $\hat{2}$ and the neapolitan sixth chord
- The augmented-sixth chord

Rhythm:

- Characteristic dance rhythms

In this chapter you'll learn to:

- Recognize and perform melodies that feature the neapolitan sixth chord and the augmented-sixth chord
- Improvise a melody to a waltz that features modal mixture
- Perform the rhythms of characteristic dances

Improvisation 27.1: The Neapolitan Sixth Chord _____

Write Roman numerals in the blanks below the bass pitches. Improvise an accompaniment to this waltz while a second performer improvises a melody, singing with solfège syllables or scale-degree numbers.

Variations

- Create an interesting texture for the accompaniment. For example, arpeggiate the chords instead of playing them as block harmonies.

- Once you have analyzed the chords, perform them by looking at only the Roman numerals.

- Create a different type of dance by changing the meter to simple quadruple.

Quick Composition Notate your favorite improvisation and create a score to show all parts using a grand staff for the keyboard plus a single staff above for the soloist. Align the parts so all players can both see and hear each other's parts. Include the correct key and meter signatures. Exchange with a peer and sing each other's parts with solfège syllables, scale-degree numbers, or letter names.

Lowered $\hat{2}$ and the Neapolitan Sixth Chord

Sing these études to learn the sound of the Neapolitan sixth chord. Stems-down pitches represent bass lines; listen especially to these notes or have a partner sustain them while you sing the melody.

$I-V^4_3-I^6-N^6-V-I$

1084

1085

1086 Berlioz, *Symphonie fantastique*, Op. 15, Funeral March

1087 Mendelssohn, "Des Mädchens Klage" ("The Maiden's Lament")

1088 Brahms, *Liebeslieder Walzer*, Op. 65, No. 9

1089 Jack Gold and John Barry, "Midnight Cowboy"

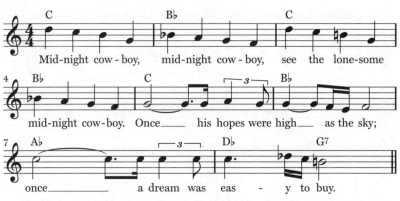

Mid-night cow - boy, mid-night cow - boy, see the lone-some
mid-night cow-boy. Once___ his hopes were high___ as the sky;
once_____ a dream was eas - y to buy.

1090 John Barry and Don Black, "Thunderball"

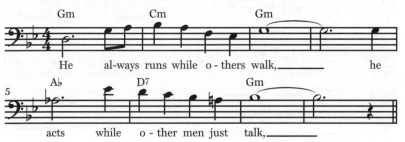

He al-ways runs while o - thers walk,___ he
acts while o - ther men just talk,___

1091 Stephen Schwartz, "Turn Back, O Man"

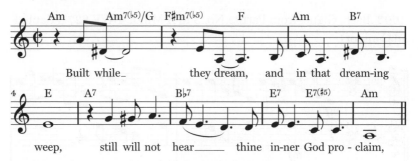

Built while they dream, and in that dream-ing

weep, still will not hear thine in-ner God pro - claim,

1092 Mahler, "Nun will die Sonn' so hell aufgeh'n" (Now the Sun Will Rise as Brightly"), from *Kindertotenlieder* (adapted)

Ensemble Melodies

1093 Bach, Gigue, from Partita No. 3 in A Minor, BWV 827 (adapted in C minor)

1094 Bach, Badinerie, from Suite No. 2 for Orchestra, BWV 1067
(adapted)

1095 Bach, Sonata IV, from *Six Trio Sonatas*, BWV 528a

♯4̂, ♭6̂, and Augmented-Sixth Chords

Sing these études to learn the sound of the German augmented-sixth chord. Stems-down pitches represent bass lines; listen especially to these notes or have a partner sustain them while you sing the melody. Alter the pitches in measure 4 to create the French augmented-sixth chord and the Italian augmented-sixth chord.

$$I-V\frac{4}{2}/IV-IV^6-Ger^{+6}-V^{8\,7}_{6\,5}{}^{4\,3}-I$$

1096

$$i-V\frac{4}{2}/iv-iv^6-Ger^{+6}-V^{8\,7}_{6\,5}{}^{4\,3}-i$$

1097

Ensemble Melodies

1098 Bach, Kyrie, from *Mass in B Minor*

1099 Beethoven, Bagatelle No. 1 in G Minor, from *Eleven Bagatelles*, Op. 119 (adapted)

1100 Wolf, "Ein stündlein wohl vor Tag" ("Just Before the Dawn") (adapted)

1101 Hensel, "Lust'ge Vögel" ("Happy Birds")

1102 Beethoven, String Quartet in G Major, Op. 18, No. 2, third
movement (Trio)

1103 Haydn, String Quartet in F Major, Op. 74, No. 2, first movement (adapted)

Study the accidentals to determine the local keys.

1104 Mozart, Piano Sonata in F Major, K. 332, first movement (adapted)

Characteristic Dance Rhythms

For each of the following rhythms note the characteristic meter, tempo, and rhythmic motives of each dance type. For example, Viennese waltzes often feature triple meter in a relatively fast tempo, and a short anacrusis before the downbeat.

1105

Viennese waltz

1113

Mazurka (♩ = 126)

1114

Tango (♩ = 60)

1115

Tango (♩ = 60)

1120

Polonaise (♩ = 88)

1121

Polonaise (♩ = 100)

1122

CHAPTER 28

Melody:

- Melodies from the literature (sixteenth to nineteenth centuries)

Rhythm:

- More syncopation: ragtime

In this chapter you'll learn to:

- Perform melodies from the vocal repertoire
- Perform syncopated rhythms from ragtime pieces
- Improvise ragtime melodies
- Recognize and perform melodies that feature the neapolitan sixth chord and the augmented-sixth chord (review)

Improvisation 28.1: Ragtime

While one person plays a ragtime accompaniment based on the following outline, a second person improvises a melody. The accompanist should also improvise, embellishing the outline and imitating the soloist when possible. Each person should improvise a solo and accompany.

Listen to this accompaniment and practice singing your improvisation with the recording.

Strategies

- According to Scott Joplin, rags should never be played fast. Try a nice strolling tempo of MM = 72.

- Create a motive that features rhythms characteristic of rags, such as these:

- Perform the motive each time the opening chord progression recurs. Use the motive in other places.

- In measure 8, one or both performers should create a lead-in to the next phrase. (The bass line is a good place for the lead-in!)

Quick Composition Notate your favorite improvisation and create a score to show all parts using a grand staff for the keyboard plus a single staff above for the soloist. Align the parts so all performers can both see and hear each other's parts. Include the key signature and meter signature. Exchange with a peer and sing each other's part with solfège syllables, scale-degree numbers, or letter names.

Vocal Melodies for Harmonization

Perform each of the following melodies a cappella, taking note of specific harmonic and melodic features of each. For example, the first modulates to the relative major; the second presents several half cadences approached from ♭6 melodically, and so on. Then create a simple accompaniment for each and perform them again.

1123 Schubert, "Der Jäger" ("The Hunter"), from *Die schöne Müllerin*

1124 Schubert, "Venetianisches Gondellied" ("Song of a Venetian Gondolier")

1125 "Love Grows Under a Wide Oak Tree" (traditional)

Love grows un - der a wide oak tree. Su-gar flows like can - dy. Top of the moun-tain shines like gold when you kiss your lit - tle hon - ey sort - a han - dy.

Dreams, dreams, sweet dreams, un - der the wide oak tree,___ dreams, dreams, sweet dreams, one for you and me!___ Oh,

1126 "Every Time I Feel the Spirit" (traditional)

Sing measures 1-16. After measure 16, return to the beginning (*da capo*, or *D.C.*) and sing until the first note in measure 8 (*Fine*).

Ensemble Melodies

1127 Beethoven, Gloria, from *Mass in C*, Op. 86

Remember that pitches notated on a treble clef with an "8" beneath it sound one octave lower than written.

1128 Mozart, *Exsultate, jubilate*, third movement

Remember that F♯ is called *di* (♯1̂).

1129 Gibbons, "O Lord, Increase My Faith"

1130 Morley, "April Is in My Mistress' Face"

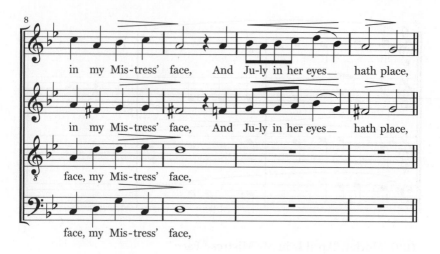

in my Mis-tress' face, And Ju-ly in her eyes___ hath place,

in my Mis-tress' face, And Ju-ly in her eyes___ hath place,

face, my Mis-tress' face,

face, my Mis-tress' face,

This is an entire vocal composition whose features recall many of the challenges you have worked hard to master.

1131 Bruckner, "Locus Iste"

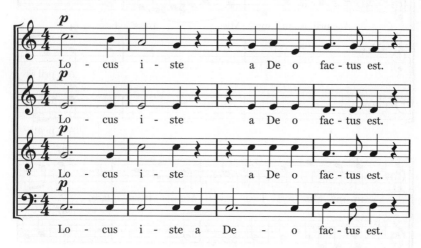

Lo - cus i - ste a De o fac - tus est.

Lo - cus i - ste a De o fac - tus est.

Lo - cus i - ste a De o fac - tus est.

Lo - cus i - ste a De - o fac - tus est.

Translation: This place was made by God, a priceless sacrament, beyond reproach.

Rhythms: Syncopation in Ragtime Music

Perform in *tempo giusto* (strict time), without swing or *rubato*.

1132 Scott Joplin, "The Easy Winners"

1133

Andante

1134

Not fast

1135 Joplin, "Solace" (adapted)

Very slow march time

1136 Joplin, "Bethena" (adapted)

Cantabile

rit.

1137 Joseph Lamb, "Bohemia" (adapted)

Moderately

1138

Andante

1139

Moderato

1140

Slow march tempo

Ensemble Rhythms

1141

Slowly

1142

1143 Joplin, "Solace" (adapted)

Review: The Neapolitan Sixth Chord and the Augmented-Sixth Chord

1144 Schubert, "Der stürmische Morgen" ("The Stormy Morning"), from *Winterreise*

1145 Schubert, "Die Liebe hat gelogen" ("Love Has Proved False")

Translation: Love has proved false, sorrow weighs heavily.

1146 Hensel, "Schon kehren die Vögel" ("Even the Birds Return")

1147 Bach, Agnus Dei, from *Mass in B Minor*

CHAPTER 29

Melody:

- Rock and popular music

Rhythm:

- Swung rhythms
- Syncopation and swing in jazz

In this chapter you'll learn to:

- Perform melodies from popular music
- Perform swung rhythms found in jazz music
- Improvise the verse of a song in a classic rock style

Improvisation 29.1: Rock _____

Use the following progression as a basis for the verse of a song in a classic rock style.

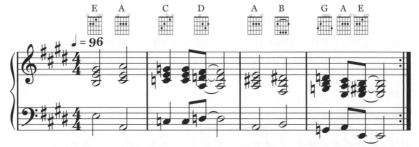

Listen to this accompaniment and practice singing your improvisation with the recording.

Variations

- Accompany yourself on keyboard or guitar.
- Initially, play the music as written. Later, embellish the rhythm, but keep a steady, driving beat.
- Add other instruments (percussion and bass) to create an ensemble.
- Assemble a vocal quintet. While four people sing the progression, a fifth person improvises a melody. Exchange parts each time, so each person has a chance to improvise.
- Improvise a chorus, then perform ‖: verse, verse, chorus :‖.

Quick Composition Notate your favorite improvisation and create a score to show all parts using a grand staff for the keyboard plus a single staff above for the soloist. Or, notate the vocal quintet as a five-part score. Align the parts so all performers can both see and hear each other's parts. Include the key signature and meter signature. Exchange with a peer and sing each other's part with solfège syllables, scale-degree numbers, or letter names.

Rhythms: Syncopation and Swing in Jazz

The following rhythms should be "swung," with a long-short division of the beat, similar to that of a compound meter's ♩ ♪ rhythm. Where no swing is indicated, perform the rhythm as written.

Strategies for swung rhythms

- Perform the rhythm in strict time, then "relax" the offbeats.
- Experiment by accenting the offbeats.
- Swing the rhythm from the start; set a tempo and conduct a few measures while imagining the written rhythm in its swung fashion.

1148

Bright swing

1149 Johnny Green, "Body and Soul" (adapted)

1150 Billy Strayhorn, "Take the 'A' Train" (adapted)

1151

1152 Antonio Carlos Jobim, "One Note Samba" (adapted)

1153 Phil Woods, "Waltz for a Lovely Wife" (adapted)

1154

1155 Thelonious Monk, "'Round Midnight" (adapted)

1156

1157

1158

1159

Popular Song

1160 Pete Seeger, "Turn! Turn! Turn! (To Everything There Is a Season)"

1161 "Auld Lang Syne" (traditional)

1162 Joe Burke, "Tiptoe Through the Tulips"

Harmonize the beginning with a chromatic 5–6 sequence. (Use a half-note harmonic rhythm.) On beat 4 of measure 4, use a borrowed chord.

1163 Don Hecht and Alan W. Block, "Walkin' After Midnight"

I'll go out walk-in'___ af - ter mid-night___ in___ the

moon-light___ just like we used to do. I'm al-ways

walk-in'___ af - ter mid-night search-in' for you.___

1164 Dave Loggins, "Please Come to Boston"

Hey ram - blin' boy,___ now won't you set - tle down

Bos-ton ain't your kind of town___ There ain't no gold___ and there

ain't no - bod-y like me.___

1165 "How Can I Keep from Singing?" (traditional)

1166 Jerome Kern and Oscar Hammerstein II, "All the Things You Are"

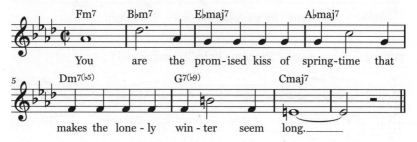

Fm7   B♭m7   E♭maj7   A♭maj7

You   are   the prom-ised kiss of spring-time that

Dm7(♭5)   G7(♭9)   Cmaj7

makes the lone - ly win - ter seem long.___

1167 George Gershwin and DuBose Heyward, "Summertime," from *Porgy and Bess*

Your___ dad-dy's rich___ and your mam-ma's good

look - in'___ so hush lit-tle ba - by don't___ you cry.___

1168 John Denver, "Annie's Song"

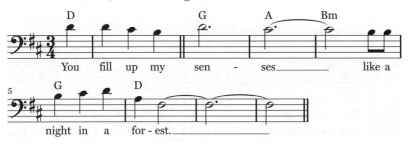

You fill up my sen - ses___ like a

night in a for - est.___

1169 Frank Perkins and Mitchell Parish, "Stars Fell on Alabama"

We lived our lit-tle dram - a. We kissed in a field of

white and stars fell on A-la - ba - ma last night.___

1170 "Niño precioso" ("Precious Baby") (traditional)

1171 James Taylor, "Carolina in My Mind"

Kar-en she's_ a sil-ver sun,_ you'd best walk her_ way and watch it shine. Watch her watch_____ the morn-ing come._

1172 Robert Henning and Heinz Provost, "Intermezzo"

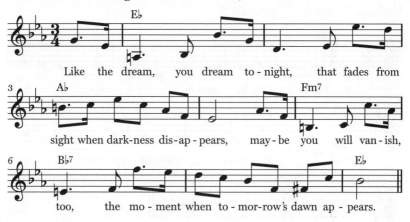

Like the dream, you dream to-night, that fades from sight when dark-ness dis-ap-pears, may-be you will van-ish, too, the mo-ment when to-mor-row's dawn ap-pears.

1173 Richard Rodgers and Oscar Hammerstein II, "Sixteen Going on Seventeen," from *The Sound of Music*

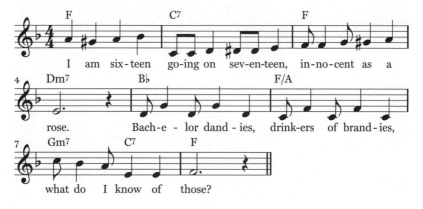

I am six-teen go-ing on sev-en-teen, in-no-cent as a rose. Bach-e-lor dand-ies, drink-ers of brand-ies, what do I know of those?

1174 Joe Satriani, "Flying in a Blue Dream"

1175 Paul Francis Webster and Dimitri Tiomkin, "The Green Leaves of Summer

Variation: In measure 7, play an A^6.

CHAPTER 30

Melody:

- More chromaticism
- Melody harmonization
- The blues

Rhythm:

- Asymmetric meters 1: two unequal beats per measure

In this chapter you'll learn to:

- Perform melodies while harmonizing them with chromatic chords
- Perform melodies that present a variety of chromatic pitches
- Perform twelve-bar blues excerpts
- Improvise over the twelve-bar blues
- Perform rhythms in which the measure is divided into two unequal beats

Improvisation 30.1: The Blues

While one person performs the chords of the twelve-bar blues on keyboard or guitar, a soloist improvises, drawing from pitches of the blues scale. Switch roles and perform again. Soloists may sing their improvisations or play them on an instrument.

To get started, review the C blues scale and progression found in Keyboard Lesson 29.1.

Variation: Transpose the blues scale and progression to the key of F. Ask multiple soloists to improvise over the accompaniment. The first soloist performs a four-measure motive based on the blues scale. The second imitates the motive, adjusting for the chord change. The third makes a variation of the motive and cadences in measure 11.

Quick Composition Notate your favorite improvisation and create a score to show all parts using a grand staff for the keyboard plus a single staff above for the soloist. Align the parts so all performers can both see and hear each other's part. Include the key signature and meter signature. Exchange with a peer and sing each other's part with solfège syllables, scale-degree numbers, or letter names.

Harmonization with Chromatic Chords

Harmonize the following melodies as indicated while you sing.

1176 Hensel, Song No. 6 for Piano

In measures 4 and 8, harmonize the melody with A⁶-V. In measure 6, use A⁶-V in the key of VII. To accommodate the extended instrumental range, find places to change register (for example, the second beat of measure 2 and the first beat of measure 7).

1177 Johann Strauss Jr., "The Beautiful Blue Danube" (adapted)

Conclude your hamonization with A⁶-V in the key of vi.

1178 "My Country, 'Tis of Thee" (traditional)

In measure 4, harmonize with a chromatic cadential $^6_4$ followed by a deceptive resolution. Try another variation: harmonize measures 4-6 with I-V$^6_5$/vi-V$^6_5$/V-V$^6_4$-$^6_5$-I.

1179 Jean Thielemans, "Bluesette"

Chromatic Melodies

1180 Tchaikovsky, Symphony No. 5, third movement (adapted)

1181 Brahms, Piano Trio No. 2, Op. 87 (adapted)

1182 Mozart, Piano Sonata in B♭ Major, K. 282, second movement

1183 Schumann, "Der Ring a meinen Finger," from *Dichterliebe*, Op. 42

1184 Wagner, "Noch bleibe denn unausgesprochen" ("For a Short While Still"), from *Tannhäuser*

Ensemble Melody

1185 Haydn, String Quartet in F Major, Op. 74, No. 2, first movement (adapted)

Study the accidentals to determine the local keys.

The Blues

Sing the following melodies first without harmony, and then play the blues progressions indicated as another student sings the melody. Finally, sing the melodies while accompanying yourself.

1186 Hart A. Wand, "Dallas Blues"

1187 Joel Phillips, "Blues for Norton"

1188 W. C. Handy, "Memphis Blues"

1189 J. Brandon Walsh, "The Broadway Blues" (adapted)

Rhythm: Asymmetric Meters 1:
Two Unequal Beats Per Measure

The beat divisions of asymmetric meters are unequal. Thus, meters of five or seven may sound like alternations between two or three different meters. Meters of five usually have two beats (dividing into 3 + 2 or 2 + 3). Meters of seven can have two beats (4 + 3 or 3 + 4) or three (3 + 2 + 2, 2 + 2 + 3, or 2 + 3 + 2). When a meter's bottom number is 8, beams help to indicate the grouping; when the bottom number is 4, analyze the longest and shortest note values of each measure to reveal any grouping patterns.

Perform the following two preparatory exercises by conducting in two throughout, while keeping the eighth note steady and constant.

- In measures 3-4, change your conducting to a compound pattern followed by a simple pattern.

- Make sure that the beats in measures 3-4 are *not* of the same duration; the second beat will feel "square" in comparison with the "round" feel of the first beat.

- Tap eighth notes with one hand while conducting the meter with the other.

1190a

1190b

1200

Sehr schnell

1201

Ruhig

1202

Moderato

CHAPTER 31

Melody:

- Chromatic modulation
- Modulation to distantly related keys

Rhythm:

- Asymmetric meters 2: two or three beats per measure

In this chapter you'll learn to:

- Perform études that feature enharmonic modulations to distantly related keys
- Perform melodies that present modulations to distantly related keys
- Improvise over a soprano-bass framework that features modal mixture, the Neapolitan sixth chord, and the augmented-sixth chord
- Perform rhythms in which the measure is divided into two or three unequal beats

---

Improvisation 31.1: Review of Mixture, Neapolitan Sixth, and Augmented-Sixth Chords

Improvise a waltz from the following melodic and harmonic outline. While one person realizes the figured bass at the keyboard, the partner improvises a melody. Sing with solfège syllables and scale-degree numbers that reflect the modal mixture.

Beat 3 of measure 6 may be performed two ways. Until you become comfortable with A6 chords, ignore the parenthetical figure and perform only the ♭5. Once you learn A6 chords, perform both figures—the parenthetical ♯6 and the ♭5.

Quick Composition Notate your favorite improvisation and create a score to show all parts using a grand staff for the keyboard plus a single staff above for the soloist. Align the parts so all performers can both see and hear each other's parts. Include the key signature and meter signature. Exchange with a peer and sing each other's parts with solfège syllables, scale-degree numbers, or letter names.

Chromatic Modulation

The études that follow feature chromatic (enharmonic) modulations to keys in a chromatic mediant relationship to the starting key. Sing each étude with solfège syllables or scale-degree numbers to learn how chords can be reinterpreted so that they can function in another key. Stems-down pitches represent bass lines; listen especially to these notes or have a partner sustain them while you sing the melody. Note the following:

- These modulations can appear visually quite complicated! By contrast, their sound is quite smooth and subtle.

- Measures 4 and 5 will sound exactly the same, but should be sung with different solfège syllables or scale-degree numbers to reflect the chord's function in each key.

The dominant seventh chord is reinterpreted as the Ger^{+6} chord.

The fully diminished seventh chord is reinterpreted in a different inversion.

1206

b: i   vii°6   i6

vii°$^6_{4\ 3}$ g: vii°$^6_{5\ 3}$/V   V$^8_6{}_4$

$^7_3$ i

1207 Beethoven, Symphony No. 5, Op. 67, second movement (adapted)

In this melody C♯ is the common tone between the dominant chord (V) and F♯ major.

1208 Schumann, "Widmung" (Dedication") (adapted)

Innig, Lebhaft

mf

Grab,   in   das   hin - ab   ich   e   -   wig

ritard.   *p*

mei-nen Kum - mer gab!   Du   bist die

Ruth,   du   bist____ der Frei - den.

Translation: [O you, my] grave, into which I eternally pour my sorrow. You are rest, you are peace.

1209 Schubert, 36 *Originaltänze*, D. 365, No. 3

1210 Schubert, "Wehmuth," Op. 22, No. 2 (adapted)

1211 Strauss, Overture to *Die Fledermaus* (adapted)

1212 Schubert, "Der Flug der Zeit" ("The Flight of Time"), D. 515 (adapted)

1213 Brahms, Neue Liebeslieder, Op. 65, No. 6 (adapted)

In the next melody, F is the common tone between F major (reached in m. 21) and D♭ major.

1214 Beethoven, Symphony No. 4 in B♭ Major, Menuetto (adapted)

In the next melody, G is the common tone between C major and E♭ major.

1215 Schubert, Zwölf Ländler, D. 790, No. 1 (adapted)

1216 Schubert, "Agnus Dei," from *Mass in A♭*, D. 678

A - gnus De - i, a - gnus De - i, qui tol - lis pec-

- ca - ta, pec - ca - ta mun - di,

Ensemble Melody

In this excerpt the E♭ in measure 14 plays a crucial role in both the starting key of G major and the concluding key of A minor. How would this chord be spelled in A minor?

1217 Haydn, String Quartet, Op. 76, No. 6, second movement (adapted)

Rhythm: Asymmetric Meters with Two or Three Beats Per Measure

Remember that, like compound meters in moderate or faster tempos, the lower number in asymmetric meter signatures indicates the division of the beat; the top number must be divided asymmetrically to reveal the number of beats per measure.

1218

1219

1220

1221

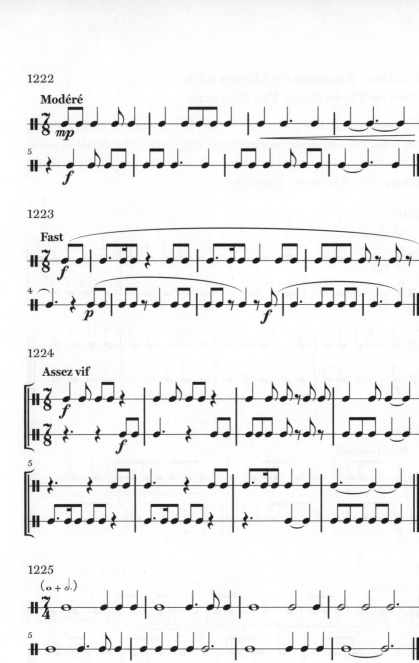

1222

Modéré

1223

Fast

1224

Assez vif

1225

$(o + \mathrel{\downarrow}.)$

1226

Calmly

CHAPTER 32

Melody:

- Themes and excerpts from sonata-form movements and concertos

Rhythm:

- Combined dissimilar beat divisions in simple meters

In this chapter you'll learn to:

- Perform instrumental melodies from sonata-form movements and concertos by yourself and in ensembles
- Perform simple-meter rhythms in which the beat or the measure features dissimilar divisions simultaneously
- Improvise melodies in chromatic descending-third sequences

Improvisation 32.1: Singing and Playing Chromatic Descending-Third Sequences

Use each sequence shown next as the basis for improvisation. Begin with the diatonic sequence (1) then, as you become more comfortable, chromaticize it (2). Play the outline at the keyboard while singing an improvised melody, or improvise on your instrument while someone improvises a keyboard accompaniment.

Strategies

- Because the patterns are sequential, think of a motive that you can perform over a two-chord segment. Then transpose this pattern down to the next segment.
- Compound melodies work beautifully over these sequences. Create motives that imply two melodic strands. For example, present a

starting motive in a higher register then a second one in a lower register, and alternate between them as the sequence progresses. Follow the strategies from Improvisation 14.1.

(1) Diatonic descending thirds

Root-position chords with a 10-5 LIP

(2) Chromatic descending thirds

Alternating $\frac{5}{3}$ and $\frac{4}{3}$ with a 10-5 LIP

Variations:

- Change to triple meter.

- Change to compound meter.

- Add melodic embellishments, such as suspensions (e.g., in sequence 2: I-V4-3-vi9-8-iii4-3, etc.).

- Assign the given soprano voice to another part to create a different linear intervallic pattern (LIP).

Quick Composition Notate your favorite improvisation and create a score to show all parts using a grand staff for the keyboard plus a single staff above for the soloist. Align the parts so all performers can both see and hear each other's part. Include the correct key and meter signature. Exchange with a peer and sing each other's part with solfège syllables, scale-degree numbers, or letter names.

Themes and Excerpts from Sonata-Form and Concerto Movements

1231 Copland, Piano Concerto, second movement

1232 Fauré, *Elégie*, Op. 24, for Cello and Orchestra

1233 Mozart, Piano Sonata in G Major, K. 283, second movement (adapted)

1234 Mozart, Piano Sonata in D Major, K. 284, third movement (adapted)

1235 Rachmaninov, Piano Concerto No. 3 in D Minor, first movement

1236 Brahms, Double Concerto in A Minor, Op. 102, first movement (adapted)

1237 Chopin, Cello Sonata in G Minor, Op. 65, first movement

Ensemble Melodies

Although the following excerpts are drawn from instrumental repertoire they lend themselves to ensemble vocal performance. Try to develop the skill of switching to a comfortable octave when the melodies extend beyond your range.

1238 Haydn, Piano Sonata No. 15 in C Major, first movement

1239 Haydn, Piano Sonata No. 14 in D Major, second movement

1240 Beethoven, Piano Sonata in D Minor, Op. 31, No. 2 (*Tempest*), first movement (adapted)

1241 Haydn, Piano Sonata No. 45 in E♭ Major, Hob. XVI:45, first movement (adapted)

1242 Schumann, String Quartet in A Minor, Op. 41, No. 1, fifth movement (adapted)

1243 Mozart, Piano Sonata in A Minor, K. 310, first movement (adapted)

1244 Mozart, Piano Concerto in C Major, K. 467, first movement (adapted)

Rhythm: Combined Beat Divisions in Simple Meters

Rhythms 1245a and 1245b help you understand kinesthetically how these two beat divisions (four groups of three and three groups of four) relate to each other.

Strategies

- Tap the lower part with your left hand and the upper part with your right hand

- Sing aloud the rhythmic syllables of the lower and upper parts as instructed by your teacher.

- Practice the exercise until the 3:4 relationship is accurate and you can sing the rhythmic syllables of either part independently.

1245a

1245b

1246

1247

1248

1249

1250

Sweetly

1251

Waltz

1252

Vif

1253

1254

1255

1256

1257

CHAPTER 33

Melody:

- Rondo

Rhythm:

- Combined dissimilar beat divisions in compound meter

In this chapter you'll learn to:

- Perform compound-meter rhythms in which the beat or the measure features dissimilar divisions simultaneously
- Improvise melodies in chromatic ascending 5-6 sequences

Improvisation 33.1: Singing and Playing Chromatic Ascending 5-6 Sequences

Use each sequence that follows as the basis for improvisation. Begin with the diatonic sequence (1) then, as you become more comfortable, chromaticize it (2). Play the outline at the keyboard while singing an improvised melody, or improvise on your instrument while someone improvises a keyboard accompaniment.

Strategies

- Because the patterns are sequential, think of a motive that you can perform over a two-chord segment. Then transpose this pattern down for the next segment.
- Compound melodies work beautifully over these sequences. Create motives that imply two melodic strands.

- Follow the strategies from Improvisation 14.1.

(1) Diatonic ascending 5-6

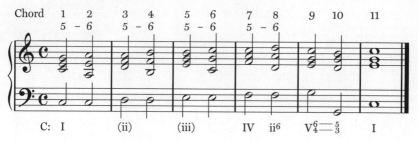

(2) Chromatic ascending 5-6

The chromatic ascending 5-6 sequence is more common than the diatonic. It is the most common ascending sequence, and appears characteristically in major keys.

Variations

- Change to triple meter.
- Change to compound meter.
- Add melodic embellishments, such as suspensions (e.g., in sequence 2: I-V$^{4-3}$-vi$^{9-8}$-iii$^{4-3}$, etc.).
- Assign the given soprano voice to another part to create a different linear intervallic pattern (LIP).

Quick Composition Notate your favorite improvisation and create a score to show all parts using a grand staff for the keyboard plus a single staff above for the soloist. Align the parts so all performers can both see and hear each other's part. Include the correct key signature and meter signature. Exchange with a peer and sing each other's part with solfège syllables, scale-degree numbers, or letter names.

Melodies: Rondo Refrains

1258 Diabelli, Sonatina, Op. 168, No. 2, third movement, Rondo
(adapted)

1259 Diabelli, Sonatina, Op. 168, No. 4, third movement, Rondo
(adapted)

1260 Mozart, Rondo, K. 485 (adapted)

Although rondo themes are often fast and light-hearted, this famous excerpt demonstrates a moderately slow, serious, and contemplative character.

1261 Mozart, Rondo, K. 511 (adapted)

1262 Mozart, Clarinet Concerto, K. 511, Rondo (adapted)

In this next melody, one phrase is elided with the beginning of the next phrase, which results in seven-measure phrases. To manage the instrumental range, return to the original register for measures 7-18 and 25-30.

1263 Brahms, Quartet for Piano and Strings, Op. 25, Rondo alla Zingarese (adapted)

The design of this five-part rondo is **A B A C A′**. The composition is presented next with its three different sections separated. (The retransition and coda are not shown here.) Practice each of its three different sections as follows:

- the melody alone
- the melody and bass as a two-part duet for individuals or groups
- in three parts for groups or individuals

Haydn, Piano Sonata No. 30 in D Major, Hob. XVI:37, third movement

A section, the theme of the rondo

1264

B section, a digression from the theme in the parallel minor

1265

***The A section returns followed by the C section, which contrasts
with both A and B, in the subdominant***

1266

The A section returns followed by the coda

1267 Haydn, Piano Trio No. 39 in G Major, third movement (adapted)

This melody is an example of a rondo.

Rhythm: Combined Beat Divisions in Compound Meters

1268

1269

Doux

1270

Allegro

1271

Flowingly

1272

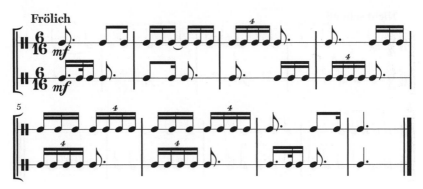

1273

1274

1275

1276

1277

PART IV

The Twentieth
Century and Beyond

CHAPTER 34

Melody:

- Pentatonic melodies revisited
- Twentieth-century modal melodies
- Precursors to atonal music: collections and sets

Rhythm:

- Quintuplets and septuplets

In this chapter you'll learn to:

- Perform traditional and twentieth-century pentatonic melodies
- Perform accompanied and unaccompanied twentieth-century modal melodies
- Perform rhythms with beats subdivided into five and seven parts
- Improvise modal melodies

Improvisation 34.1: Melodies Based on the Diatonic Modes

Improvise short melodies in the diatonic modes. Play them and sing with solfège syllables or scale-degree numbers. Refer to Chapter 5, page 65, to review the use of parallel and relative syllables, and to Chapter 9, pages 114-117, for examples of intonation formulae. Before starting, conduct in silence until you establish a comfortable, steady tempo. Always sing with attention to dynamics, and with inflection and expressiveness to make your performance musically interesting.

Dorian mode

Perform a natural minor scale and raise ♭6̂ a half step.

Call the first pitch *re* (2̂). Perform a major scale from *re* to *re* (2̂–2̂).

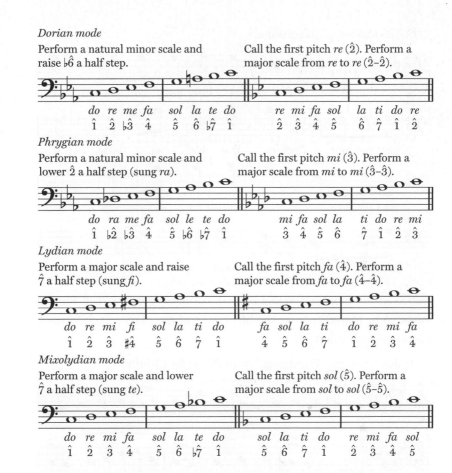

Phrygian mode

Perform a natural minor scale and lower 2̂ a half step (sung *ra*).

Call the first pitch *mi* (3̂). Perform a major scale from *mi* to *mi* (3̂–3̂).

Lydian mode

Perform a major scale and raise 7̂ a half step (sung *fi*).

Call the first pitch *fa* (4̂). Perform a major scale from *fa* to *fa* (4̂–4̂).

Mixolydian mode

Perform a major scale and lower 7̂ a half step (sung *te*).

Call the first pitch *sol* (5̂). Perform a major scale from *sol* to *sol* (5̂–5̂).

Quick Composition Notate your favorite improvisation. Choose a clef and indicate a key and meter signature. Notate the rhythm and solfège syllables of your improvisation above the staff, then convert this to notation on the staff. Exchange with a peer and sing each other's melody with solfège syllables, scale-degree numbers, or letter names.

Melodies

The Pentatonic Collection Revisited

The following melodies feature the pentatonic scale in a traditional song, in works for or about children, and in early twentieth-century works for piano.

1278 "Riddle Song" (traditional)

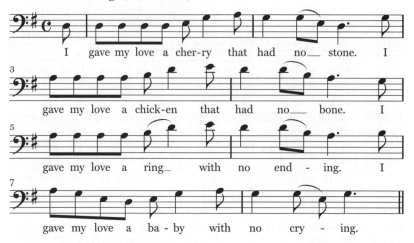

I gave my love a cher-ry that had no_ stone. I
gave my love a chick-en that had no_ bone. I
gave my love a ring_ with no end - ing. I
gave my love a ba - by with no cry - ing.

Notice in the next two melodies that the key signatures call for the music to be played only on the black keys of the piano. Each forms a pentatonic collection.

1279 Joel Phillips, "Windsong," from *Pieces for Children*

1280 Ravel, "Laideronnette, Impératice des Pagodes" ("Little Ugly Girl, Empress of the Pagodas"), from *Ma mère l'Oye* (*Mother Goose*) (adapted)

1281 Debussy, "Bruyères," from *Préludes*, Book II

1282 Debussy, "Général Lavine," from *Préludes*, Book II

Modal Melodies

1283 Bartók, *First Term at the Piano*, No. 21, "Farmer in the Dell"

1284 Chausson, "La Cigale," from *Four Songs*, Op. 13, No. 4

1285 Germaine Tailleferre, Sonata in C♯ Minor for Violin and Piano

1286 Rebecca Clarke, Sonata for Violin and Piano, first movement

Add a second performer in measure 8, when a second line enters.

1287 Ravel, "Là-bas, vers l'église" ("Near the Church")

Precursors to Atonal Music: Collections and Sets

1288 Tchaikovsky, Symphony No. 4, first movement (adapted)

1289 Wolf, "Ein Stündlein wohl vor Tag" ("Just Before Daybreak")

1290 R. Strauss, *Don Juan* (viola part)

1291 Wolf, "In der Frühe" ("At Dawn")

1292 Webern, "Am Ufer" ("On the Shore"), from *Five Songs After Poems by Richard Dehmel*

1293 Webern, "Helle Nacht" ("Bright Night"), from *Five Songs After Poems by Richard Dehmel*

1294 Berg, "Liebesode" ("Ode of Love"), from *Seven Early Songs*

Rhythms

Quintuplets

The first two preparatory rhythms present divisions and subdivisions of the beat in a graduated manner. Conduct the rhythms in duple meter throughout while keeping the same duration for each beat. Aim for equally spaced divisions and subdivisions.

1295

1296

1297

1298

1299

Stark

1300

Sustained

1301

Allegretto

1302

($\bullet. = 72$)

1303

Allegretto

1304

Ensemble Rhythms

1305

1306

Septuplets

Conduct the next two preparatory rhythms in duple meter throughout while keeping the same duration for each beat. Aim for equally spaced divisions and subdivisions.

1307

1308

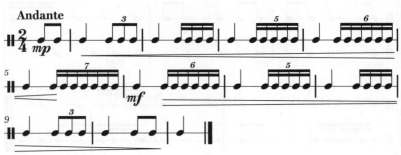

1309

1310

1311

Andante

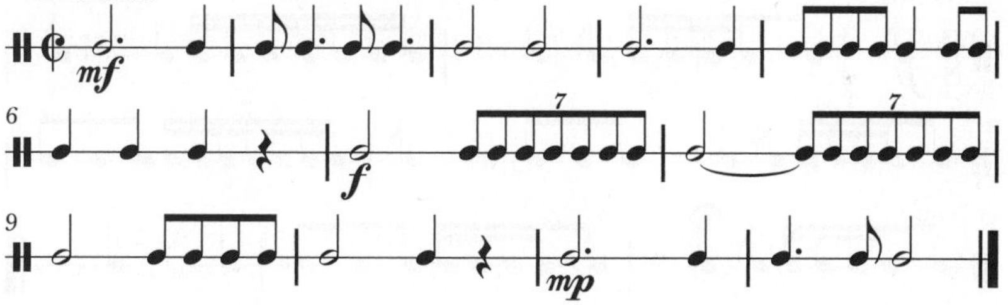

1312

Andantino

1313

Sweetly

1314

♩. = 90

1315

Joyeux

1316

Ensemble Rhythms

1317

1318

CHAPTER 35

Melody:

- Singing with integers: chromatic, whole-tone, and octatonic collections

Rhythm:

- Quintuple and septuple meters in slow tempos

In this chapter you'll learn to:

- Apply integers to the pitches of melodies
- Perform chromatic, whole-tone, and octatonic scales and melodies
- Perform rhythms in slow meters with five or seven beats per measure
- Improvise melodies with pitches from whole-tone collections

Nondiatonic Collections

Nondiatonic collections such as the chromatic scale, the whole-tone scale, and the octatonic scale may be sung using integers, with enharmonic pitches receiving the same integer name. In order to maintain accurate rhythms, abbreviate any multisyllable integers as shown.

The Chromatic Scale

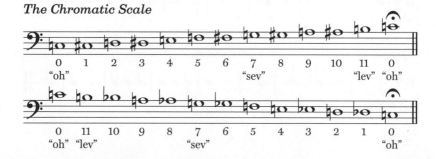

Whole-Tone Scales

Notice that whole-tone 0 uses "even" integers (0-2-4-6-8-10) while whole-tone 1 uses "odd" integers (1-3-5-7-9-11). Sing the notes of the scale with pitches grouped in strong-weak pairs, then in strong-weak-weak triplets.

Whole-Tone 0 (WT0)

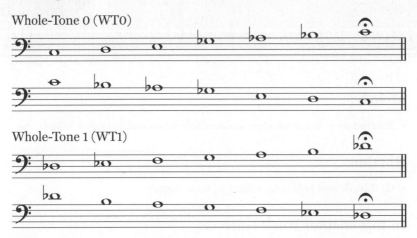

Whole-Tone 1 (WT1)

Improvisation 35.1: Melodies Based on the Whole-Tone Scale

The four given rhythms serve as the basis for improvising whole-tone melodies. In preparation for improvising your own melodies, clap, tap, or sing on a neutral syllable each rhythm while conducting. After having internalized a rhythm, improvise short melodies using the pitches of WT0 or WT1. Perform your melodies both with and without integers. Always sing with attention to dynamics, and with inflection and expressiveness, to make your performance musically interesting.

(1)

Moderato

(2)

Waltz

(3)

March

(4)

Sweetly

Sample improvisation using WT0 and rhythm (2):

Quick Composition Choose a clef and indicate the meter of your favorite improvisation. You can notate your work using accidentals or create a nontraditional key signature that indicates the sharps or flats that are included in the whole-tone collection you are using. For example, if you are using WT0, write a key signature with F♯, G♯, and A♯ indicated. Exchange with a peer and sing each other's melody with solfège syllables, scale-degree numbers or letter names.

Whole-Tone Études and Melodies

1319

1320

1321 Composers often use a non-traditional key signature to indicate a whole-tone collection.

1322

1323

1324

1325 Debussy, "Coloque sentimental" ("The Colloquy"), from *Fêtes Galantes*, Book 2

1326 Debussy, "Les ingénues" ("Innocent Young Girls"), from *Fêtes Galantes*, Book 2

1327 Ives, "September"

Octatonic Scales

Note that the ordering of pitches in these octatonic scales presents four half-step pairs. Sing the scale with notes grouped into strong-weak pairs, then with equal stress on each note.

Octatonic 01

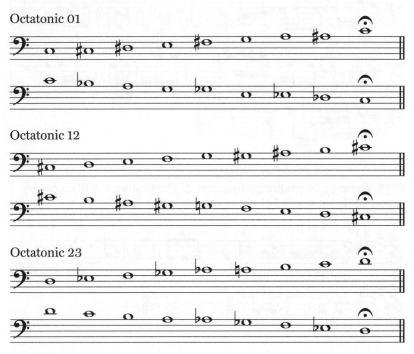

Octatonic 12

Octatonic 23

Octatonic Études and Melodies

1328

1332

1333 Scriabin, *Prelude*, Op. 74, No. 3

Ensemble Melody

The dual key signatures of this melody correspond to the octatonic 23 collection.

1334 Bartók, "Song of the Harvest"

Rhythms

Quintuple Meters at Slow Tempos

Practice the conducting patterns shown for use in slow-tempo quintuple meters. Your conducting gestures should convey any dynamic changes in the rhythm.

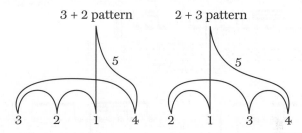

1335

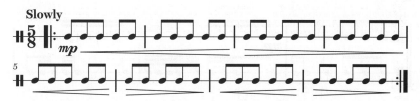

1336

1337

1338

1339

1340

Septuple Meters at Slow Tempos

Practice the following conducting patterns for use in slow-tempo quintuple meters. Notice how each pattern represents a modified triple-meter conducting pattern.

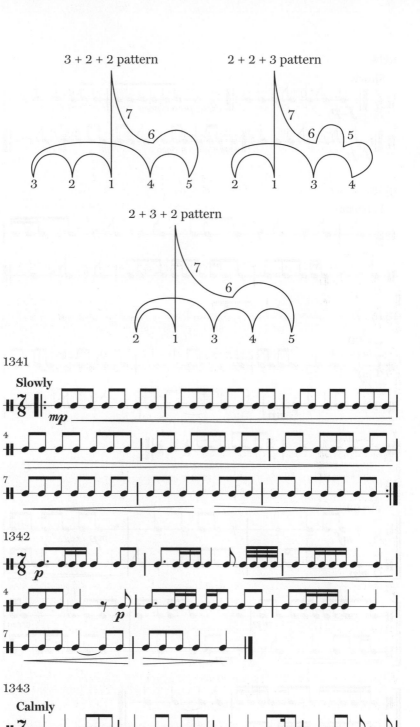

1344

1345

1346

1347

CHAPTER 36

Melody:

- Singing with solfège syllables, scale-degree numbers, and integers
- The Lydian-Mixolydian mode (overtone scale)
- The octatonic collection

Rhythm:

- Rhythms of the spoken word

In this chapter you'll learn to:

- Apply integers to the pitches of melodies
- Perform chromatic and modal melodies using solfège syllables, scale-degree numbers, or integers
- Perform a melody in the Lydian-Mixolydian mode (overtone scale)
- Perform rhythmic settings of excerpted lines from poems
- Improvise melodies with pitches from octatonic collections

Improvisation 36.1: Melodies Based on the Octatonic Scale

The following four rhythms serve as the basis for improvising octatonic melodies. In preparation for improvising your own melodies, clap, tap, or sing on a neutral syllable each rhythm while conducting. After having internalized a rhythm, improvise short melodies using the pitches of octatonic 01, 12, or 23. Perform your melodies both with and without integers. Always sing with attention to dynamics, and with inflection and expressiveness to make your performance musically interesting.

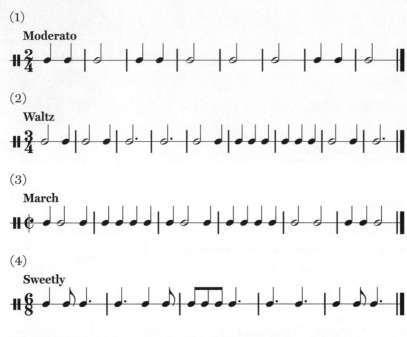

(1)

Moderato

(2)

Waltz

(3)

March

(4)

Sweetly

Sample improvisation using octatonic 01 and rhythm (3):

March

f 0 3 0   1 1 1 1   0 3 4   6 7 7 7 7 6   3 0 0

Quick Composition Choose a clef and indicate the meter of your favorite improvisation. You can notate your work using accidentals or create a nontraditional key signature that indicates the sharps or flats that are included in the octatonic collection that you are using. For example, if you are using octatonic 12, write a key signature with D♭, E♭, and G♭, and B♭ indicated. Exchange with a peer and sing each other's melodies with solfège syllables, scale-degree numbers, or letter names.

Melodies

Integers are often helpful when singing highly chromatic, atonal, and unfamiliar melodies. When performing with integers, remember that enharmonic pitches receive the same name. In order to maintain accurate rhythms abbreviate any multisyllable integer as shown in Chapter 35, page 497. For the following melodies, compare the use of solfège syllables, scale-degree numbers, and integers, and determine the most useful system for each melody. Regardless of the system that you choose, look for patterns such as scales, modes, and tetrachords to help orient your ear to unfamiliar music.

1348 Bartók, No. 10 from *44 Duets*, Vol. I

Though the melodic pitches occur in the A harmonic minor scale, *ti* ($\hat{7}$) resolves atypically.

1349 Bartók, *Mikrokosmos*, Vol. V, No. 128

1350 Ravel, "Aousa!" from *Chansons madécasses* (adapted)

1351 Reger, "Der Tod, das ist die kühle Nacht" ("Death Is the Cool Night") (adapted)

Der Tod, das ist die küh-le Nacht, das

Le - ben ist der schwü-le Tag.

1352 Prokofiev, *Visions fugitives*, No. 13, Op. 22 (adapted)

1353 Prokofiev, "Legenda," from *Ten Pieces*, Op. 12 (adapted)

1354 Prokofiev, Melody 1, from *Five Melodies*, Op. 35 (adapted)

1355 Prokofiev, Melody 4, from *Five Melodies*, Op. 35 (adapted)

1356 Bartók, No. 7 from *44 Duets*, Vol. I

Pitches 1-5 occur in the A harmonic minor scale, but here the centric pitch is D. Perform the pentachords to orient your ear to Bartók's melody, then perform the melody.

1357 Stravinsky, "Danse infernale de tous les sujets de Kastchéi" ("Dance of King Kastchéi's Subjects"), from *L'oiseau de feu* (*The Firebird*) (adapted)

Enharmonically, all the pitches belong to the E harmonic minor scale, but here B is the centric pitch. Sing the B-to-B scale to orient your ear to Stravinsky's scale, then sing his melody.

1358 Bartók, No. 44 from *44 Duets*, Vol. II (adapted)

Practice the familiar tetrachord patterns to help your intonation when singing Bartók's melody.

The Lydian-Mixolydian Mode (Overtone Scale)

1359 Joel Phillips, "Wallowtumble," from *Pieces for Children* (adapted)

Though the pitches in measures 1-6 belong to a G melodic minor scale, the centric pitch is C. This collection is called the Lydian-Mixolydian mode, or overtone scale. It is often interpreted as two interlocking dominant seventh chords. Perform the bass line while playing the upper parts or perform with two other performers or groups.

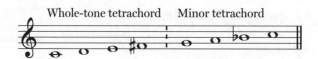

Rhythms of the Spoken Word

The following rhythms present poetic texts set for rhythmic recitation. As you perform these rhythms pay special attention to the meaning of the text.

1360 Madison Julius Cawein, "A Song of Cheer"

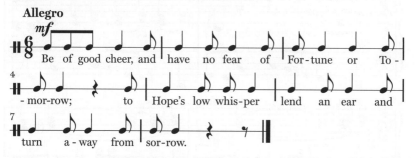

1361 Ben Jonson, "An Elegy"

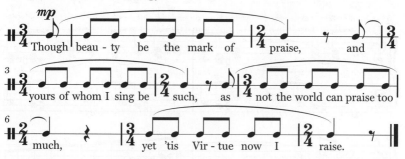

1362 Ella Wheeler Wilxoc, "A Dirge"

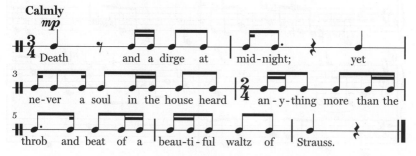

1363 Robert Frost, from "Dust of Snow"

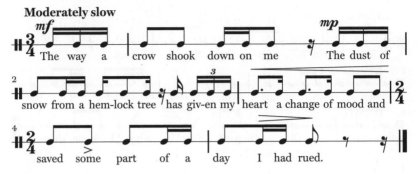

Moderately slow

mf *mp*

The way a | crow shook down on me | The dust of
snow from a hem-lock tree | has giv-en my | heart a change of mood and
saved some part | of a day | I had rued.

1364 William Shakespeare, from Sonnet XLIII

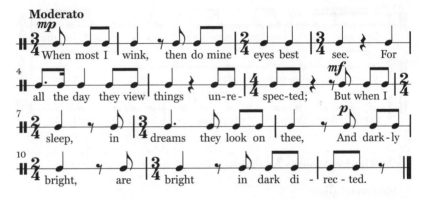

Moderato

mp

When most I | wink, then do mine | eyes best | see. For
all the day they view | things un-re- | spec-ted; | But when I
sleep, in | dreams they look on | thee, And dark-ly
bright, are | bright in dark di - | rec-ted.

mf *p*

1365 Alexander Pope, from "Ode on Solitude"

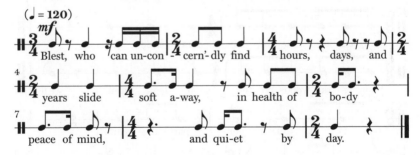

($\quad$ = **120**)

mf

Blest, who | can un-con- | cern'-dly find | hours, days, and
years slide | soft a-way, in health of | bo-dy
peace of mind, | and qui-et by | day.

1366 Christina Georgina Rosetti, "Song"

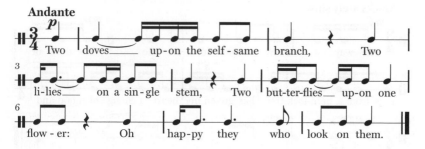

Andante

Two doves up-on the self-same branch, Two li-lies on a sin-gle stem, Two but-ter-flies up-on one flow-er: Oh hap-py they who look on them.

1367 William Ernest Henley, from "Rondel"

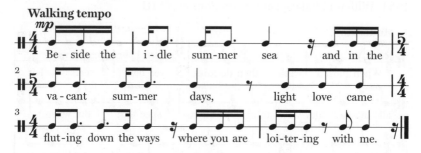

Walking tempo

Be-side the i-dle sum-mer sea and in the va-cant sum-mer days, light love came flut-ing down the ways where you are loi-ter-ing with me.

1368 Thomas Moore, "A Canadian Boat Song"

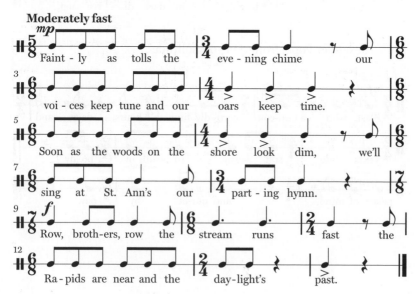

Moderately fast

Faint-ly as tolls the eve-ning chime our voi-ces keep tune and our oars keep time. Soon as the woods on the shore look dim, we'll sing at St. Ann's our part-ing hymn. Row, broth-ers, row the stream runs fast the Ra-pids are near and the day-light's past.

1369 William Blake, "Ah Sunflower"

CHAPTER 37

Melody:

- Trichord études
- Whole-tone and pentatonic collections

Rhythm:

- Changing meters 3: symmetric and asymmetric meters
- Obscured meters
- Polymeters

In this chapter you'll learn to:

- Perform the twelve trichords in prime form and in inversions
- Perform rhythms in which the meter changes, is obscured, or is combined with a contrasting one
- Improvise a duet where the pitch content alternates between whole-tone and pentatonic pitch-class sets

---

Improvisation 37.1: Whole-Tone and Pentatonic Scales as Sets

Improvise an **A B A** duet that moves from whole-tone sets to pentatonic sets, then back to whole-tone sets. Choose from the following sets, moving from one set to the next by means of the "pivot" trichord {6 8 t}. On your own, practice singing and playing the sets. Remember that you may realize the pitch classes in any octave.

Whole-tone sets: {6 8 t}, {6 8 0}, {6 t 4}, {6 8 t 0}, {6 8 t 2, {6 8 0 2}

Pentatonic sets: {1 3 6}, {1 3 8}, {6 8 t}, {1 3 6 8}, {6 8 t 1 3}

"Pivot set" to move between collections: {6 8 t}

- Performer 1 begins by improvising an ostinato based on one of the whole-tone sets.
- Performer 2 then improvises a melody based on any of the remaining whole-tone sets.
- At a predetermined signal, such as a nod of the head, both perform only pcs from the "pivot" collection {6 8 t}.
- At a second signal, they move to the pentatonic sets and repeat the process (with one performer improvising an ostinato and the other a melody).
- Return to the whole-tone sets, again by means of {6 8 t}.

Variations

- Add a percussionist to the ensemble, who plays on surfaces available in class (books, desktops, pencils, etc.).
- Add a conductor. The performers must follow the gestures of the conductor, adjusting elements of their performance such as dynamics, tempo, and texture.

Quick Composition Notate your favorite improvisation and create a score to show all parts using a staff for each performer. Align the parts so all players can both see and hear each other's part. Include the key signature (if needed) and the meter signature. Exchange with a peer and sing each other's part with solfège syllables, scale-degree numbers, or letter names.

Trichord Études

Pitches 1–3 in each trichord are the prime form; pitches 4–6 are an inverted form.

1381

Inverted Forms of the Twelve Trichords

Rhythms

Changing Meters 3: Symmetric and Asymmetric Meters

The following rhythms feature changes between symmetric and asymmetric meters. Unless indicated otherwise, these rhythms should be performed with note-value equivalence. See Chapter 22 for review.

1396

Andantino

1397

Gracieux

1398

Allegretto

1399

Ensemble Rhythms

1400

Obscured Meter

In the following rhythms the meter is obscured when accents regularly occur on weak beats of the measure. The meter that is perceived does not match the written meter.

1402

1403

1404

1405

1406

Polymeter

When two different meters are written or perceived, polymeter occurs. Often in such instances, the two meters alternate from being in and out of alignment with each other.

1407

CHAPTER 38

Melody:

- Pitch-class sets in melodies
- Ordered collections and twelve-tone music
- Octatonic scales and subsets

Rhythm:

- Tempo and meter modulation

In this chapter you'll learn to:

- Perform melodies derived from or based on pitch-class sets
- Perform melodies based on ordered collections and twelve-tone rows
- Perform rhythms in which the tempo or meter changes by combining beat-value and note-value equivalence
- Improvise a duet whose pitch content derives from subsets of the octatonic scale

---

*Improvisation 38.1: Octatonic Scales and Subsets*_____

Choose one of the following set classes and display it as pitches for the whole class. Write its transpositions and inversions as well. Add to this each of the three distinct versions of the octatonic scale (for example, scales beginning whole step/half step, that include the pc C, C♯, or D). Perform all these examples to get the sounds in your ears, voice, and fingers. Remember to think of these realizations as pitch classes that may be expressed in any octave.

4-3 [0 1 3 4]   4-9 [0 1 6 7]   4-Z15 [0 1 4 6]

5-28 [0 2 3 6 8]   5-31 [0 1 3 6 9]

- Performer 1 begins by developing an ostinato based on some version of the set.
- Performer 2 then improvises a melody based on the octatonic scale that contains the pitches of the ostinato.
- If performer 1 changes to a different transposition or inversion of the set, performer 2 should respond by adjusting to a new octatonic scale.

Variations

- At a predetermined signal, such as a nod of the head, the performers should switch their roles in the middle of the improvisation. Switch once more to give the improvisation an **A B A** design.
- Add a percussionist to the ensemble, who plays on surfaces available in class (books, desktops, pencils, etc.). The percussionist should listen to the melodic improviser and try to create a rhythmic canon.
- Add a second melodic improviser who must imitate the first improviser's melody, but in inversion, and feature pcs from the same octatonic scale.
- Add a conductor. The performers must follow the gestures of the conductor, adjusting elements of their performance such as dynamics, tempo, and texture.
- Add a speaker. The speaker might recite poetry or interject familiar maxims from music history, such as Fux's "*Mi* contra *fa* est diabolus in musica," from *Gradus ad Parnassum*. (Today we might say, "The tritone is the devil in music.")

Quick Composition Notate your favorite improvisation and create a score to show all parts using a staff for each performer. Align the parts so all performers can both see and hear each other's part. Include the correct key and meter signature. Exchange with a peer and sing each other's part with solfège syllables, scale-degree numbers, or letter names.

Pitch-Class Sets in Melodies

In addition to identifying scales and modes in the next group of melodies, practice identifying trichords. Hints are provided in the first several melodies.

1410 Ives, "Premonitions"

Overlapping versions of the [0 1 6] trichord.

1411 Bartók, No. 28 from *44 Duets*, Vol. II

Trichord [0 2 4] begins and [0 1 6] ends each six-note melodic motive.

1412 Bartók, *Two Rumanian Dances*, Op. 8a, No. 1 (adapted)

Look for the following trichords and scales: Measure 1 (beat 4): [0 1 5] trichord. Measure 6a [0 1 4] trichord. Measures 8-9: octatonic scale. Measure 10: Lydian-Mixolydian mode (overtone scale). Measures 10-end: [0 2 5], [0 2 6], and [0 2 7] trichords.

1413 Schoenberg, *Das Buch der hängenden Gärten* (*"The Book of the Hanging Gardens"*), No. XIV

Look for the following trichords and scales: Measure 1 [0 1 6] trichord outline ([0 1 6 7] subsets). Measure 1 (last eighth) to measure 3 (downbeat), and measure 10: whole-tone segments. Measures 4–5: chromatic trichords. Measures 7 and 9: "split-third triads" [0 3 4 7].

1414 Berg, Piano Sonata, Op. 1 (adapted)

Pickup and measure 5: [0 1 6]. Measures 1, 3, 6, and downbeat of measure 7: [0 4 8]. Measure 7 (beat 3) to measure 9 (beat 1): both forms of [0 1 4].

1415 Berg, "Marie's Lullaby," from *Wozzeck*

1416 Debussy, "C'est l'extase" ("Ecstasy"), from *Ariettes oubliées* (*Forgotten Little Arias*)

1417 Webern, "Himmelfahrt" ("Heavenly Journey"), from *Five Songs After Poems by Richard Dehmel*

1418 Webern, "Nächtliche Seheu" ("Nocturnal Fear"), from *Five Songs After Poems by Richard Dehmel*

Ordered Collections and Twelve-Tone Music

As you sing the following melodies, try to determine the ordered collections and the serial operations involved in each: transposition, inversion, retrograde, and retrograde-inversion.

1419 Dallapiccola, "Liriche di Antonio Machado"

Note how the row consists of hexachords comprised of subsets of octatonic scales.

1420 Schoenberg, "Unentrinnbar" ("Inescapable"), from *Four Pieces for Mixed Chorus*, Op. 27, No. 1

1421 Stravinsky, Four Trios, from *Argon*

Perform the pitches forward and backward to discover how the composer organized his twelve-tone fugue subject.

1422 Schoenberg, *De profundis (Out of the Depths)*, Op. 50B

Translation: "Out of the depths I call to You, God."

1423 Berg, Violin Concerto, first movement

The row, P_7, is the first twelve pcs. Measures 10ff are I_7. Consider pcs 1–4 and
5–8 to be ordered segments: the second is T_2, of the first. Consider pcs 9–12 to be
another ordered segment: the whole-tone tetrachord, 4–21 [0 2 4 6].

1424 Schoenberg, *Variations for Orchestra*, Op. 31

1425 Schoenberg, *Suite for Piano*, Op. 25, Trio

Rhythms: Tempo and Meter Modulation

Using Common Divisions to Change Tempo and Meter

The first rhythm presents tempo modulation that gradually slows. Conduct the melody in duple meter throughout. As indicated, keep the value of the beat divisions constant. Notice the indicated tempo changes, and determine how these are calculated mathematically. For example if the ♩ = 135, the ♪ (twice as fast) = 270, and the ♩. (three times as slow) = 90.

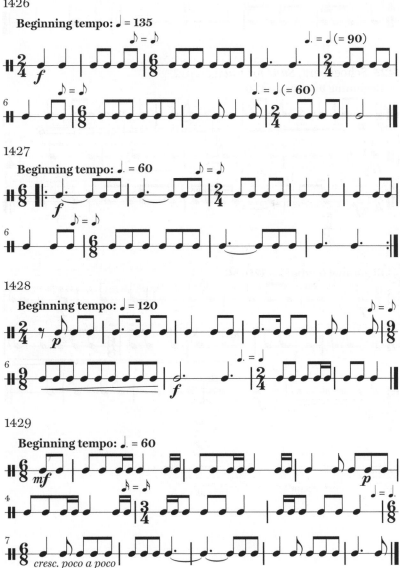

1430

Beginning tempo: ♪ = 60

1431

Beginning tempo: ♩ = 120

1432

Beginning tempo: ♩ = 120, 80

1433

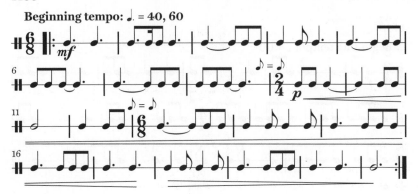

1434

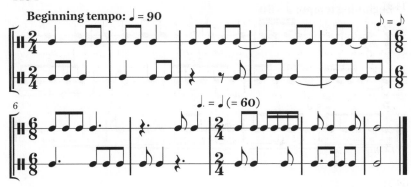

1435

1436

1437

1438

1439

1440

1441

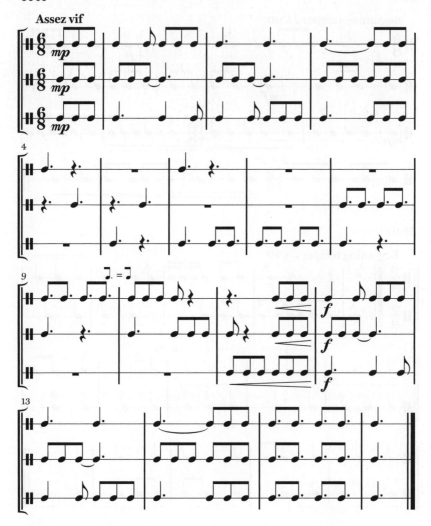

CHAPTER 39

Melody:

- More rhythmic challenges
- Modes, sets, and rows

Rhythm:

- Ametric rhythms
- Non-retrogradable rhythms
- Rhythms with added values

In this chapter you'll learn to:

- Perform rhythms that have no meter signature, that are the same when performed forward and backward, and in which small durations are added to disrupt a regular pattern
- Perform melodies that feature many of the rhythmic challenges encountered throughout this text
- Improvise polymetric duets

Improvisation 39.1: Polymetric Duets _____

Create a polymetric ostinato. First, take two meters, $\frac{3}{4}$ and $\frac{4}{4}$, and multiply their beats (the top number in the signature): multiply 3 times 4. Your ostinato will be twelve *beats* long—four measures of 3 and three measures of 4, heard at the same time.

- Performer 1 begins by improvising a four-measure rhythmic ostinato in $\frac{3}{4}$ meter.
- Once the ostinato is established, performer 2 enters, improvising a three-measure ostinato in $\frac{4}{4}$ as the first performer continues.

- To make the meters more audible, each person should choose a contrasting timbre, choose rhythmic patterns common to the meters, and emphasize the metric accent.

- Following the same procedure, combine other meters.

Quick Composition Notate your favorite improvisation on a two-line rhythm staff with upward stems. Align the parts so all players can both see and hear each other's part. Exchange with a peer and sing each other's part with solfège syllables, scale-degree numbers, or letter names.

Rhythms

Ametric Rhythms

The following rhythms have no meter signature. Perform them while quietly tapping the shortest note value as you sing multiples of this value. Alternately, sing the shortest note value on a neutral syllable while you tap the rhythm.

1442

1443

1444

1445

Non-Retrogradable Rhythms

The following rhythms are palindromes, that is, the same forward and backward.

1446

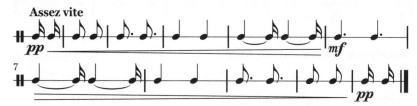

1447

1448

1449

Rhythms with Added Values

In the following rhythms a short note or rest value is added to a pattern to disrupt the regularity of the rhythm. Such rhythms are often written without a meter signature. Perform these rhythms while quietly tapping the shortest note value as you sing multiples of this value. Alternately, sing the shortest note value on a neutral syllable while you tap the rhythm.

1450

Melodies

The following melodies feature rhythmic variety typical of music from the last hundred years. They also manipulate pitches in all the various ways you have studied so far—from the use of modes, to sets and rows. Consider singing with solfège syllables, scale-degree numbers, or integers and determine the most appropriate system to perform each.

1455 Stravinsky, "Royal March," from *L'histoire du soldat* (*The Soldier's Tale*) (adapted)

Lydian mode

1456 Stravinsky, Theme and Variations, from *Octet for Wind Instruments* (adapted)

Octatonic scale

1457 Messiaen, "Danse de la fureur" ("Dance of Fury"), from *Quatour pour le fin du temps* (*Quartet for the End of Time*)

Measures 1-4 are predominantly whole-tone, and measures 5-6 are octatonic.

1458 Webern, "Dies ist ein Lied für dich allein" ("This Is a Song for You Alone"), from *Five Songs from "Der siebente Ring"* of Stefan George

1459 Webern, "Ave Regina Coelorum" ("Hail, Queen of Heaven"), Op. 18, No. 3

There are three row forms: P_4, I_4, and RI_4. The last pc of I_4 (G♯, in m. 7) is also the first pc of RI_4.

1460 Webern, "Im Morgentaun" ("In the Morning Dew"), from *Five Songs from "Der siebente Ring" (The Seventh Ring) of Stefan George*

wie ein Hauch

1461 Hindemith, *Concert Music for Strings and Brass*, Op. 50

Listen for subsets of the octatonic scale.

1462 Berg, *Lyric Suite*, first movement (adapted)

1463 Webern, "In der Fremde" ("In a Foreign Land"), from *Four Songs for Soprano and Orchestra*, Op. 13

This melody may sound similar to that of Webern's twelve-tone melodies, but it is not twelve-tone. This technique was a natural outgrowth of the atonal musical language composers were already developing in their music.

1464

Ensemble Melodies

1465 Bartók, No. 29 from _44 Duets_, Vol. II

This melody moves from Dorian to Mixolydian.

1466 Joel Phillips, "Holiday Round 2009" (round in 3 parts)

This melody is also Dorian.

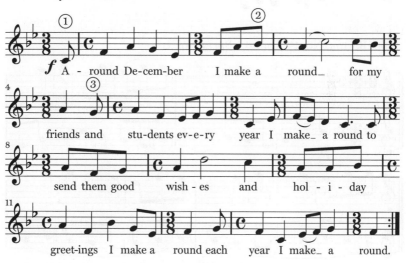

1467 Bartók, No. 30 from *44 Duets*, Vol. II

1468 Bartók, No. 19 from *44 Duets*, Vol. I

1469 Phillips, *Wild Nights!* (adapted)

This melody is based on the minor pentatonic scale.

1470 Stravinsky, Gloria, from *Mass*

CHAPTER 40

Melody:

- Music composed after 1950

Rhythm:

- Feathered beams
- Isorhythm and serialized durations
- Rhythms from the literature

In this chapter you'll learn to:

- Perform rhythms with repeated patterns and serialized durations
- Perform rhythms with feathered beams
- Perform literature melodies composed after 1950
- Improvise a twelve-tone dance on your choice of instrument

Improvisation 40.1: Twelve-Tone Dance _____

Create a row of your own. Select at least two forms of the row to use in an improvisation—a short dance movement—that you will perform on a pitched instrument of your choice. Display your choices of row forms for the whole class. Select one of the following dance rhythms for the motivic rhythm of your improvisation.

- Practice the row forms and the rhythm separately before putting them together.
- Remember, these are pcs, so practice them in every octave available on your instrument.
- Practice expressing the intervals in both conjunct and disjunct lines. Many twelve-tone melodies express each interval in the series as a leap.

Quick Composition Notate your favorite improvisation and create a score that accommodates your choice of instrument. Do not use a key signature, but instead notate the pitches of the row using accidentals.

Rhythms

Feathered Beams

The next five rhythms feature "feathered beams," which indicate an increase or decrease in tempo *within* the beat while the overall tempo remains constant. Conduct throughout, keeping strict time. Aim for clear accelerations and decelerations that do not lengthen or shorten the quarter-note beat.

1471

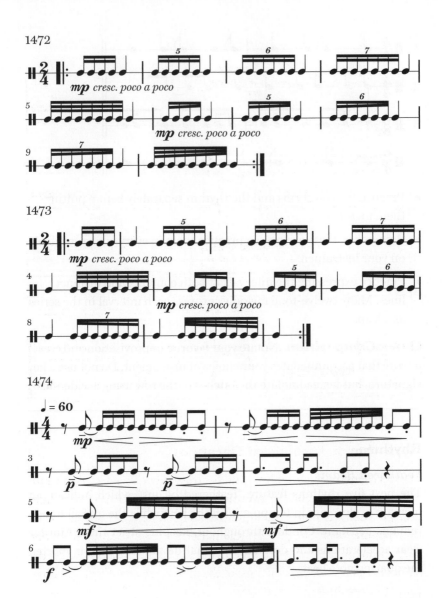

1472

1473

1474

1475

Isorhythm and Serialized Durations

The technique of isorhythm can be traced back to the thirteenth century. Composers of the twentieth and twenty-first centuries have utilized this technique to organize and shape their music. With isorhythmic technique, a rhythmic pattern is usually repeated in one part; although the pitches of this rhythmic pattern usually change, the pattern does not. The repetitions of the pattern frequently do not align with the downbeat of a measure.

Serialized Durations

Note in the following exercise that the series of note values in the first three measures of the upper part is presented in its original order and in retrograde throughout the excerpt.

1478

Rhythms from the Literature

1479 Messiaen, "Danse de la fureur" ("Dance of Fury"), from *Quatour pour le fin du temps* (*Quartet for the End of Time*) (adapted)

1480 Carter, *Eight Etudes and a Fantasy for Woodwind Quartet*, No. 9, Fantasy (adapted)

1481 Dallapiccola, *Goethe-Lieder*, No. 2 (adapted)

1482 Debussy, *Syrinx* (adapted)

1483 Varèse, *Density 21.5* (adapted)

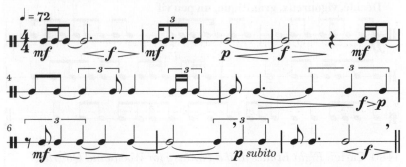

1484 Ives, Sonata for Violin and Piano, third movement, "The
Revival" (adapted)

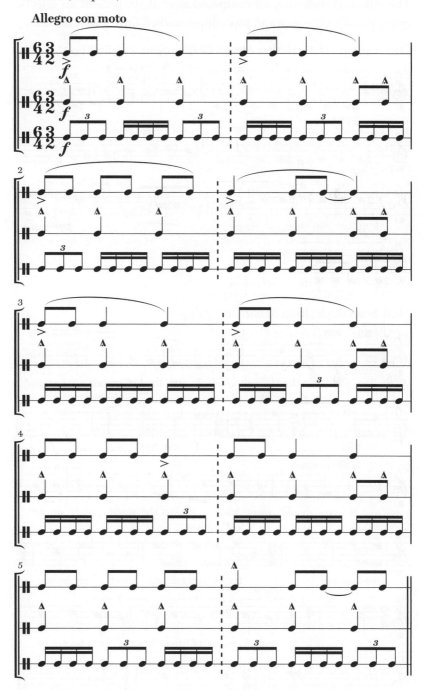

Melodies

The following melodies, all composed after 1950, present an eclectic collection of techniques and procedures studied throughout the text.

1485 Crumb, "Dark Mother Always Gliding Near with Soft Feet"

1486 Sean Doyle, from *Samaritan* (adapted)

1487 Morton Gould, *Jekyll and Hyde Variations for Orchestra*

If the excerpt were to continue, which pitch class would occur next?

1488 Sean Doyle, from *A Satire to Decay*

O, how this spring of love re - sem - bleth the un - cer-tain glo - ry of an Ap - ril day, Which now shows all the beau-ty of the sun, and by and by a cloud takes all a-way, a - way,

1489 Deborah Koenigsberg, String Quartet, third movement (adapted)

1490 Rebecca Oswald, *Finding the Murray River*

1491 Douglas Ovens, "The Queen," text by Pablo Neruda (translated)

and a hymn fills the world. a hymn fills the world.

On-ly you and I on-ly you and I my love, lis-ten to it.

1492 Sean Doyle, from *Harlequin Redux*

Freely moving, like a ballad: ♩. = approx. 58

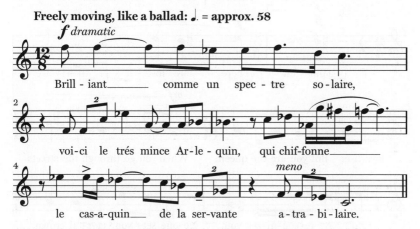

Brill - iant____ comme un spec - tre so - laire,

voi - ci le trés mince Ar - le - quin, qui chif-fonne____

le cas-a-quin___ de la ser-vante a - tra - bi - laire.

1493 Sean Doyle, from *Harlequin Redux*
(second verse of the above; similar, but a little simpler)

A - fin____ d'a-pai-ser sa co-lère,

Il fait_ mir-oi-ter_ un se-quin. Brill - iant____ comme

_ un spec-tre so-laire,_ voi-ci____ le très mince Ar-le-quin

Ensemble Melodies

1494 Joel Phillips, "Reflections," from *Pieces for Children* (adapted)

1495 Andrew Carter, *Nunc dimittis* (*Now Let Your Servant Depart*)

1496 Hanson, "How Excellent Thy Name"

1497 Joel Phillips, "Two Lazy Cats," from *Pieces for Children*

1498 Joel Phillips, *Libera me, Domine!* (*Deliver Me, Lord!*)

1499 Joel Phillips, "Gambolroister," from *Pieces for Children* (adapted)

This free use of all diatonic pitches is called pandiatonicism.

1500 Bernstein, *Kaddish* (Symphony No. 3) (adapted)

This work features a twelve-tone ground bass set to an asymmetrical meter.

1501 Dallapiccola, *Quaderno musicale di Annalibera* (*Musical Notebook of Annalibera*), No. 4

Treat this melody as a duet or play one part while singing the other.

1502 Joel Phillips, *The All Too Big Throne of Heaven*

Keyboard Lessons

Elements of Music

KB 1: Orientation to the Keyboard

A. Finding and Identifying Pitches

(1) C is the white key immediately to the left of paired black keys. The C in the middle of a piano is called middle C or C4. One octave higher is C5; one octave lower is C3; and so forth. Find and identify each C on the piano. Include the octave number.

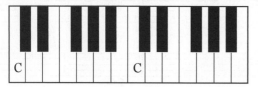

(2) Notes between Cs use the octave number of the lower C. Begin with C4 and play each white key up to C5. These pitches are C4-D4-E4-F4-G4-A4-B4-C5. Begin with a different C and repeat the process.

(3) Play the following pitches.

(a) C4	(b) A3	(c) F4	(d) G3	(e) E5	(f) G2
(g) B5	(h) D3	(i) A4	(j) D5	(k) F3	(l) B4
(m) C3	(n) B4	(o) F3	(p) E5		

(4) Work with a partner. One person places a pitch; the other identifies it including its octave number.

B. Whole and Half Steps, Accidentals, and Enharmonic Spelling

(1) Any two adjacent keys create a half step (H). When raising a white-key note, add a sharp to its name; when lowering one, add a flat (e.g., H↑C is C♯; H↓G is G♭). Play and identify half steps above and below the notes in A(3).

(2) Two successive half steps (H + H) make a whole step (W). Generally, whole steps use adjacent letter names (e.g., W↑A is B; W↓E♭ is D♭). Half steps can be figured similarly (e.g., H↑C is D♭ and H↓G is F♯). Play and identify whole steps above and below the notes in A(3) using adjacent letter names. Repeat the exercise and identify half steps.

(3) Enharmonic spelling calls the same key by different names. (e.g., C♯ and D♭; G♭ and F♯). Complete exercises B(1) and B(2) again. Provide enharmonic spellings for each answer.

KB 2: Reading Pitches and Spelling Half and Whole Steps

A. Reading and Identifying Pitches

(1) Work in pairs. One person should play the given pitches at the keyboard while the other checks for accuracy. Switch roles.

(2) Using the pitches in A(1), first play the pitch, then play and spell H and W steps above and below it. Ask a partner to check your work as you perform. Switch roles and perform again.

B. Multi-Pitch Segments

(1) Start with your right-hand thumb and play five-pitch white-key segments beginning with those shown and continuing until you reach C again. As you play, sing with letter names in a comfortable range. Identify each adjacent pair as half (H) or whole (W) step. Variation: Begin with your left-hand little finger and double the right hand with your left one octave lower.

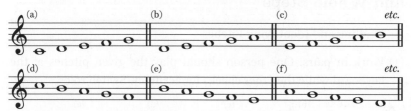

(2) Begin with the starting pitches for B(1), but change the whole- and half-step pattern to those shown in (a) and (b). While playing each new pattern, sing in a comfortable range with letter names, which may include accidentals.

(a) W-W-H-W   (b) W-H-W-W

(3) Begin with the starting pitches for B(1), but use only pitches 1-3 of each exercise when applying each of the following interval patterns.

(a) W-W   (b) W-H   (c) H-W

(4) Begin with the starting pitches for B(1), but use only pitches 1-4 of each exercise when applying each of the following interval patterns.

(a) W-W-H   (b) W-H-W   (c) H-W-W

KB 3: Major Pentachords, Tetrachords, and Scales

For all of the following exercises, sing with note names, solfège syllables, and scale-degree numbers as you play up and down the patterns.

C major pentachord with right- and left-hand fingering

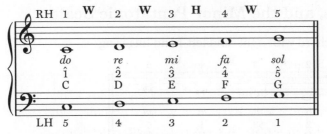

C major scale contructed from two major tetrachords (C major tetrachord + G major tetrachord)

A. Play major pentachords in octaves with both hands from the starting pitches listed.

(1) A   (2) F   (3) G   (4) E♭   (5) F♯   (6) E

(7) C♯   (8) A♭   (9) B♭   (10) B   (11) G♭   (12) D♭

Musical challenges! (13) A♯   (14) D♯   (15) F♭

B. Beginning on the starting pitches listed in exercise A, play major tetrachords in octaves with both hands.

C. Play an ascending major scale starting on each of the following tonic pitches. As you play each pitch, sing its name.

(1) D   (2) F   (3) A♭   (4) B/C♭   (5) E♭   (6) F♯/G♭

(7) A   (8) C   (9) E   (10) G   (11) B♭   (12) D♭/C♯

Musical challenges! (13) G♯   (14) F♭   (15) D♯

KB 4: Major Pentatonic Scales

Compared with major scales, major pentatonic scales omit *fa* ($\hat{4}$) and *ti* ($\hat{7}$). Using the following example as a guide, perform the major scales, followed by the major pentatonic scales. Begin on each of the pitches in KB 3: A.

KB 5.1: Minor Pentachords, Tetrachords, and Scales, and the Minor Pentatonic Scale

C minor pentachord with right- and left-hand fingering

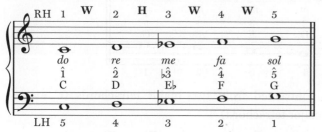

To make the minor tetrachord, perform the first four notes of the minor pentachord.

Natural minor scale (the same notes found in the minor key signature)

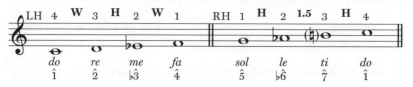

Harmonic minor scale (Think of the minor key signature, and raise ♭$\hat{7}$.)

Ascending melodic minor scale (Play a major scale, but lower $\hat{3}$ a half step; or think of the minor key signature, and raise ♭$\hat{6}$ and ♭$\hat{7}$.)

Descending melodic minor scale (same as natural minor)

A. Play minor pentachords in octaves with both hands from the starting pitches listed in KB 1: A(3). Play minor tetrachords from the same pitches.

B. For each pitch in KB 1: A(3), play the natural, harmonic, and melodic minor scale, ascending and descending.

C. Compared with natural minor scales, minor pentatonic scales omit *re* (2̂) and *le* (♭6̂). Using the following example as a guide, perform the natural minor scales, followed by the minor pentatonic scales. Begin on each of the pitches in KB 1: A(3).

KB 5.2: Diatonic Modes

You already know two diatonic modes: the major mode, also called the Ionian mode; and the natural (descending melodic) minor mode, also called the Aeolian mode. Next are the remaining common diatonic modes with two different ways to remember them.

Dorian mode

Perform a natural minor scale and raise ♭6̂ a half step.

Call the first pitch *re* (2̂). Perform a major scale from *re* to *re* (2̂-2̂).

Phrygian mode

Perform a natural minor scale and lower 2̂ a half step (sung *ra*).

Call the first pitch *mi* (3̂). Perform a major scale from *mi* to *mi* (3̂-3̂).

Lydian mode

Perform a major scale and raise 4̂ a half step (sung *fi*).

Call the first pitch *fa* (4̂). Perform a major scale from *fa* to *fa* (4̂-4̂).

Mixolydian mode

Perform a major scale and lower $\hat{7}$ a half step (sung *te*).

Call the first pitch *sol* ($\hat{5}$). Perform a major scale from *sol* to *sol* ($\hat{5}$-$\hat{5}$).

do	re	mi	fa	sol	la	te	do		sol	la	ti	do	re	mi	fa	sol
$\hat{1}$	$\hat{2}$	$\hat{3}$	$\hat{4}$	$\hat{5}$	$\hat{6}$	$\flat\hat{7}$	$\hat{1}$		$\hat{5}$	$\hat{6}$	$\hat{7}$	$\hat{1}$	$\hat{2}$	$\hat{3}$	$\hat{4}$	$\hat{5}$

Beginning on the given pitch, play the mode specified, ascending and descending.

(1) D Dorian   (2) F Mixolydian   (3) G♯ Aeolian

(4) B Phrygian   (5) B♭ Lydian   (6) F♯ Phrygian

(7) A Lydian   (8) D Mixolydian   (9) E♭ Lydian

(10) G Mixolydian   (11) B♭ Ionian   (12) E Dorian

KB 6: Intervals

A. Intervals from the Major Scale and the Phrygian Mode

Sing the entire scale or mode, then sing each interval above and below C as shown. Perform each interval four times, singing with solfège syllables, scale-degree numbers, note names, and interval names. (For example: "*do-do*, $\hat{1}$-$\hat{1}$, C-C, perfect unison"; "*do-re*, $\hat{1}$-$\hat{2}$, C-D, major second"; etc.)

C major scale: Major and perfect intervals above C; minor and perfect intervals below C

do do	do re	do mi	do fa	do sol	do la	do ti	do do
$\hat{1}$ $\hat{1}$	$\hat{1}$ $\hat{2}$	$\hat{1}$ $\hat{3}$	$\hat{1}$ $\hat{4}$	$\hat{1}$ $\hat{5}$	$\hat{1}$ $\hat{6}$	$\hat{1}$ $\hat{7}$	$\hat{1}$ $\hat{1}$
PU	M2	M3	P4	P5	M6	M7	P8

do do	do ti	do la	do sol	do fa	do mi	do re	do do
$\hat{1}$ $\hat{1}$	$\hat{1}$ $\hat{7}$	$\hat{1}$ $\hat{6}$	$\hat{1}$ $\hat{5}$	$\hat{1}$ $\hat{4}$	$\hat{1}$ $\hat{3}$	$\hat{1}$ $\hat{2}$	$\hat{1}$ $\hat{1}$
PU	m2	m3	P4	P5	m6	m7	P8

C Phrygian mode: Minor and perfect intervals above C; major and perfect intervals below C

do do	do ra	do me	do fa	do sol	do le	do te	do do
1̂ 1̂	1̂ ♭2̂	1̂ ♭3̂	1̂ 4̂	1̂ 5̂	1̂ ♭6̂	1̂ ♭7̂	1̂ 1̂
PU	m2	m3	P4	P5	m6	m7	P8

do do	do te	do le	do sol	do fa	do me	do ra	do do
1̂ 1̂	1̂ ♭7̂	1̂ ♭6̂	1̂ 5̂	1̂ 4̂	1̂ ♭3̂	1̂ ♭2̂	1̂ 1̂
PU	M2	M3	P4	P5	M6	M7	P8

Imagine the given pitch to be the lowest or highest note of either a major scale or Phrygian mode, as in exercise A. Sing up or down with solfège syllables, scale-degree numbers, letter names, and interval names until you reach the interval specified. Play the two notes of the interval simultaneously as a harmonic interval. Then, play the lower pitch and sing the higher one; switch and play the higher pitch and sing the lower one.

B. Ascending Major and Perfect Intervals

   (1) M6 above D   (2) M2 above A♭   (3) M3 above F♯

   (4) M7 above D♭   (5) P5 above B♭   (6) P4 above B

   (7) M7 above E♭   (8) M6 above C♯   (9) M3 above G♭

 (10) P8 above G   (11) M3 above A   (12) P5 above A♭

 (13) M2 above F   (14) P4 above F   (15) M6 above B

 (16) M3 above C♯

C. Descending Minor and Perfect Intervals

   (1) m2 below A   (2) m2 below C♯   (3) P8 below A♯

   (4) m7 below E♭   (5) m2 below B♭   (6) P4 below D♭

   (7) m7 below B   (8) m3 below F♯   (9) m6 below E

 (10) m3 below F   (11) m3 below A♭   (12) P5 below F

 (13) m3 below C♯   (14) P4 below B♭   (15) P5 below A

 (16) m6 below D

D. Ascending Minor and Perfect Intervals

  (1) m3 above E   (2) P5 above B   (3) m2 above D

  (4) m6 above A   (5) m2 above C♯   (6) m6 above B♭

  (7) P4 above F   (8) m7 above E♭   (9) m2 above A

(10) m3 above F♯   (11) m7 above A♭   (12) P5 above D♭

(13) m3 above G♯   (14) m7 above D   (15) m6 above F

(16) m3 above E♭

E. Descending Major and Perfect Intervals

  (1) M2 below D   (2) M6 below E♭   (3) M3 below B♭

  (4) M7 below F♯   (5) M2 below D♭   (6) P4 below G

  (7) M7 below B   (8) M3 below F♯   (9) M6 below E

(10) M3 below F   (11) M3 below A♭   (12) P5 below C

(13) M3 below C♯   (14) M6 below B♭   (15) M2 below A

(16) M7 below E

F. Ascending and Descending Major, Minor, and Perfect Intervals
Beginning on G, E, D♭, B, and G♭, play and sing all of the following intervals.

  (1) M6 above   (2) M3 below   (3) P5 above

  (4) m2 below   (5) m7 above   (6) m6 below

  (7) M7 above   (8) P5 below   (9) P4 above

(10) m7 below   (11) M3 above   (12) M7 below

(13) m2 above   (14) P4 below   (15) M2 below

(16) m7 above

G. Augmented and Diminished Intervals

(1) Change the following perfect and major intervals to an augmented
    interval.

    • Play the given interval, then raise the upper pitch a half step;
      name the new interval.

    • Play the given interval again, then lower the bottom pitch a half
      step; name the new interval.

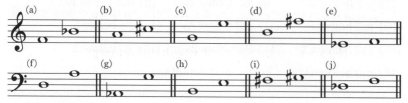

(2) Change the following perfect and minor intervals to a diminshed interval.

- Play the given interval, then lower the upper pitch a half step; name the new interval.
- Play the given interval again, then raise the bottom pitch a half step; name the new interval.

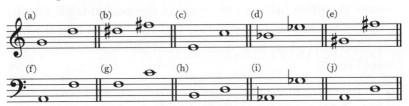

H. Augmented/diminished interval pairs and their resolutions often occur between particular scale degrees. Using the following model, perform and resolve pairs A6/d3, d7/A2, and d5/A4 in the following minor keys.

(1) A   (2) E   (3) D   (4) B   (5) G   (6) F♯   (7) F

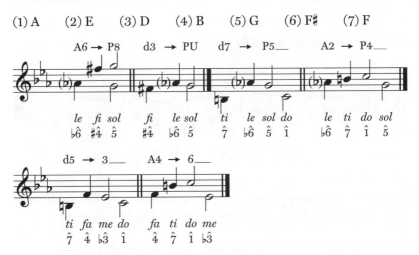

KB 7: Triads

A. Major and Minor Triads

For each of the following tonic pitches, perform a major pentachord and triad, then a minor pentachord and triad. The triad is the first, third, and fifth notes of the pentachord. Perform the patterns in both simple and compound meters.

- Recall the key signature associated with each tonic pitch.
- Play the patterns in both hands simultaneously.
- Sing with solfège syllables, scale-degree numbers, and letter names.

(1) G   (2) F   (3) Ab   (4) B   (5) Eb   (6) C#

(7) A   (8) C   (9) E   (10) Bb   (11) F#   (12) Gb

Musical challenges! (13) A#   (14) G#   (15) D#

B. Augmented and Diminished Triads

(1) For each pitch given in exercise A, perform a major triad, then *raise the fifth* a half step to create an augmented triad. Finally, resolve the augmented fifth up a half step. If you sing the first pitch as *do* ($\hat{1}$), hear how the augmented fifth lies between *sol* and *la* ($\hat{5}$ and $\hat{6}$).

(2) For each pitch in exercise A, perform a minor triad. Then *lower the fifth* a half step to create a diminished triad.

(3) Diminished triads in minor-key music: We hear the diminished triad as the supertonic chord in minor keys and as the leading-tone chord in both major and minor keys. Sing the following example to hear how the pitches of a diminished fifth resolve toward each other into a third.

Example: The given tonic is B.

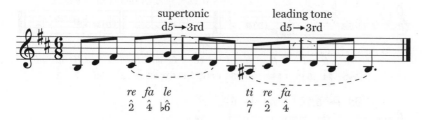

Transpose the preceding example to begin on A, E, G, C#, and F. Sing with solfège syllables, scale-degree numbers, and letter names.

C. Performing Triads on Major- and Minor-Key Scale Degrees

Consider each given note as the tonic. Using the notes from its major scale, play triads in your right hand on $\hat{1}$, $\hat{2}$, $\hat{3}$, and so on, as shown. If the quality of the triad is major or minor, play its root in your left hand. If its quality is diminished, play its third in your left hand. Perform again using notes from the natural minor. However, for the triads on the fifth and seventh scale degrees use *ti* ($\hat{7}$) instead of *te* ($\flat\hat{7}$).

(1) C   (2) G   (3) F   (4) A   (5) D   (6) E

KB 8: Seventh Chords

For each of the roots E, A, C, F♯, and G, play a major triad with the root doubled at the octave. Then lower one chord tone at a time to create all five common seventh chords on the root.

Example: The root is B.

KB 9: Connecting Intervals in Note-to-Note Counterpoint

A. Note-to-Note Species Counterpoint

(1) Harmonize a melody with imperfect consonances.

(a) First, play and sing the melody.

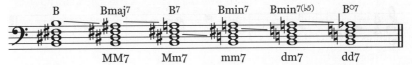

(b) Next, play the melody while singing thirds below it.

(c) This time, play the melody while singing sixths below it.

(2) For lines to be truly contrapuntal, they must sometimes move with the melody and other times against it, so that the parts will sound independent of each other. Mix the thirds and sixths this time, and add a few perfect consonances (PU, P5, or P8). These may also appear in the middle of phrases, but not as often as thirds and sixths and never in succession.

(3) Follow all the same steps to harmonize, and add counterpoint to the following melody. Remember to employ pitches from the melodic minor scale, raising ♭6̂ and ♭7̂ when ascending and lowering 6̂ and 7̂ when descending.

KB 10: Melodic and Rhythmic Embellishments in Two-Voices

A. Second-Species Counterpoint: Passing Tones, Neighbor Tones, and Consonant Skips and Steps

(1) Perform each of these first-species exercises, (a)-(c), as written. Sing one part while playing the other, then switch parts.

(2) Convert each exercise to second species by replacing the half notes in the higher part with two quarter notes. The first quarter must be the same pitch as the half note it replaces.

Try the following embellishments in the counterpoint wherever possible, and choose the ones that sound best.

- a passing tone placed between skips
- a neighbor tone added between repeated notes
- a consonant skip or step (CS) added between steps

First-species example

One possible second-species solution

(a)

(b)

(c)

B. Performing Suspensions

(1) Perform the following consonant sixths, then the displaced sixths (shown with arrows) to hear 7-6 suspensions. Note that the dissonance (7) occurs on the strong part of the beat and the resolution (6) on the weak part.

Consonant sixths

6   6   6   6   6   6   8

Displaced sixths become 7-6 suspensions.

6   6   6   6   7 – 6   7 – 6   8

(2) In a series of thirds, either the upper or lower part may be displaced (shown with arrows). A delayed upper part creates 4-3 suspensions; a delayed lower part creates 2-3 (bass) suspensions. Perform the consonant thirds, then each type of suspension. Again, the dissonance (4 or 2) occurs on the strong part of the beat and the consonance (3) on the weak part.

Consonant thirds

1   3   3   3   3   3   3   3   1

Displaced upper part becomes a chain of 4-3 suspensions.

1   3   3   3   3   4-3   4-3   4-3   1

Displaced lower part becomes a chain of 2-3 (bass) suspensions.

1   3   3   3   3   2-3   2-3   2-3   1

(3) Taking exercises (1) and (2) as models, embellish the following exercises to include suspensions when possible. The 2-3 suspension may occur only in the lower part, but the other suspensions may occur in either part. Play the original twice, singing first the lower part, then the upper part. Next, play the lower part while singing the upper part. Finally, sing the lower part while playing the upper part.

(a)

(b)

(c)

(d)

Diatonic Harmony and Tonicization

KB 11.1: Keyboard Style and SATB

For playing harmonies and accompanying improvisations, keyboard style has several advantages: it is easier to play, bass parts are easier to hear, and spacing errors are impossible. Keyboard style places three parts in the treble clef and one in the bass clef. Change keyboard style (KB) to SATB in one of two ways: (1) drop the alto part one octave, or (2) if Part 3 is already in the tenor range, simply notate it in the bass clef.

Converting keyboard style to SATB

Method 1	Method 2
Drop the alto one octave.	If the tenor is in range, notate it in bass clef.

Apply It

A. Revisit KB 7: C and perform the triads as specified. Convert each keyboard-style triad to SATB, as shown next. Limit the ranges of your soprano, alto, tenor, and bass pitches between C4-G5, G3-E5, C3-G4, and E2-C4, respectively.

KB 11.2: Embellishing Tones

Several Keyboard Lessons that follow ask you to improvise melodic variations of the soprano voice in each new progression you learn. The following example in Exercise A(1) presents a harmonic procedure that will reappear in later chapters, but may also be applied to any accompanied or unaccompanied melody.

Apply It

A. Follow the procedure given next to improvise melodic variations of a progression's soprano voice.

Practice each type of embellishment—neighbor tone (N), chordal skip (CS), chordal skip plus passing tone (CS + P), and double neighbor (DN)—separately then mix them to create "free" improvisations.

(1) Learn the progression that is the basis of your improvisation. While playing the progression, sing the melody. Listen for these original melodic pitches as guide tones during each embellishment that follows.

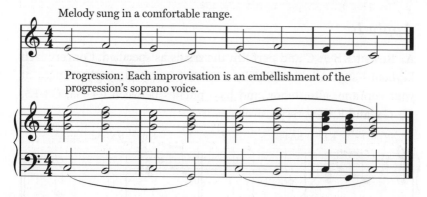

(2) Perform neighbor tone (N) études.

Upper N (UN or just N)

Lower N (LN or just N)   Chromatic lower N (CLN or just N)

(3) Perform chordal skip (CS) études.

Chordal skip (CS) down-up contour   Chordal skip (CS) up-down contour

(4) Perform a passing tone (P) étude by filling in the chordal skip (CS) étude from exercise (3).

Chordal skip plus passing tone (CS + P)

Chordal skip plus passing tone (CS + P)

(5) Perform double neighbor (DN) études.

Double N (DN or just N) up-down contour

Chromatic double N (CDN or just N) up-down contour. Use only the CLN.

Double N (DN or just N) down-up contour

Chromatic double N (CDN or just N) down-up contour. Use only the CLN.

(6) Create "free" improvisations by mixing the embellishments you practiced in the études.

Perform a transcription of one such possibility. Note that the rhythm has been varied. In addition you could add rests, change dynamics or articulations, and so on, to make your improvisation unique.

KB 12.1: Root-Position I-V-I

Memorize the four parts of the progression by singing them as a continuous melody. Sing each part in a comfortable range.

Apply It

A. Perform I-V-I in keyboard style with each of the three possible sopranos voices.

Each part indicates a melody. A voice is conveyed by the part numbers, from high (soprano) to low (bass).

Parts 1-3 may appear in the soprano (S), alto (A), or tenor (T) voice. The bass part (B) remains constant.

Example 12.1a

Example 12.1b

Example 12.1c

(1) If Part 1 is the soprano, perform Example 12.1a.

(2) If Part 2 is the soprano, Parts 3 and 1 become the alto and tenor, respectively. Perform Example 12.1b.

(3) If Part 3 is the soprano, Parts 1 and 2 become the alto and tenor, respectively. Perform Example 12.1c.

B. Create the following variations.

(1) Perform the bass pitch for chord 2 down one octave.

(2) Perform in the parallel minor key. Remember to raise the leading tone.

(3) Transpose to other keys (e.g., with key signatures ranging from three flats to three sharps).

(4) Convert from keyboard style to SATB (see KB 11.1: A).

(5) Create longer phrases by repeating measure 1.

(6) Embellish the rhythm and/or meter (e.g., play with an alternation of the bass and the chords).

(7) While playing the chords, sing embellishments of the soprano voice (e.g., neighbor tones) per KB 11.2.

C. Use the memorized pattern (from the beginning of KB 12.1) to employ proper voice-leading or in aural or visual identification.

(1) In G major notate the progression I-V-I in four-part SATB style.

Solution: Beginning with the bass part, sing each part and notate it.

(2) Realize the bass line in four-part SATB style.

Solution: Beginning with the bass part, sing each part and notate it.

(3) Work in pairs. One person creates and performs a progression from KB 12.1: A, while the partner listens and responds by singing, playing, and notating what was performed. Switch roles.

KB 12.2: Root-Position I-V$^{8\text{-}7}$-I

Memorize the four parts of the progression by singing them as a continuous melody. Sing each part in a comfortable range. If Part 2 is the soprano, *ti* ($\hat{7}$) must lead to *do* ($\hat{1}$). Otherwise, *ti* ($\hat{7}$) may fall to *sol* ($\hat{5}$) or rise to *do* ($\hat{1}$).

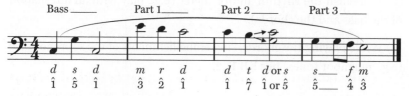

Apply It

A. Perform Example 12.2 in keyboard style following the procedure given.

Example 12.2: The Tonic-Dominant-Tonic (T-D-T) Model

For   *Perform chords as indicated.*

triads only	• 1-2a-1 as written (IAC) creates a progression identical to Example 12.1a.
	• 1-2a-1 with Part 2 as the soprano (PAC) creates a progression identical to Example 12.1b.
	• 1-2a-1 with Part 3 as the soprano (IAC) creates a progression identical to Example 12.1c.
V$^{8-7}$	• 1-2a-3a or 3b as written (PAC).
	• 1-(2a)-2b-3a or 3b as written (PAC).
	• 1-(2a)-2b-3a or 3b with Part 3 as the soprano (IAC).
	• 1-(2a)-2b-3b with Part 2 as the soprano (PAC with tripled root).

B. Follow the procedures in KB 12.1: B to create variations of Example 12.2.

C. Follow the guidelines given to perform the following cadences.

For this cadence:	*Perform a progression that concludes with chord:*
Half cadence (HC)	2a
Imperfect authentic (IAC)	3a or 3b with Part 3 in the soprano
Perfect authentic (PAC)	3a or 3b with Part 1 in the soprano; 3b with Part 2 in the soprano

D. Call and Response

Following the procedure in KB 12.1: C, use the memorized patterns when voice-leading or aurally "imagine" these parts over this bass line. Work in pairs. One person creates and performs a progression from

KB 12.2: A, while the partner listens and responds by singing, playing, and notating what was performed. Switch roles.

Listening Strategies for Root-Position Tonic- and Dominant-Function Chords

Always listen from the bottom to the top voice, focusing first on the bass part.

- If the bass is *do* ($\hat{1}$), write I or i.
- If the bass is *sol* ($\hat{5}$), write V, then listen for these possibilities.
  - If above the bass you hear *sol-fa* ($\hat{5}$-$\hat{4}$), add 8-7 to create V⁸⁻⁷.
  - If above the bass you hear just *fa* ($\hat{4}$), add 7 to create V⁷.

KB 13.1: Resolving Inversions of V⁷

Memorize the four parts of the progression by singing them as a continuous melody. Sing each part in a comfortable range.

Apply It

A. Perform chords 1, 2, and 3 in keyboard style to resolve V⁶₅, V⁴₂, or V⁴₃.

Example 13.1a

Example 13.1b

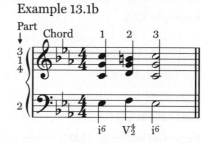

Example 13.1c

Any part, 1-4, may appear in the soprano, alto, or tenor voice.
Parts 4, 1, and 2 may appear in the bass voice.

- Perform Part 4 in the bass to produce i-V$^6_5$-i (Example 13.1a).
- Perform Part 1 in the bass to produce i^6-V$^4_3$-i^6 (Example 13.1b).
- Perform Part 2 in the bass to produce i-V$^4_2$-i (Example 13.1c).

B. Perform the following variations.

(1) Perform each example with each possible soprano voice (e.g., Example 13.1a with Part 2 as the soprano, then Part 3 as the soprano).

(2) Perform major-key versions of those just given.

- Change Roman numeral i to I to reflect the change in chord quality.
- Adjust solfège syllables and scale-degree numbers to reflect major-key solmization.

(3) Transpose to other keys (e.g., with key signatures ranging from three flats to three sharps).

(4) Convert from keyboard style to SATB (see KB 11.1: A).

(5) Create longer phrases (e.g., begin with Example 13.1a, measure 1 then conclude with all of Example 12.2).

(6) Embellish the rhythm and/or meter (e.g., play as arpeggiated chords in compound duple meter.).

(7) While playing the chords, sing embellishments of the soprano voice (e.g., chordal skips) per KB 11.2 (6).

C. Following the procedure in KB 12.1: C, use the memorized patterns when voice-leading or aurally "imagine" these parts over this bass line.

D. Call and Response

Work in pairs. One person creates and performs a progression from KB 13.1: A or B, while the partner listens and responds by singing, playing, and notating what was performed. Switch roles.

KB 13.2: Harmonizing the *do-re-me* Bass Line with I-V$^4_3$ or V$^6_4$-I^6

Memorize the four parts of the progression by singing them as a continuous melody. Sing each part in a comfortable range. Parts B, 2, and 3 are constant. Part 1 changes to create parallel or contrary motion above its bass.

Apply It

A. Perform the following keyboard-style harmonizations of the *do-re-me* bass.

Example 13.2a   Example 13.2b

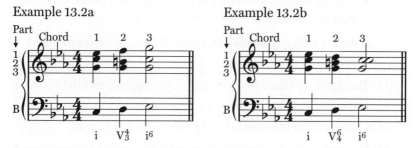

Parts 1–3 may appear in the soprano, alto, or tenor voice, but Part 1 in the soprano is the most common.

- If Part 1 moves parallel to the bass voice, bass pitch *re* ($\hat{2}$) is harmonized with V$^4_3$ (Example 13.2a).

- If Part 1 moves contrary to the bass voice, bass pitch *re* ($\hat{2}$) is harmonized with V$^6_4$ (Example 13.2b).

Parallel Tenths	*Contrary Motion (Voice Exchange)*
Passing V$^4_3$	Passing V$^6_4$

B. Perform the following variations.

(1)–(4) Follow the procedures in KB 13.1: B(1–4) to create variations employing these progressions.

(5) Create longer phrases (e.g., begin with Example 13.2a or 13.2b chords 1-2-3-1, then perform Example 12.2).

(6) Embellish the rhythm and/or meter (e.g., play Alberti figuration in the right hand—lowest note, highest, middle, highest).

(7) While playing the chords, sing embellishments of the soprano voice (e.g., chromatic lower neighbors) per KB 11.2.

C. Follow the procedures outlined in KB 13.1: C and D.

KB 14.1: Incorporating the Cadential $^6_4$ (V^{6-5}_{4-3} and V^{8-7}_{6-5}–I) into the T-D-T Model
$_{4-3}$

The cadential $^6_4$ is a melodic embellishment of V. Strong-beat pitches *mi* and *do* ($\hat{3}$ and $\hat{1}$) delay chord tones *re* and *ti* ($\hat{2}$ and $\hat{7}$) of V, which resolve on a metrically weaker beat. The four parts are identical to those you memorized in KB 12.1.

Apply It

A. Perform Example 14.1 in keyboard style following the procedure given.

Example 14.1 (Compare this with Example 12.2.)

For   *Perform the following chord progressions, which conclude with the cadence indicated.*

triads only	• 1-2b-1 as written (IAC) creates a progression identical to KB 12.1, Example 12.1a.
	• 1-2b-1 with Part 2 as the soprano (PAC) creates a progression identical to KB 12.1, Example 12.1b.
	• 1-2b-1 with Part 3 as the soprano (IAC) creates a progression identical to KB 12.1, Example 12.1c.
	• 1-2b-3a as written (PAC).
$V^{8\text{-}7}$	• 1-(2b)-2c-3a as written (PAC).
	• 1-(2b)-2c-3a with Part 3 as the soprano (IAC).
	• 1-(2b)-2c-3b with Part 2 as the soprano (PAC with tripled root).
	• Create longer progressions [e.g., 1-2b-1-2b (HC) 1-2b-1-2c-3a (PAC)]
	• Perform minor-key versions of those just given.

Perform the following chord progressions, which conclude with the cadence indicated.

V^{6-5}_{4-3}

- 1-2a → 2b-1 as written (IAC) (Chord 2a must continue to 2b.)
- 1-2a → 2b-1 with Part 2 as the soprano (PAC).
- 1-2a → 2b-1 with Part 3 as the soprano (IAC).
- 1-2a → 2b-3a as written (PAC).

$V^{8-7}_{\substack{6-5\\4-3}}$-I

- 1-2a → 2c-3a as written (PAC) (Chord 2a must continue to 2c.)
- 1-2a → 2c-3a with Part 3 as the soprano (IAC).
- 1-2a → 2c-3b with Part 2 as the soprano (PAC with tripled root).
- Create longer progressions [e.g., 1-2b-1-2b (HC) 1-2b-1-2c-3a (PAC)]
- Perform minor-key versions of those just given.

B. Follow the guidelines given to perform the following cadences.

For this cadence:	Perform a progression that concludes with chord:
Half cadence (HC)	2b
Imperfect authentic (IAC)	3a or 3b with Part 3 in the soprano
Perfect authentic (PAC)	3a or 3b with Part 1 in the soprano; 3b with Part 2 or 3 in the soprano
Perfect authentic (PAC)	3a or 3b with Part 1 in the soprano

C. Memorize the parts of $V^{8-7}_{\substack{6-5\\4-3}}$ (measure 2) to make voice-leading and aural identification easier.

(1) In G major notate V^{6-5}_{4-3} in four-part SATB style.

Solution: Beginning with the bass part, sing each part and notate it.

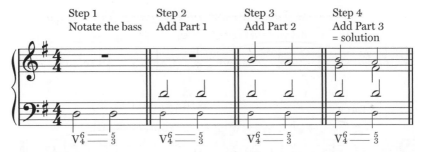

Step 1	Step 2	Step 3	Step 4
Notate the bass	Add Part 1	Add Part 2	Add Part 3 = solution

$V_4^6 - \frac{5}{3}$ $V_4^6 - \frac{5}{3}$ $V_4^6 - \frac{5}{3}$ $V_4^6 - \frac{5}{3}$

(2) Realize the patterns V_{4-3}^{6-5} and $V_{6-\frac{3}{3}}^{8-7}$ in major and minor keys from three flats to three sharps.

D. Call and Response

Work in pairs. One person creates and performs a progression from KB 14.1: A, while the partner listens and responds by singing, playing, and notating what was performed. Switch roles.

Listening Strategies for Root-Position Tonic- and Dominant-Function Chords

Always listen from the bottom to the top voice, focusing first on the bass part.

- If the bass is *do* ($\hat{1}$), write I or i.
- If the bass is *sol* ($\hat{5}$), write V, then listen for these possibilities.
  - If above the bass you hear *sol-fa* ($\hat{5}$-$\hat{4}$), add 8-7 to create V8-7.
  - If above the bass you hear just *fa* ($\hat{4}$), add 7 to create V7.
  - If above the bass you hear *mi-re* ($\hat{3}$-$\hat{2}$) or *do-ti* ($\hat{1}$-$\hat{7}$), add $\frac{6-5}{4-3}$ to create V_{4-3}^{6-5}.
  - If bass *sol* ($\hat{5}$) rises to *la* ($\hat{6}$) or *le* ($\flat\hat{6}$), write vi or VI, respectively, beneath the bass.

KB 14.2: Adding Predominant Chords (P) to the T-D-T Model = T-P-D-T

Memorize the four parts of the progression by singing them as a continuous melody. Sing each part in a comfortable range. If Part 2 is the soprano, *ti* ($\hat{7}$) must lead to *do* ($\hat{1}$). Otherwise, *ti* ($\hat{7}$) may fall to *sol* ($\hat{5}$) or rise to *do* ($\hat{1}$).

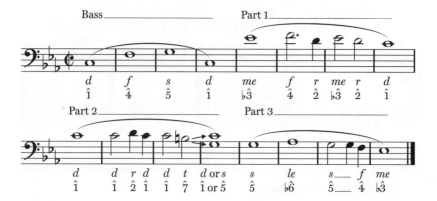

Bass_____ Part 1_____

	d	f	s	d	me	f	r	me	r	d
	$\hat{1}$	$\hat{4}$	$\hat{5}$	$\hat{1}$	$\flat\hat{3}$	$\hat{4}$	$\hat{2}$	$\flat\hat{3}$	$\hat{2}$	$\hat{1}$

Part 2_____ Part 3_____

	d	d	r	d	d	t	d or s	s	le	s___	f	me
	$\hat{1}$	$\hat{1}$	$\hat{2}$	$\hat{1}$	$\hat{1}$	$\hat{7}$	$\hat{1}$ or $\hat{5}$	$\hat{5}$	$\flat\hat{6}$	$\hat{5}$___	$\hat{4}$	$\flat\hat{3}$

Apply It

A. Perform in keyboard style with each of the three possible soprano voices following the procedure given.

Example 14.2

For

Perform the following chord progressions, which conclude with the cadence indicated.

triads only

- 1a-2a (or 2b)-3b-1 as written (IAC).

- 1a-2a (or 2b)-3b-1 with Part 2 as the soprano (PAC).

- 1a-2a (or 2b)-3b-1 with Part 3 as the soprano (IAC).

- 1a-2a (or 2b)-3b-4a as written (PAC).

add iiϕ^6_5 and V$^{8\text{-}7}$

- 1a-2a, b, or c-3c-4a as written (PAC).

- 1a-2a, b, or c-3c-4a with Part 3 as the soprano (IAC). In major, 1-2b creates parallel P5s.

- 1a-2a, b, or c-3c-4b with Part 2 as the soprano (PAC with tripled root).

add V^{6-5}_{4-3}	• 1a-2a, b, or c-3a → 3b-1 as written (IAC).
	• 1a-2a, b, or c-3a → 3b-1 with Part 2 as the soprano (PAC).
	• 1a-2a, b, or c-3a → 3b-1 with Part 3 as the soprano (IAC). In major, 1-2b creates parallel P5s.
	• 1a-2a, b, or c-3a → 3b-4a as written (PAC).
add $V^{8-7}_{6-5}_{4-3}$	• 1a-2a, b, or c-3a → 3c-4a as written (PAC).
	• 1a-2a, b, or c-3a → 3c-4a with Part 3 as the soprano (IAC). In major, 1-2b creates parallel P5s.
	• 1a-2a, b, or c-3a → 3c-4b with Part 2 as the soprano (PAC with tripled root).
neighboring $^6_4$ (pedal $^6_4$)	• In any progression just performed, replace 1a with 1a-1b-1c.
passing $^6_4$	• Review Example 13.2b.

B. Create the following variations of Example 14.2.

(1) Create longer progressions [e.g., 1-2a, b, or c-3a → 3b (HC) 1-2a, b, or c-3a → 3c-4a (PAC)].

(2) Perform major-key versions of those just given.

    (a) If using chords 1-2b, don't employ Part 3 as the soprano to avoid parallel P5s.

    (b) Change Roman numerals to reflect changes in chord quality (e.g., I, IV, ii6, ii$^6_5$).

    (c) Adjust solfège syllables and scale-degree numbers to reflect major-key solmization.

(3) For chords 1-2b or c begin chord 1 with Part 1 as the soprano. From chord 2b or c, finish with Part 2 as the soprano.

(4) While playing the chords, sing embellishments of the soprano voice with N, CLN, CS, and CS + P per KB 11.2.

C. Call and Response

Work in pairs. One person creates and performs a progression from KB 14.2: A, while the partner listens and responds by singing, playing, and notating what was performed. Switch roles.

Strategies for Distinguishing Predominant-Function Chords

Always listen from the bottom to the top voice, focusing first on the bass part. If bass pitch *fa* (4̂) rises to *sol* (5̂) the chord above *fa* (4̂) is predominant and that above *sol* (5̂) is dominant.

The following table summarizes various ways to discern one predominant chord from another.

Example 14.2 chord	2a	2b	2c	3a–c*
Possible key type(s)	M key; m key	M key; m key	M key; m key	
Chord quality	M; m	m; d	mm7; dm7	
Distinguishing melodic pitch(es)	*do* (1̂)	*re* (2̂)	*do* + *re* (1̂ + 2̂)	
Common tone with tonic?	yes, *do* (1̂)	no	yes, *do* (1̂)	
Common tone with V?	no	yes; *re* (2̂)	yes; *re* (2̂)	
Tritone?	no	no; yes	no; yes	
Chord symbol	IV; iv	ii6; ii°6	ii°$^6_5$; ii⌀$^6_5$	V*
Bass pitch	*fa* (4̂) —————————————————————			*sol* (5̂)

*Strategies for distinguishing root-position dominant-function chords (see KB 14.1).

KB 15.1: Incorporating Plagal and Deceptive Resolutions into the T-P-D-T Model

Memorize the four parts by singing them as melodies.

Example 15.1 (Compare with Example 14.2.)

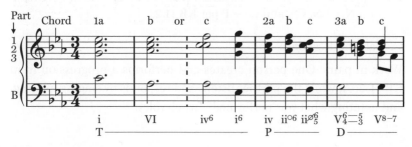

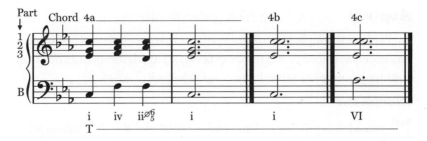

(1) Plagal extension: Perform Example 15.1 4a with Parts B, 1, 2, 3 (e.g., *d-f-f-d, d-d-d-d, s-l-l-s, me-f-r-me*).

(2) Deceptive resolutions or cadences: Perform Example 15.1 3b-3c-4c with parts B, 2, 1, 3 (e.g., *s-d, t-d, r-d, s-f-me*).

Apply It

A. Perform Example 15.1 following the procedures from KB 14.2: A and include these three additions.

(1) For chord 1a substitute 1a-1b or 1a-1c to create the two common tonic expansions in Example 15.1 (e.g., 1a-2a-3b becomes 1a-1b-2a-3b or 1a-1c-2a-3b).

(2) For a plagal extension of chord 4a's PAC play the entire two measures. Choose iv, ii°⁶₅, or both.

(3) For a deceptive cadence conclude with 4c (e.g., 1a-2b-3a-3c-4c).

B. Follow the example of KB 14.2: B and C to create variations and paired exercises based on Example 15.1.

KB 15.2: The Phrygian (Half) Cadence

Sing the following parts to memorize the voice-leading for iv⁶-V⁶⁻⁵₄⁻₃, the Phrygian (half) cadence (Example 15.2, mm. 3-4).

Apply It

A. Perform Example 15.2 to create phrases that conclude with a Phrygian half cadence. Chord 2b is a minor v^6 because bass descents from *do* ($\hat{1}$) in a minor key employ natural minor—*do-te-le-sol* ($\hat{1}$-$\flat\hat{7}$-$\flat\hat{6}$-$\hat{5}$).

Example 15.2

(1) Play first without these parenthetical chords—1a-(1b-1c)-2a or b-3-(4a →)-4b, then include them.

(2) To perform a passing $^6_4$ choose chord 2a.

(3) To perform a cadential $^6_4$ choose chord 4a, which must resolve to 4b.

(4) Compare measure 1 of Example 15.2 with Example 13.1a.

(5) If you perform Parts 2 or 3 as the soprano, always keep Part 1 above Part 2 to avoid parallel P5s in iv^6-V.

B. Create the following variations of Example 15.2.

(1) The Phrygian half cadence is found in minor-key progression. Transpose to other minor keys from three flats to three sharps.

(2) While playing the chords, sing embellishments of the soprano voice with N, CLN, CS, CS + P, and DN per KB 11.2.

C. Following the procedure in KB 14.1: C, use the memorized parts from measures 3-4 when voice-leading or aurally "imagine" them over the Phrygian half cadence's *le-sol* ($\flat\hat{6}$-$\hat{5}$) bass line.

D. Follow the example of KB 14.2: B and C to create variations and paired exercises based on KB 15.1.

KB 16: Delayed Resolutions
Apply It

A. Follow the procedure given next to create delayed resolutions.

Revisit KB 12-15. Sustain each dominant-function chord over the change of bass to tonic to create delayed resolutions—retardations and suspensions—like those shown next.

Example 16: Delayed Resolutions Based on Previous KB Lessons

Example 12.1a

Example 12.2

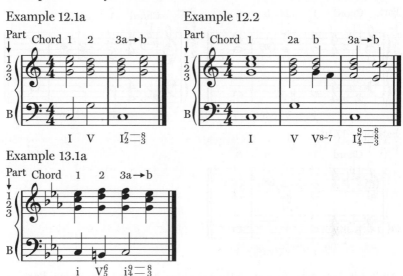

Example 13.1a

B. Work in pairs to create and identify examples of delayed resolution.

(1) Person 1 performs a delayed resolution based on examples from KB 12–15.

(2) Person 2 sings, plays, and notates what person 1 performs.

(3) Person 2 listens and identifies the type—retardation or suspension—and the two-number figure of each (e.g., in KB 12.1a above, identifies "retardations" and gives the figure for each: 2-3 and 7-8.)

KB 17.1: Dominant-Function Seventh Chords— viiᴼ⁷ Chord Equivalents of V_5^6, V_2^4, and V_3^4

Memorize the four parts of the progression by singing them as a continuous melody. Sing each part in a comfortable range.

Apply It

A. Perform chords 1-2b-3 to resolve viiᴼ⁷ chord equivalents of V_5^6, V_2^4, and V_3^4. These equivalent forms merely substitute *le* ($\flat\hat{6}$) for *sol* ($\hat{5}$) in Part 3. Compare KB 17.1 with KB 13.1.

Example 17.1a

Example 17.1b

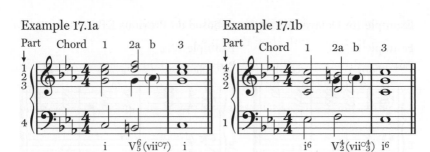

$$i \quad V_5^6(\text{vii}^{\circ}7) \quad i \qquad\qquad i^6 \quad V_2^4(\text{vii}^{\circ}_3^4) \quad i^6$$

Example 17.1c

$$i \quad V_3^4(\text{vii}^{\circ}_5^6) \quad i$$

Any part, 1-4, may appear in the soprano, alto, or tenor voice. Parts 4, 1, and 2 may appear in the bass voice.

- Perform Part 4 in the bass to produce i-vii°7-i as shown in Example 17.1a.

- Perform Part 1 in the bass to produce i⁶-vii°$_3^4$-i⁶ as shown in Example 17.1b.

- Perform Part 2 in the bass to produce i-vii°$_5^6$-i as shown in Example 17.1c.

B. Create the following variations.

(1) Perform each example with each possible soprano voice (e.g., Example 17.1a with Part 2 as the soprano, then Part 3 as the soprano).

(2) Perform major-key versions of those just given.

- Change Roman numerals to reflect changes in chord quality (e.g., I, vii$^{\emptyset}$7).

- Adjust solfège syllables and scale-degree numbers to reflect major-key solmization.

- In major keys, vii$^{\emptyset}$7 occurs infrequently. If you use it, keep Part 2 above Part 3 to avoid parallel P5s.

(3) Transpose to other keys (e.g., with key signatures ranging from three flats to three sharps).

(4) Convert from keyboard style to SATB (See KB 11.1: A).

(5) Create longer phrases (e.g., begin with Example 17.1a, measure 1 then conclude with all of Example 12.2).

(6) Embellish the rhythm and/or meter (e.g., play as arpeggiated chords in compound duple meter).

(7) While playing block chords, sing embellishments of the soprano voice per KB 11.2.

C. Call and Response

Following the procedure in KB 12.1: C, use the memorized patterns when voice-leading or aurally "imagine" these parts over this bass line. Work in pairs. One person creates and performs a progression from KB 17.1: A or B, while the partner listens and responds by singing, playing, and notating what was performed. Switch roles.

Strategies for Distinguishing Dominant-Function Seventh Chords

Always listen first for the bass part. The essence of dominant-function seventh chords is their *ti-fa* ($\hat{7}$-$\hat{4}$) dyad. If either one of these is the bass pitch and the other is above it, the chord is a dominant-function seventh chord. The bass pitch of a dominant-function seventh chord is harmonized with one of these chords:

ti ($\hat{7}$)	V^6_5 or vii°7
re ($\hat{2}$)	V^4_2 or vii°$^4_3$
fa ($\hat{4}$)	V^4_3 or vii°$^6_5$

Discerning V7 from vii°7			
Chord	V7	vii⌀7	vii°7
Example 17.1 chord number	2a	2b	2b
Possible key type(s)	major or minor	major	minor
Chord quality	Mm7	dm7	dd7
Tritones	1	1	2
Distinguishing melodic pitch	*sol* ($\hat{5}$)	*la* ($\hat{6}$)	*le* ($\flat\hat{6}$)
Common tone with tonic?	yes, *sol* ($\hat{5}$)	no	no

*Review the strategies for distinguishing root-position dominant-function chords (see KB 14.1).

KB 17.2: Harmonizing the *do-re-me* Bass Line

Memorize the four parts of the progression by singing them as a continuous melody. Sing each part in a comfortable range. Note that three parts remain constant. Part 1 changes to create parallel or contrary motion above its bass.

Apply It

A. Perform the following keyboard-style harmonizations of the *do-re-me* bass.

Parts 1-3 may appear in the soprano, alto, or tenor voice, but Part 1 in the soprano is most common.

Example 17.2

Parallel tenths
Dominant-function seventh

Contrary motion (voice exchange)
Dominant-function triad

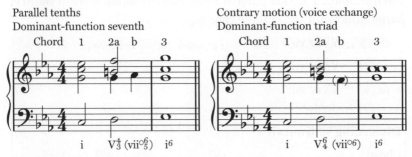

- If Part 1 moves parallel to the bass, harmonize bass pitch *re* ($\hat{2}$) with V$^4_3$ or vii$^{\circ 6}_5$ (Example 17.2, 2a).

- If Part 1 moves contrary to the bass, harmonize bass pitch *re* ($\hat{2}$) with V$^6_4$ or vii$^{\circ 6}$ (Example 17.2, 2b).

B. Perform the following variations.

(1)-(4) Follow the procedures in KB 17.1: B(1-4) to create variations employing these progressions.

(5) Create longer phrases (e.g., begin with Example 17.2, 2a or 2b chords 1-2-3-1, then perform Example 12.2).

(6) Embellish the rhythm and/or meter.

(7) While playing block chords, sing embellishments of the soprano voice (e.g., for double neighbor tones refer to KB 11.2).

C. Follow the procedures outlined in KB 17.1 C.

KB 18: Creating Parallel and Contrasting Periods

Distinct rhythms, contours, and pitches make motives memorable. As you or a partner play the chords, consider these three attributes when embellishing the soprano voice per KB 11.2. For parallel periods, begin phrase 2 with the same or a similar motive as phrase 1. For contrasting periods, begin phrase 2 with a different motive.

Apply It

A. Create parallel and contrasting periods from previous KB lessons as specified.

(1) Use Examples 14.2 and 15.1 [e.g., 1-2a, b, or c-3a → 3b (HC) 1-2a, b, or c-3a → 3c-4a (PAC)].

(2) Perform major-key versions of those just given.

    (a) If using chords 1-2b, don't employ Part 3 as the soprano to avoid parallel P5s.

    (b) Change Roman numerals to reflect changes in chord quality (e.g., I, IV, ii^6, ii$^6_5$).

    (c) Adjust solfège syllables and scale-degree numbers to reflect major-key solmization.

(3) For chords 1-2b or c begin chord 1 with Part 1 as the soprano. From chord 2b or c, finish with Part 2 as the soprano.

(4) Employ Example 15.2 for phrase 1 and Example 15.1 for phrase 2 in minor keys only.

B. Call and Response

Work in pairs. One person creates and performs a period from KB 18: A, while the partner listens and responds by singing, playing, notating, and/or identifying what was performed. Switch roles.

KB 19: Sequences

Sequences have five attributes—pattern, direction, interval, steps, and LIP—and a technical name—such as *descending fifths* (KB 19.1), *descending thirds* (KB 19.2), *descending parallel* $^6_3$ *chords* (KB 19.3), and *ascending 5-6* (KB 19.4).

- *Patterns* "measure" how much music is repeatedly transposed (e.g., 2-chord pattern, 1-bar pattern, etc.).
- *Direction* is overall contour that either *descends* or *ascends* by some *interval* (e.g., by step, by third, etc.)
- *Steps* are the number of times the pattern is transposed (e.g., 4 steps, 3 steps, etc.).
- *Linear Intervallic Patterns* (*LIPs*) are recurring intervals between the bass and soprano (e.g., a 10-8 LIP).

Apply It

For KBs 19.1-19.4 perform the following activities.

(1) Memorize the parts of the sequence by singing them as a continuous melody. Sing each part in a comfortable range.

(2) Perform the sequence with each of its possible soprano voices.

(3) Describe the attributes of the sequence (e.g., descending-fifth sequences in Example 19.1).

  (a) Example 19.1a comprises two-chord patterns that descend by step in four steps with a 10-8 LIP.

  (b) Example 19.1b comprises two-chord patterns that descend by step in three and a half steps with a 10-8 LIP.

(4) Transpose the sequence to different major and minor keys. In minor keys adjust the solmization and Roman numerals.

(5) While playing block chords, sing melodic embellishments of the soprano voice per KB 11.2.

KB 19.1: Descending Fifths

In Example 19.1a, compare Pattern 1 with Example 14.2 (1a-2a) and Pattern 4 with Example 12.1b. A common variant of 19.1a includes passing tones in Part 1 between patterns (e.g., Part 1 becomes | *m-f-m*| *r-m-r*| *d* . . ., etc.).

Example 19.1a Root-Position Triads

Example 19.1b Root-Position Seventh Chords

KB 19.2: Descending Thirds

Compare Pattern 1 with Example 12.1. A common variant swaps Parts 2 and 4 in Patterns 1-3 but keeps measure 4 as written. In minor employ natural minor in Patterns 1-3 but keep *ti* ($\hat{7}$) in the cadential V chord.

Example 19.2

KB 19.3: Descending Parallel $^6_3$ Chords

Measure 1 employs a 5-6 technique. Descending parallel $^6_3$ chords appear often in three parts that include a series of 7-6 suspensions. In minor use natural minor but employ *ti* ($\hat{7}$) in the first ending and the penultimate chord.

Example 19.3

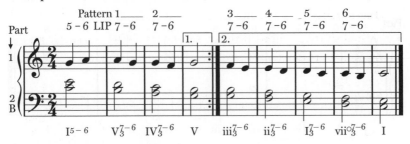

KB 19.4: Ascending 5-6

Each sequential pattern features a 5-6 technique. In minor use natural minor but employ *ti* ($\hat{7}$) in the penultimate chord. For a three-part sequence omit Part 3 but in the last chord include $\hat{3}$.

Example 19.4

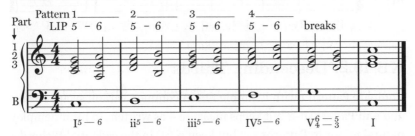

KB 20.1: Tonicizing V

If V is tonicized, *fi* (#$\hat{4}$) functions like *ti* ($\hat{7}$) in the key of V and belongs to a secondary dominant chord that employs the same pitches, voice-leading, and solmization that would occur if the key of V were tonic. These three notations—colon, bracket, and slash—all mean "of V."

$$\text{V: I V}^6_5\text{ I} \qquad \underset{\text{V}}{\underline{\text{I V}^6_5\text{ I}}} \qquad \text{V V}^6_5\text{/V V}$$

Apply It

Problem: In C major perform a progression that tonicizes V.

Solution:

(1) Perform a T-D-T progression in the tonic (Example 12.1b in major).

(2) Perform a second T-D-T progression in the tonic (Example 13.1a in major).

(3) Transpose and perform the second progression to $\hat{5}$. Its leading tone requires an accidental.

(4) Embellish the V chord with the secondary T-D-T and perform the expanded progression.

Example 20.1a

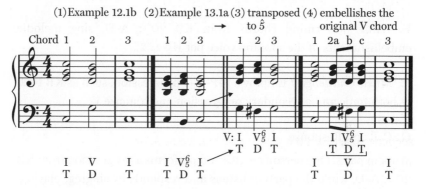

A. Follow the model just provided to tonicize V in the given keys. Remember to raise *ti* ($\hat{7}$) in minor keys.

(1) F major   (2) D major   (3) G major   (4) B♭ major

(5) E♭ major   (6) C minor   (7) A minor   (8) G minor

(9) D minor   (10) B minor

B. Follow the same procedure and use the same keys as in KB 20.1: A, but use Example 12.1a as the first tonic progression.

Hint: Examine the V chord in Example 12.1a; its root is the bass, and the fifth is the soprano. In Example 13.1a place Part 3 in the soprano to match this position. When transposed, Example 13.1a matches perfectly.

Example 20.1b

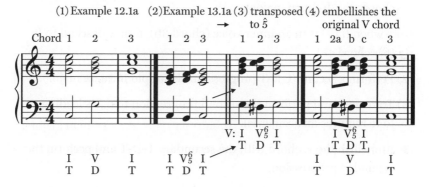

C. Follow the same procedure as in KB 20.1: A and B, but use Example 12.1c as the first tonic progression.

D. Perform minor-key versions of those just given. Use Example 17.1a as the secondary pattern to create secondary leading-tone seventh chords (e.g., the progression i-V-I becomes i-V-vii°7/V-V-i).

E. While performing chords from KB 20.1: A-D, sing melodic embellishments of the soprano voice per KB 11.2.

F. *Music Challenges!* Employ a T-P-D-T progression, such as KB 14.2, as both tonic and a secondary progression and tonicize V.

G. Call and Response

Work in pairs. One person creates and performs a progression from KB 20.1: A-D, while the partner listens and responds by singing, playing, and notating what was performed. Switch roles.

KB 21.1: Tonicizing Nontonic Chords

Any major or minor nontonic chord may be tonicized following the method from KB 20.1.

Apply It

Problem: In C major perform a progression that tonicizes vi.

Solution:

(1) Perform a progression that concludes on a vi chord (Example 15.1, chords 1a-3b-4c, in major).

Note when *ti* ($\hat{7}$) is in an inner voice (chord 3b), it may descend to *la* ($\hat{6}$) (chord 4c).

(2) Perform a second T-D-T progression (Example 13.1a, in major).

(3) Transpose and perform the second progression to $\hat{6}$. Its leading tone requires an accidental.

(4) Embellish the vi chord with the secondary T-D-T and perform the expanded progression.

Example 21.1

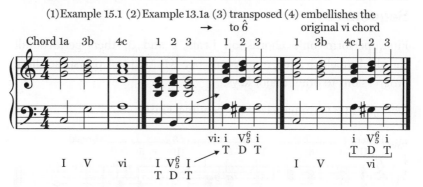

(1) Example 15.1 (2) Example 13.1a (3) transposed (4) embellishes the
                           →   to $\hat{6}$ original vi chord

A. Complete KB 20.1: A-F, but tonicize vi, IV, and ii. Raise *ti* ($\hat{7}$) in V in minor keys.

KB 21.2: Chromaticized Descending-Fifth Sequences

Perform variants of the descending-fifth and descending-third sequences first without, then with the parenthetical chromatic pitches and chords. Embellish the progressions per KB 11.2 and transpose these progressions to other major and minor keys.

Example 21.2 Chromaticized Descending Fifths

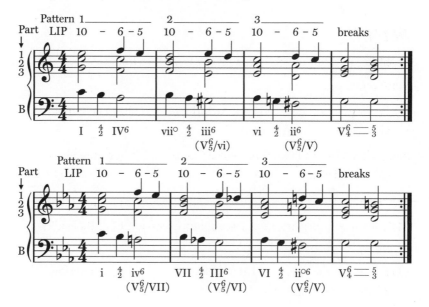

KB 21.3: Chromaticized Descending-Third Sequences

First, perform only chords on beats 1 and 3, then perform all chords. Embellish the progressions per KB 11.2 and transpose these progressions to other major keys.

Example 21.3 Chromaticized Descending Thirds

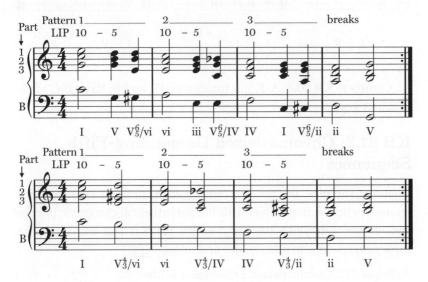

Chromatic Harmony and Form

PART III

KB 22: Modulation

To modulate, establish the tonic key, link to the new key, and establish the destination key.

Apply It

Example 22a: In C major modulate from I → V.

Example 22b: In C major modulate from I → vi.

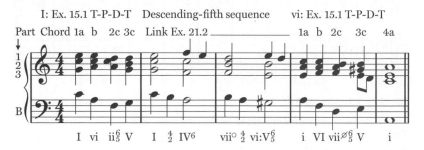

Example 22c: In C minor modulate from i → III.

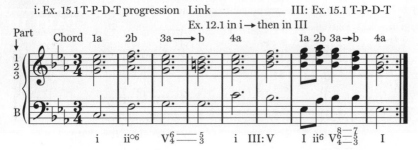

A. Use one of the preceding examples to create the specified modulation.

(1) G major: I → V   (2) F major: I → vi   (3) D major: I → V

(4) B♭ major: I → vi   (5) A major: I → V   (6) G major: I → vi

(7) A minor: i → III   (8) D minor: i → III   (9) E minor: i → III

KB 23: Binary Compositions

KB 23 combines previous keyboard lessons to create binary compositions.

Apply It

A. Create minor-key pieces that move from tonic to the mediant and back.

Example 23.1: Minor key ‖: i → III :‖‖: III → i :‖

Section 1, mm. 1-8 (= Example 22c)

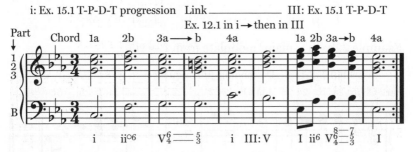

Section 2.1, mm. 9-16

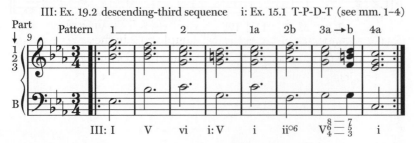

Section 2.2, mm. 9-16

(1) For a piece that incorporates descending thirds, perform Example 23.1, sections 1 and 2.1.

(2) For a piece that incorporates descending fifths, perform Example 23.1, sections 1 and 2.2.

B. Create pieces that move to the dominant and back in both minor and major keys.

Example 23.2: Minor or Major Key ‖: i → v :‖‖: v → i :‖

(1) For a minor-key piece, perform Example 23.2 as written.

(2) For a major-key piece, perform Example 23.2 in the parallel major. Retain *fi* (♯4̂) and adjust Roman numerals and solmization to those of major.

C. While one person performs, a partner embellishes the soprano voice per KB 11.2. Switch roles.

D. *Musical Challenge!* Transpose any of the binary pieces to other keys.

KB 24: Developing a Contrapuntal Motive

Motives may be transformed in many ways—such as transposition, fragmentation, inversion, sequence, or rhythmic augmentation.

Apply It

These exercises are based on J. S. Bach's Invention no. 1. Perform 1-3. Then play and notate each specified motive transformation. Check your work by looking at the specified measure in Bach's score.

(1) Invention 1 motive (m. 1)   (2) Head (fragment)

(3) Tail (fragment)

(4) Transpose the motive to the dominant pitch (m. 2).

(5) Invert the motive from A5 (m. 3).

(6) Begin with E4 and invert the tail (m. 5).

(7) Begin with E4 and sequence the inverted tail in three rising steps (m. 5). Conclude on D5 (m. 6).

(8) Begin with B3 and rhythmically augment the head (m. 3).

(9) Copy (5) and (8) on the following staff. Beginning with the copied music perform a sequence that descends by thirds in two additional steps (mm. 3-4).

(10) Use invertible counterpoint (i.e., place the upper part on the lower staff, and the lower part on the upper staff) from (9) to begin with the given pitches in D minor. Perform a sequence that descends by thirds in three steps (mm. 11-12).

KB 25: Sectional and Figural Variations

KB 25 builds on earlier work to create sectional and figural variations.

Apply It

(1) Create the structure.

- Perform Example 23.1, sections 1 and 2.1, to create an a¹-a²-b-a³ structure for the theme.

(2) Create a theme.

- Per KB 11.2 embellish the structure's soprano voice to find ideas that you like.

- Notate your favorite ideas as the theme. Use the same motive to begin phrases a¹, a², and a³.
- While performing the chord structure again, sing your theme.

(3) Create figural variations of your theme.

- From KB 11.2 choose one type of embellishment.
- Apply that embellishment to each long note of your theme to create a figural variation.
- While performing the chord structure again, sing this figural variation of your theme.
- Repeat this procedure, but choose a different melodic embellishment to create a new figural variation.

KB 26: Modal Mixture

Modal mixture "borrows" chords, typically from the parallel minor key.

Apply It

A. Follow the procedures of KB 15.1 to perform T-P-D-T progressions that employ modal mixture.

Example 26

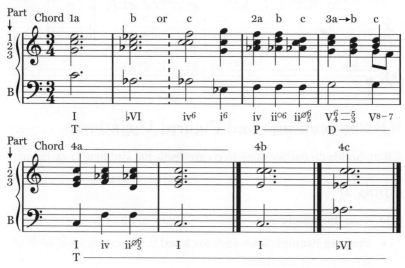

B. Transpose the progression to other major keys from three flats to three sharps.

C. Play block chords and sing melodic embellishments of the soprano voice per KB 11.2.

D. Call and Response

Work in pairs. One person performs, while the partner listens then responds by playing, singing, or notating what was performed. Switch roles.

KB 27.1: The Neapolitan Sixth (N⁶) and Other Predominant Chords

The N⁶ chord voice-leading is identical to that for ii○⁶. Though N⁶ may go directly to V, it is often followed by a secondary dominant-function seventh chord.

Apply It

A. Follow the method of KB 14.2 to perform in keyboard style with each of the three possible soprano voices.

Example 27.1

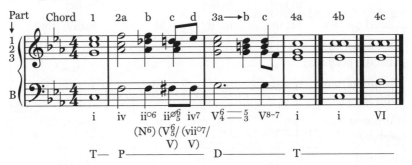

(1) For diatonic predominant chords, perform 2a, b, c, or d as notated.

(2) For N⁶, perform parenthetical notations for 2b.

(3) For V$^6_5$/V or vii○7/V, perform parenthetical notations for either 2c or 2d.

(4) Chord 3a, the cadential $^6_4$, must continue to 3b or 3c.

(5) For a deceptive resolution, perform 4c.

B. Create the following variations.

(1) Create longer progressions (e.g., 1-2b-2d-3a → 3b [HC] 1-2b-2d-3a → 3b-4a [PAC]).

(2) From Chord 1 begin with Part 1 as the soprano. From Chord 2, finish with Part 2 as the soprano.

(3) Play the chords and sing melodic embellishments of the soprano voice per KB 11.2.

(4) Perform in minor keys ranging from three flats to three sharps.

C. Call and Response

Work in pairs. One person performs a progression based on Example 27.1, while the partner listens then responds by singing, playing, or notating what was played. Switch roles.

Strategies for Distinguishing Predominant-Function Chords

Always listen from the bottom to the top voice, focusing first on the bass part. If bass-pitch *fa* ($\hat{4}$) rises to *sol* ($\hat{5}$), the chord above *fa* ($\hat{4}$) is predominant and that above *sol* ($\hat{5}$) is dominant.

The following table summarizes various ways to discern one predominant chord from another.

Possible key(s)	M key; m key	M key; m key	M key only	M key; m key
Chord quality	M; m	m; d	M	mm7; dm7
Distinguishing melodic pitch(es)	*do* ($\hat{1}$)	*re* ($\hat{2}$)	*ra* ($\flat\hat{2}$)	*do* + *re* ($\hat{1}$ + $\hat{2}$)
Common tone with tonic?	yes, *do* ($\hat{1}$)	no	no	yes, *do* ($\hat{1}$)
Common tone with V?	no	yes; *re* ($\hat{2}$)	no	yes; *re* ($\hat{2}$)
Tritone?	no	no; yes	no	no; yes
Chord symbol	IV; iv	ii^6; ii^{o6}	N^6	ii$^6_5$; ii$^{o6}_5$ V*
Bass pitch	*fa* ($\hat{4}$) ────────────────→ *sol* ($\hat{5}$)			

*To review strategies for distinguishing root-position dominant-function chords see KB 14.1.

KB 27.2: Augmented-Sixth (A6) Chords (Chromaticized Phrygian Resolution)

Though the three A6 chords chromaticize the Phrygian resolution, the voice-leading remains the same.

Apply It

A. Follow the method of KB 15.2 to perform in keyboard style.

Example 27.2

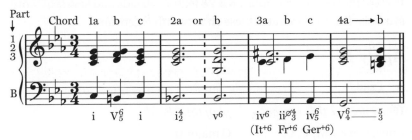

(1) For diatonic predominant chords, perform 3a, b, or c as notated.

(2) For A6 chords, perform parenthetical notations for Chord 3.

(3) Chord 4a, the cadential $^6_4$, must continue to 4b.

(4) Chord 3c, iv$^6_5$, may continue directly to 4b. These parallel fifths are characteristic.

B. Look at measures 3-4 to learn this quick method for playing A6 chords.

(1) Place your right-hand thumb on a minor key's *do* ($\hat{1}$) and your ring finger on *fi* ($\sharp\hat{4}$).

(2) Place your left-hand ring finger on *le* ($\flat\hat{6}$). *Le* ($\flat\hat{6}$) + *fi* ($\sharp\hat{4}$) = A6 interval.
    (a) double *do* ($\hat{1}$) = It^{+6} (b) *do* ($\hat{1}$) + *re* ($\hat{2}$) = Fr^{+6}
    (c) *do* ($\hat{1}$) + *me* ($\flat\hat{3}$) = Gr^{+6}

(3) *Le* ($\flat\hat{6}$) + *fi* ($\sharp\hat{4}$) → *sol* ($\hat{5}$). Resolve one *do* ($\hat{1}$) ↓ *ti* ($\hat{7}$), the other *do*, *re*, or *me* ($\hat{1}, \hat{2}$, or $\flat\hat{3}$) ↑ *re* ($\hat{2}$).

C. Construct a period by performing Example 27.2 as the antecedent phrase and Example 27.1 as the consequent.

(1) Work in pairs. One person performs, while the partner listens then responds by playing, singing, or notating what was performed. Switch roles.

(2) Transpose to minor keys from three flats to three sharps.

(3) Play chords while singing an embellishment of the soprano voice per KB 11.2.

KB 28: Realizing Popular-Music Chord Symbols

Songs are often accompanied by instrumentalists who realize chords from popular-music symbols. KB 28 features triads and seventh-chord symbols. KB 29 elaborates these chords with extensions.

Apply It

A. Triads

When you see this symbol	*play this chord.*
Cmaj, Cma, CM, C, C△	C major triad
Dmin, Dmi, Dm, d, D-	D minor triad
B°, B dim	B diminished triad
G+, G Aug	G augmented triad

B. Seventh Chords

When you see this symbol	*play this triad and seventh*	*or recall its traditional designation.*
Cmaj7, Cma7, CM7, C△7	C major triad + M7	MM7
Dmin7, Dmi7, Dm7, Dm7, D-7	D minor triad + m7	mm7
DØ7, Dmin7(♭5), Dmi7(♭5), Dm7(♭5), D-7(♭5)	D diminished triad + m7	dm7
B°7, Bdim7	B diminished triad + d7	dd7
G7	G major triad + M7	Mm7

C. Review the method for realizing all five common seventh chords from a given root in KB 8.

D. Realize the following chords from the given symbols, playing the root in your LH and the other pitches in your RH.

(1) Gma7	(2) Emi7	(3) A7	(4) A♭ma	(5) Ami7
(6) D7	(7) B♭ma7	(8) Gmin7(♭5)	(9) Bmi7	(10) E♭ma
(11) E7	(12) C♯°7	(13) Fmi	(14) Ema7	(15) F+
(16) G♯mi7	(17) E°7	(18) FØ7	(19) Cmi7	(20) F♯7

E. From a lead sheet that uses triads and seventh chords, realize the chords and perform, while accompanying yourself (or a partner).

The following examples appear in *The Musician's Guide to Aural Skills: Sight-Singing*:

(1) "All Quiet Along the Potomac Tonight," Chapter 16, page 212

(2) "Love Grows Under a Wide Oak Tree," Chapter 28, page 400

(3) "Stars Fell on Alabama," Chapter 14, page 196

(4) "The Song Is You," Chapter 16, page 211

KB 29.1: The Blues Scale and Progression

The blues scale is a minor pentatonic scale plus a "flatted fifth" (e.g., in C, the F♯ or G♭). The accidentals in the scale, called **blue notes**, are a form of modal mixture. Despite the accidentals, blues compositions use the major-key signature of its tonic pitch.

C blues scale

In its simplest harmonization, the blues progression features Mm7 chords on 1̂, 4̂, and 5̂. The slashes in the notation mean to keep time as you prolong and embellish each chord. Play first without the parenthetical chords (keep playing the previous chord), then with them to make a typical variant.

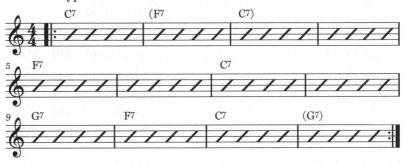

Apply It

A. Play and sing the C blues scale, then those on B♭, F, G, D, A, and E♭.

B. Perform the blues progression.

(1) In your LH play the root of each chord. In your RH play the other three pitches.

(2) Parallel chords are characteristic (for example, in measures 9-10, play parallel fifths, octaves, and sevenths!).

C. Pair work

One person performs the previous progression, while the partner sings motives from the blues scale. Switch roles.

D. Call and Response

Work in pairs. One person performs, while the partner listens then responds by playing, singing, or notating what was performed. Switch roles.

KB 29.2: Realizing Chords from Popular-Music Chord Symbols

To the popular-music symbols for triads and seventh chords you can add additional pitches called **extensions**. In popular music, extensions can be chord members, equal in importance to the root, third, fifth, and seventh.

Apply It

A. Perform each of the following.

Extensions to major or minor triads

Lead-sheet notation	What to play
Cmaj^6, Cma^6, CM^6, C^{add6}, C^{+6}, C$^{\triangle6}$, C^6	C major triad + M6
Cmin^6, Cmi^6, Cm^6, C^{-6}, c^{add6}	C minor triad + M6
Cmaj$^9_6$, Cma$^9_6$, CM$^9_6$, C$^{\triangle9}_6$, C$^9_6$	C major triad + M6 + M9
Cmin$^9_6$, Cmi$^9_6$, Cm$^9_6$, C$^{-9}_6$, c$^9_6$	C minor triad + M6 + M9
Csus^4, Csus	C, F, and G (the fourth displaces the third)

Extensions to seventh chords

Lead-sheet notation	What to play
Cmaj^9, Cma^9, CM^9, C$^{\triangle9}$	Cma^7 + M9 (MM7 + M9)
Dmin^9, Dmi^9, Dm^9, d^9, d^{-9}	Dmi^7 + M9 (mm7 + M9)
Dmin^{11}, Dmi^{11}, Dm^{11}, d^{11}, d^{-11}	Dmi^7 + M9 + P11 (mm7 + M9 + P11)
G^9	G^7 + M9 (Mm7 + M9)

Extensions to dominant seventh (Mm7) chords

Extensions appear most frequently with the Mm7 chord. Look at the following table, and play each extension of G7.

Lead-sheet notation	Play this Mm7 chord . . .	plus these interval(s).	Optional additional interval(s)
G7(♭9)	complete G7 (G-B-D-F)	m9 (A♭)	
G7(♯9)	complete G7	A9 (A♯)	
G7(♭5)	incomplete G7 (G-B-F)	d5 (D♭)	M9 or m9 (A or A♭)
G7(♯5)	incomplete G7	A5 (D♯)	M9 (A)
G7(♯11)	complete G7	M9 + A11 (A + C♯)	M13 (E)
G13	complete or incomplete G7	M9 + M13 (A + E)	
G7(♭13)	incomplete G7	M9 + m13 (A + E♭)	

The ♭5 and ♯11 are enharmonic equivalents, but are notated differently to indicate the way they tend to resolve. The same concept applies to ♯5 and ♭13. A quick way to get satisfying voicings is to put the root, seventh, and third in the bass clef and the remaining tones in the treble clef. Play these voicings of extended dominant harmonies.

Realize each of the following chords, and voice each one several different ways. Some chords have four voices, but many require more.

(1) Bmi7   (2) C♯maj9   (3) F7(♭9)   (4) A7(♯11)   (5) A♭maj$^9_6$

(6) Dma9   (7) B♭mi9   (8) E♭7(♭13)   (9) Emi11   (10) F♯13

(11) Ami9   (12) E7(♯9)   (13) Cmi7   (14) Gadd6   (15) D7(♯5)

KB 30.1: Common-Tone Embellishing Chords

Common-tone (CT) embellishing chords prolong a major chord by embellishing its third and fifth with chromatic neighbor tones.

Example 30.1a: CT°7   Example 30.1b: CT A6

Apply It

A. Perform Examples 30.1a and 30.1b in keyboard style with each of the three possible soprano voices as written, then beginning on bass pitches C, F, G, E♭, and A♭. Note in the CT A6 the fifth is doubled in the major chord.

B. Expand Examples 30.1a and 30.1b into longer progressions by replacing each common-tone chord with measure 1 of Example 14.2 or Example 15.1, transposed to the new key.

KB 30.2: Chromatic Voice Exchange and Cadential $^6_4$

Chromaticizing the end of a voice exchange or cadential $^6_4$ dramatically emphasizes the next chord.

Apply It

A. Perform Example 30.2 in all the following ways:

(1) For the diatonic chords, perform without any parenthetical notations.

(2) For a chromatic voice exchange, perform 3a-b-c with the parenthetical notations.

(3) For a chromatic cadential $^6_4$, perform 4a-b with the parenthetical notations.

(4) Transpose the progressions to other majors keys and perform them.

(5) Construct a complete phrase by performing Example 30.2 then measure 2 and following from Example 15.1.

Example 30.2

B. Call and Response

Work in pairs. One person performs a progression based on Example 30.1 or 30.2, while the partner listens then responds by singing, playing, or notating what was played. Switch roles.

KB 31: Chromatic Modulations

Three easy ways to effect chromatic modulation are to employ common tones, modal mixture, or enharmonic spelling.

Apply It

A. Common-Tone Modulation

Holding a tone common to two keys is an easy way to modulate. Perform Example 15.1 or 14.2 as written and end with a PAC. Hold *do* ($\hat{1}$) in the soprano voice where it becomes *mi* ($\hat{3}$) in the key of VI. Perform Example 15.1 or 14.2 again, this time in the key of VI.

B. Modulation using Modal Mixture

Perform Example 15.1 or 14.2 in the parallel major key and conclude with a deceptive cadence on ♭VI. Perform Example 15.1 or 14.2 again, this time in the key of ♭VI.

C. Employing Enharmonics to Modulate to the Neapolitan

Perform Example 27.2 with a Gr+6 chord. Reimagine *fi* (♯$\hat{4}$) as *se* (♭$\hat{5}$) and the Gr+6 becomes V7/N. In the key of the Neapolitan perform Example 15.1 or 14.2 and conclude with a PAC.

KB 32: Chromatic Descent

A passacaglia (ground bass) is a common way to employ chromatic descents. See KB 15.2 to review the Phrygian resolution then review Chapter 25, Improvisation 25.1, as you complete this lesson.

Apply It

A. Perform the following variations.

Example 32: Chromatic Descent Based on the Phrygian Resolution.

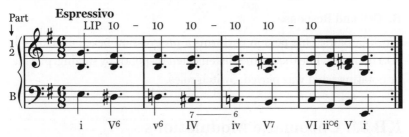

(1) While playing Example 32 sing melodic variations of the soprano voice per KB 11.2.

(2) Perform this as a trio, with each person singing a figural variation of his or her part. With each repetition change the figural variation.

(3) Transpose to other minor keys.

(4) Transpose to the parallel major, and perform as you did in questions (1) and (2).

KB 33: Chromatic Sequences

Chromatic descending-fifth and ascending 5-6 sequences are frequently the basis for transitions between sections. In chromatic descending-fifth sequences each secondary leading tone is canceled to become the next chord's seventh. In chromatic ascending 5-6 sequences the 5-6 often appears in a inner part.

Apply It

A. Perform the following variations.

Example 33.1a: Chromatic Descending-Fifth Sequence

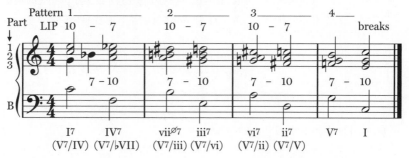

Example 33.1b: Chromatic Ascending 5-6 Sequence

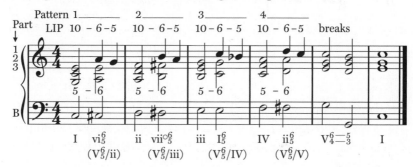

(1) For diatonic sequences, perform without the parenthetical notations.

(2) For chromatic sequences, perform with the parenthetical notations.

(3) For the ascending 5-6 sequence, omit the quarter note on beat 3 of each pattern.

(4) Transpose these sequences to other major keys.

B. Review Example 21.2. Then perform it again and continue the sequence beyond the dominant.

C. Call and Response

Work in pairs. One person performs a progression based on Example 33.1a or 33.1b, while the partner listens then responds by singing, playing, or notating what was played. Switch roles.

The Twentieth Century and Beyond

PART IV

KB 34.1: Major and Minor Pentatonic Scales

Review KB 4: A (Major Pentatonic Scales) and KB 5.1: C (Minor Pentatonic Scales).

Apply It

A. Play major pentatonic scales ascending and descending starting on the following pitches. Play them each once using the procedure given in KB 4: A, then a second time using your thumb on the white keys that precede and follow the black keys, and your other fingers to play the black keys.

(1) E   (2) G   (3) F   (4) C

(5) B♭   (6) D   (7) A   (8) A♭

(9) D♭   (10) B   (11) E♭   (12) F♯

Musical Challenges!   (13) D♯   (14) G♯   (15) A♯

B. Play minor pentatonic scales ascending and descending starting on the pitches just given. Play them each once using the procedure given in KB 5.1: C, then a second time using your thumb on the white keys that precede and follow the black keys, and your other fingers to play the black keys.

KB 34.2: The Diatonic Modes

Review KB 5.2.

Apply It

A. Beginning on the given pitch, play the untransposed mode specified ascending and descending using the procedure given in KB 5.2.

(1) D Dorian   (2) C Ionian   (3) A Aeolian   (4) G Mixolydian

(5) E Phrygian (6) B Locrian   (7) F Lydian

B. Beginning on the given pitch, play the transposed mode specified ascending and descending. Play them each once using the procedure given in KB 5.2, then a second time using your thumb on the white keys that precede and follow the black keys and your other fingers to play the black keys.

(1) G Dorian	(2) F Mixolydian	(3) C Phrygian
(4) D Lydian	(5) C Aeolian	(6) E Locrian
(7) G Ionian	(8) D Phrygian	(9) A Mixolydian
(10) E♭ Dorian	(11) F Phrygian	(12) C Lydian
(13) B♭ Mixolydian	(14) A Locrian	(15) C♯ Phrygian
(16) F Dorian		

KB 34.3: The Lydian-Mixolydian Mode

Combining the distinctive features of both the Lydian and Mixolydian modes creates the Lydian-Mixolydian mode, sometimes called the "Lydian dominant" or "overtone scale." This mode is formed from the lower pentachord of the Lydian mode and the upper tetrachord of the Mixolydian mode (for example, C D E F♯ G A B♭ C). Notice that this mode forms two interlocking dominant seventh chords, here, C7 and D7.

Apply It

Beginning on the given pitch, play the Lydian-Mixolydian mode ascending and descending. Play them each once divided into two tetrachords each, as in KB 3, then a second time using your thumb on the white keys that precede and follow the black keys and your other fingers to play the black keys.

(1) C   (2) F   (3) G   (4) D   (5) A   (6) E♭   (7) B♭   (8) E

KB 35.1: Integer Notation and Sets

It can be helpful to visualize the twelve pitch classes on a clock face, with 0 (C) at the top and 6 (F♯/G♭) at the bottom. Notice that for 10 and 11 the letters t and e are used respectively.

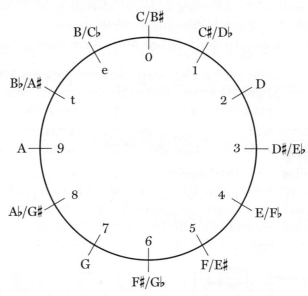

Apply It

Play the following pitch classes and sets in ascending and descending fashion, and then simultaneously, while making associations with note names and familiar harmonic structures.

(a) 6   (b) 2   (c) 8   (d) e   (e) 1

(f) 2 6   (g) 0 7   (h) 2 e   (i) 4 5   (j) 1 t

(k) 3 7 t (l) 2 5 9 (m) 6 9 0 (n) 1 5 9 (o) 0 4 7

(p) 7 e 2 5 (q) 2 5 9 0 (r) 0 4 7 e (s) 1 3 7 t (t) e 2 5 9

KB 35.2: Whole-Tone Scales

Whole-tone scales are made up of six distinct pitch classes that, when listed in scale order, are a whole step apart. Using integer notation to identify such collections avoids potential confusion in recognizing pitch classes that are a whole step apart, (for example, F♯ and A♭). There are only two possible whole-tone collections, the one that contains 0 (C) and the one that contains 1 (C♯/D♭: WT0 {0 2 4 6 8 t} and WT1

{1 3 5 7 9 e}. Notice that WT0 contains only even-numbered pitch classes while WT1 contains only odd-numbered ones.

Apply It

A. Play each of the following scales in ascending and descending fashion while singing pitch-class integers. Position your thumb on a white key so that you can play the black keys with your remaining fingers.

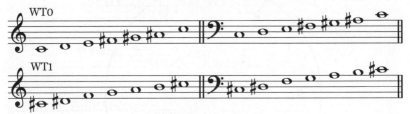

B. Before playing, identify the scale presented in each phrase, while singing pitch-class integers. In general, use your thumb on the white keys that precede and follow the black keys and your other fingers to play the black keys.

KB 35.3: Octatonic Scales

The octatonic scale consists of eight pitch classes that alternate whole and half steps. There are three possible octatonic collections, beginning on pc (pitch class) 0, 1, or 2: {0 1 3 4 6 7 9 t}, {1 2 4 5 7 8 t e}, and {2 3 5 6 8 9 e 0}. (If you begin an octatonic scale on any other pc, it simply duplicates the pcs of one of these collections.) The scales are referred to by their initial two pcs: OCT 01, OCT 12, and OCT 23.

Apply It

A. Play each of the following scales in ascending and descending fashion while singing pitch-class integers. In general, use your thumb on the white keys that precede and follow the black keys and your other fingers to play the black keys.

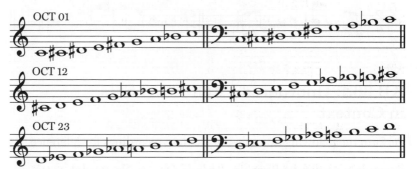

B. Next, the pitch classes of octatonic scales are notated with beams that reveal an organization of two interlocking fully diminished seventh chords. Separately play each pair of beamed notes with your thumb (RH) or fifth finger (LH) on the lowest note. Then play the scale ascending and descending using the fingering strategy just given for the octatonic scales.

C. The following melodic fragments are grouped into pairs of fully diminished seventh chords. Identify the scales presented then play each excerpt as written using the fingering strategy given for the octatonic scales.

KB 36.1: Unordered Pitch-Class Sets in Context

Perform the following examples, or listen to recordings for reference.

Example 1: Alexander Scriabin, *Prelude*, Op. 59, No. 2 (mm. 1–3a)

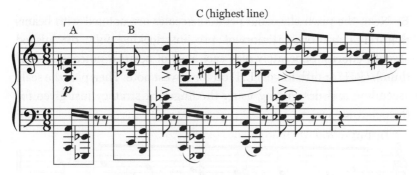

Example 2: Scriabin, *Prelude*, Op. 59, No. 2 (mm. 12–13a)

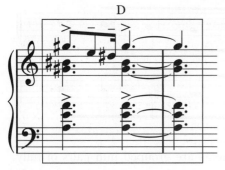

Example 3: Scriabin, *Prelude*, Op. 67, No. 2 (mm. 1-3)

In Examples 1 and 3, compare sets A and B. Your ears (and eyes) reveal them to be the same collections, though reversed in order. Since these preludes were composed years apart, clearly Scriabin treats sets A and B as distinct sonorities—unordered pitch-class sets (pcsets).

The pcs of set A are identical in each prelude, as are the pcs of set B. But what if you hear two sets that sound alike but have different pcs? How do you find the relationship between them?

KB 36.2: Unordered Pitch-Class Sets Related by Transposition

Perform Example 1 again; consider its highest line to be set C. Perform Example 2; consider all of its pitches as set D. Play each in its original order, then from lowest to highest. Can you hear that D is a transposition of C by six semitones?

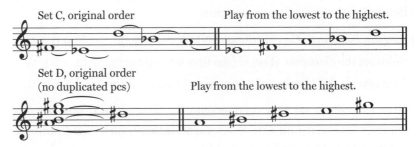

Until you become familiar with sounds like these, it may be hard to hear such relationships. One method that will help is to find each set's **normal order**: its most compact form.

Finding a set's normal order: To find the normal order of set C, first play its pitches in order from lowest to highest, as before. Then play and notate each rotation of set C (move the lowest pitch to the top for each new rotation). The rotation that ascends from D is the normal order, because it has the smallest outside interval (from D to Bb). Write the pc integers beneath each pitch of the normal order. Notate normal order with curly braces: C {2 3 6 9 t}.

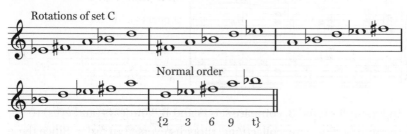

Now play the rotations of set D to find its normal order.

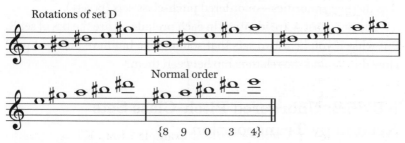

The rotation with the smallest outside interval ascends from G♯: {8 9 0 3 4}. Play the normal order of sets C and D, and listen to the interval succession for each: +1, +3, +3, +1. Sets whose normal orders have the same succession of intervals are related by *transposition*. To determine their exact transposition:

List the elements of set D (the second set you hear).   {8 9 0 3 4}
Subtract the elements of set C (the first set you hear). −{2 3 6 9 t}
This reveals the number of semitones of transposition.   6 6 6 6 6

If an element in set D is smaller than the element in C that is being subtracted from it, add 12 to D's element: rather than 0-6, 3-9, and 4-t, subtract 12-6, 15-9, and 16-t (mod 12).

Notating sets equivalent by transposition: Notate this relationship as $D = T_6C$. Note that T stands for "transposition," and the number after indicates the interval of transposition in semitones.

KB 37.1: Unordered Pitch-Class Sets Related by Inversion

Play Example 3 from KB 36.1 again (reproduced here); consider the first five distinct pitches of its highest line to be set E.

Example 3: Scriabin, *Prelude*, Op. 67, No. 2 (mm. 1-3)

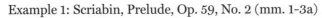

Now compare set E with set A from Example 1 from KB 36.1 (reproduced again here).

Example 1: Scriabin, Prelude, Op. 59, No. 2 (mm. 1-3a)

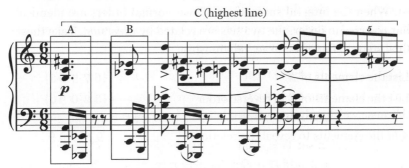

First, realize A's pcs within the span of one octave then play the rotations of A to find its normal order. One possibility appears next.

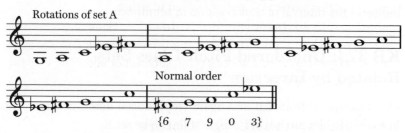

Rotations of set A

Normal order

{6 7 9 0 3}

Best normal order: Three rotations have the same smallest outside interval. When this happens, choose as best normal order the rotation with the smallest intervals (often semitones) closely packed at one end or the other. In this case, the rotation that ascends from F♯ has a semitone between the first two pitches, making it the best normal order: A {6 7 9 0 3}.

Now perform the rotations of set E to find its normal order.

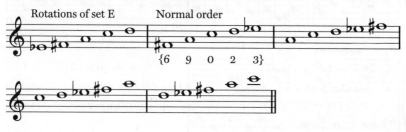

Rotations of set E   Normal order

{6 9 0 2 3}

Here too, three rotations show the same smallest outside interval. In this case, the rotation that ascends from F♯ has a semitone between the last two pitches, making it the best normal order: E {6 9 0 2 3}.

Compare the successive pitch intervals of the sets: for set A, the pitch intervals ascend +1, +2, +3, +3; and for E, they ascend +3, +3, +2, +1. When the interval successions of two normal orders are identical but *reversed* in order, the two sets are related by *inversion*. Take these final steps to find their exact relationship:

List the elements of A.   {6 7 9 0 3}

List the elements of E in reverse order   +{3 2 0 9 6}
(because we already know E is related by inversion).

Add the elements to reveal the relation.   9 9 9 9 9

Notating sets equivalent by inversion: Notate this relationship as $E = T_9IA$. The I indicates "inversion" and $_9$ is the **index number**—the number obtained when the pcs are added together.

Again, with transpositions you subtract the elements, and with inversions you add them. In performing these operations, if you get a number larger than 11 or smaller than 0, subtract or add 12 to keep the result between 0 and 11.

KB 37.2: Interval-Class Vectors

At the keyboard, play new trichord sets F {7 9 2} and G {2 4 9}. One possible realization is shown next. To identify an interval class (ic), find the shortest possible distance between two pcs as measured in semitones. For example, in set F the pcs G and D might be separated by 19, 7, or 5 semitones. Because 5 is the smallest distance, G and D are members of ic 5. Now determine all the interval classes by playing each pair of pitches. In each trichord, you will hear one ic 2 and two ic 5s.

An **ic vector** summarizes the interval-class content of any set. To make one, write interval classes 1-6 in one row and the number of occurrences of each ic underneath.

Interval class:	ic1	ic2	ic3	ic4	ic5	ic6
Number of occurrences:	0	1	0	0	2	0

Once you complete this tally, take the bottom row as the ic vector: [010020]. Because sets F and G share the same ic vector, they share the same interval content, which means they sound alike.

KB 38.1: Ordered Segments and Serialism (Basic Transformations)

Familiarize yourself with the following serial transformations of ordered segments:

- T (transposition): the pitch-interval sequence is identical to that of the prime segment;

- I (inversion): the direction of each pitch-class interval (pci) in the prime segments is inverted (e.g., pci +9 transforms to pci –3);

- R (retrograde): the pcs of the prime segments are reversed in order, and the original pitch-interval sequence is inverted and reversed in order;

- RI (retrograde inversion): the pcis of I are reversed in order, and the pitch-interval sequence of the prime segment is reversed in order.

Apply It

A. Play each notated transformation of the given segment.

<0 7 6>

B. Play each transformation of the given P_0 segments.

(1) <0 2 5>   (2) <0 t 8>   (3) <0 3 7>

$P_0 \ P_6 \ I_0 \ R_0 \ RI_0$ $P_0 \ P_5 \ I_5 \ R_5 \ RI_5$ $P_0 \ P_{10} \ I_{10} \ R_{10} \ RI_{10}$

KB 38.2 Combining Transposition with Other Transformations

A. The transformations I(nversion), R(etrograde), and R(etrograde) I(nversion) are typically combined with T(ransposition). Note that transformations are deciphered in relation to P_0. For the segment <9 5 t>, first determine P_0 then play each of the indicated transformations as notated.

<9 5 t>

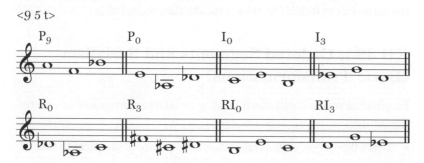

B. Play each transformation of the given transposed segments.

(1) <3 4 e 6>

$P_0\ I_0\ I_3\ R_0\ R_3\ RI_0\ RI_3$

(2) <2 4 9 4 7>

$P_0\ I_0\ I_4\ R_0\ R_4\ RI_0\ RI_4$

(3) <4 8 t 5 6 2>

$P_0\ I_0\ I_5\ R_0\ R_5\ RI_0\ RI_5$

KB 38.3 Twelve-Tone Rows

A. After playing the given twelve-tone row, play the indicated transformations. The processes are the same as for trichords and so on. Additional suggestions are presented to manage these larger segments.

P_0

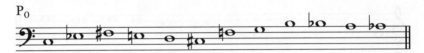

P_4: Transpose each pc up four half steps (= M3).

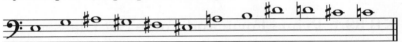

I_0: Play the inversion of each pci (e.g., pci +9 transforms to pci −3). Note that when working from P_0 (only), the pitch classes (pcs) will have the same designation as the pitch-class integers (pcis). Thus, for example, pc 9 above C will invert to pc 3 below C.

I_4: Play I_0 transposed four half steps (= M3) higher.

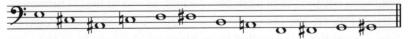

R_0: Play P_0 in reverse order.

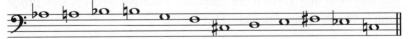

R_4: Play R_0 transposed four half steps (= M3) higher.

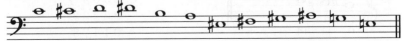

RI_0: Play I_0 in reverse order.

RI_4: Play I_4 in reverse order.

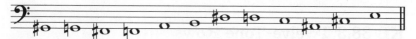

B. Play the following twelve-tone row, and then play each of the indicated transformations. It will be helpful to notate P_0 first before proceeding to other transformations.

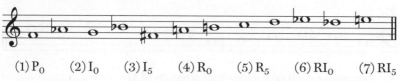

(1) P_0 (2) I_0 (3) I_5 (4) R_0 (5) R_5 (6) RI_0 (7) RI_5

KB 39.1: Prime Form and Forte Set Classes

A **set class** (SC) consists of all transpositions and inversions of a particular pcset. Since it would be cumbersome to refer to a SC by listing all its members, one pcset—called its **prime form**—represents the entire group.

Identifying Transpositions of the Prime Form

Play Example 1, and review how you found the normal order of set C {2 3 6 9 t}. Then play the first pc of the normal order, but call it 0. Play up the chromatic scale from the first pc, counting the number of semitones between each pitch and the first, as shown next. These numbers, 01478, are the pcs of the prime form—Forte SC 5-22. Counting from zero in this way is called "movable zero." You can obtain the same result by subtracting the first element of set C from every element, but movable zero may seem more musically intuitive. Write a set's prime form between square brackets: [0 1 4 7 8].

"Movable zero"

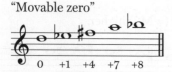

    0   +1   +4   +7   +8

Subtracting the first element

C {2 3 6 9 t}
- 2 2 2 2 2
0 1 4 7 8

Now play Example 2 and review how you found the normal order of set D {8 9 0 3 4}. Apply movable zero or subtract D's first element from each element to determine the prime form. Like C, D also belongs to Forte SC 5-22 [0 1 4 7 8].

KB 39.2: Inversions of the Prime Form

Play Example 3 and review how you found the normal order for set E {6 9 0 2 3}. Recall that E's smallest outside interval occurred between its last two pcs, or to its *right* side. Prime forms, however, all show the smallest intervals to the *left* of the set, so set E must be inverted. Call its last pc zero and play *down* the chromatic scale, counting the number of semitones between each element and the highest, as shown next. The prime form for Set E is [0 1 3 6 9], Forte SC 5-31.

Set E: The smallest interval is to the right.

Play set E from its highest to lowest pitch, counting the semitones between each element and the highest pitch.

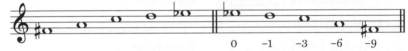

Earlier you discovered that set E was equivalent to (an inversion of) set A {6 7 9 0 3}, so A must be a member of the same set class. Apply what you have learned to prove this fact. The traditional way of finding the prime form of an inverted set is as follows.

Reverse the elements of E:	{3 2 0 9 6}
Write the mod12 inverse of each element:	{9 t 0 3 6}
Subtract the first element from each pc in the set:	− 9 9 9 9 9
The result is the inverted set's prime form:	[0 1 3 6 9]

For a few set classes, both the normal and inverted form must be subjected to this procedure to determine the prime form.

KB 40: Five Examples for Analysis at the Keyboard

For each of the five examples that follow, work through the process at the keyboard (or other instrument) in order to learn to recognize the sets both aurally and kinesthetically. After you have completed the exercises, check your work against the solutions, which begin on page 662.

Example 1: Anton Webern, "Nachts" ("At Night"), from *Sechs Lieder* (*Six Songs*), Op. 14

dein ro-ter Mund be - sei-gel-des des Freun-des Um-nach - tung.

Translation: Your red mouth sealed the friend's madness.

Set A Normal order {__ __ __}   ic vector [__ __ __ __ __ __]

prime form [__ __ __]   Forte SC 3-__

Set B Normal order {__ __ __}   ic vector [__ __ __ __ __ __]

prime form [__ __ __]   Forte SC 3-__

Set C Normal order {__ __ __}   ic vector [__ __ __ __ __ __]

prime form [__ __ __]   Forte SC 3-__

Set D Normal order {__ __ __}   ic vector [__ __ __ __ __ __]

prime form [__ __ __]   Forte SC 3-__

(1) How are sets A and D equivalent? (For example, A = T_xD or A = T_xID; D = T_xA or D = T_xIA.)

(2) How are sets B and C equivalent?

On your own paper, show the steps you took to answer each question.

Example 2: Webern, "Wiese im Park" ("Meadows in the Park"), from *Four Songs for Voice and Orchestra*, Op. 13

Die vie - len Glock-en - blu - men!

Translation: The many bluebells!

Set E Normal order {__ __ __}   ic vector [__ __ __ __ __ __]

prime form [__ __ __]   Forte SC 3-__

Set F Normal order {__ __ __}   ic vector [__ __ __ __ __ __]

prime form [__ __ __]   Forte SC 3-__

How are sets E and F equivalent? Show the steps you took to determine their equivalence.

Example 3: Igor Stravinsky, "Action rituelle des ancêtres" ("Ritual Dance of the Elders"), from *The Rite of Spring*

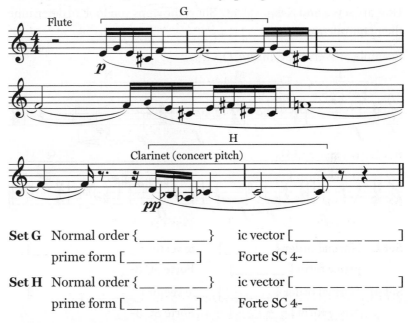

Set G   Normal order {_ _ _ _}   ic vector [_ _ _ _ _ _]
          prime form [_ _ _ _]   Forte SC 4-__

Set H   Normal order {_ _ _ _}   ic vector [_ _ _ _ _ _]
          prime form [_ _ _ _]   Forte SC 4-__

(1) How are sets G and H equivalent? Show the steps you took to determine their equivalence.

(2) Combine the pcs of sets G and H to make a scale. What is the name of this scale?

Example 4: Stravinsky, "Rondes printanières" ("Spring Rounds") and "Action rituelle des ancêtres," from *The Rite of Spring*

Set J Normal order {__ __ __ __} ic vector [__ __ __ __ __ __]

prime form [__ __ __ __] Forte SC 4-__

Set K Normal order {__ __ __ __} ic vector [__ __ __ __ __ __]

prime form [__ __ __ __] Forte SC 4-__

How are sets J and K equivalent? Show the steps you took to determine their equivalence.

Example 5: Webern, *Cantata*, Op. 29

Set L Normal order {__ __ __} ic vector [__ __ __ __ __ __]

prime form [__ __ __] Forte SC 3-__

Set M Normal order {__ __ __} ic vector [__ __ __ __ __ __]

prime form [__ __ __] Forte SC 3-__

Set N Normal order {__ __ __} ic vector [__ __ __ __ __ __]

prime form [__ __ __] Forte SC 3-__

Set O Normal order {__ __ __} ic vector [__ __ __ __ __ __]

prime form [__ __ __] Forte SC 3-__

Set P Normal order {__ __ __} ic vector [__ __ __ __ __ __]

prime form [__ __ __] Forte SC 3-__

Set Q Normal order {__ __ __} ic vector [__ __ __ __ __ __]

prime form [__ __ __] Forte SC 3-__

For each of the following questions, show the steps you took to determine their equivalence.

(1) How are sets M and L equivalent?

(2) How are sets N and L equivalent?

(3) How are sets O and L equivalent?

(4) How are sets P and L equivalent?

(5) How are sets Q and L equivalent?

Solutions

Example 1: Anton Webern, "Nachts" ("At Night"), from *Sechs Lieder* (*Six Songs*), Op. 14

Set A Normal order {6 7 8} ic vector [210000]
     prime form [0 1 2] Forte SC 3-1

Set B Normal order {9 0 1} ic vector [101100]
     prime form [0 1 4] Forte SC 3-4

Set C Normal order {t e 2} ic vector [101100]
     prime form [0 1 4] Forte SC 3-4

Set D Normal order {e 0 1} ic vector [210000]
     prime form [0 1 2] Forte SC 3-1

(1) How are sets A and D equivalent?

$$\begin{array}{ll} \text{D } \{e\ 0\ 1\} & \text{A } \{6\ 7\ 8\} \\ -\text{A } \underline{\{6\ 7\ 8\}} \quad \text{or} & -\text{D } \underline{\{e\ 0\ 1\}} \\ \text{T } \overline{5\ 5\ 5} & \text{T } \overline{7\ 7\ 7} \\ \text{D} = \text{T}_5\text{A} & \text{A} = \text{T}_7\text{D} \end{array}$$

(2) How are sets B and C equivalent?

$$\begin{array}{l} \text{C } \{t\ e\ 2\} \\ +\text{B } \underline{\{1\ 0\ 9\}} \text{ (elements reversed)} \\ \text{index } \overline{e\ e\ e} \\ \quad \text{B} = \text{T}_e\text{IC or C} = \text{T}_e\text{IB} \end{array}$$

Example 2: Webern, "Wiese im Park" ("Meadows in the Park"), from *Four Songs for Voice and Orchestra*, Op. 13

Set E Normal order {2 3 8} ic vector [100011]
     prime form [0 1 6] Forte SC 3-5

Set F Normal order {7 0 1} ic vector [100011]
     prime form [0 1 6] Forte SC 3-5

How are sets E and F equivalent?

$$\begin{array}{l} \text{E } \{2\ 3\ 8\} \\ +\text{F } \underline{\{1\ 0\ 7\}} \text{ (elements reversed)} \\ \text{index } \overline{3\ 3\ 3} \\ \quad \text{E} = \text{T}_3\text{IF or F} = \text{T}_3\text{IE} \end{array}$$

Example 3: Igor Stravinsky, "Action rituelle des ancêtres" ("Ritual Dance of the Elders"), from *The Rite of Spring*

Set G Normal order {1 4 5 7}   ic vector [112101]
        prime form [0 2 3 6]   Forte SC 4-12
Set H Normal order {8 t e 2}   ic vector [112101]
        prime form [0 2 3 6]   Forte SC 4-12

(1) How are sets G and H equivalent?

$$G \ \{1\ 4\ 5\ 7\}$$
$$+ H \ \{2\ e\ t\ 8\} \ \text{(elements reversed)}$$
$$\text{index} \ \overline{3\ 3\ 3\ 3}$$

$$G = T_3IH \ \text{or} \ H = T_3IG$$

(2) Combine the pcs of sets G and H to make a scale. What is the name of this scale? octatonic

Example 4: Stravinsky, "Rondes printanières" ("Spring Rounds") and "Action rituelle des ancêtres," from *The Rite of Spring*

Set J Normal order {t 0 1 3}   ic vector [122010]
        prime form [0 2 3 5]   Forte SC 4-10

Set K Normal order {8 t e 1}   ic vector [122010]
        prime form [0 2 3 5]   Forte SC 4-10

How are sets J and K equivalent?

$$J \ \{t\ 0\ 1\ 3\}$$
$$+ K \ \{1\ e\ t\ 8\} \ \text{(elements reversed)}$$
$$\text{index} \ \overline{e\ e\ e\ e}$$

$$J = T_eIK \ \text{or} \ K = T_eIJ$$

or

$$J \ \{t\ 0\ 1\ 3\} \qquad K \ \{8\ t\ e\ 1\}$$
$$- K \ \{8\ t\ e\ 1\} \qquad - J \ \{t\ 0\ 1\ 3\}$$
$$T \ \overline{2\ 2\ 2\ 2} \qquad T \ \overline{t\ t\ t\ t}$$

$$J = T_2K \ \text{or} \ K = T_t J$$

Example 5: Webern, *Cantata*, Op. 29

Set L Normal order {5 8 9}   ic vector [101100]
        prime form [0 1 4]   Forte SC 3-3

Set M Normal order {7 t e}   ic vector [101100]
        prime form [0 1 4]   Forte SC 3-3

Set N Normal order {0 1 4}   ic vector [101100]
        prime form [0 1 4]   Forte SC 3-3

Set O Normal order {2 3 6}   ic vector [101100]
        prime form [0 1 4]   Forte SC 3-3

Set P   Normal order {4 5 8}   ic vector [101100]
           prime form [0 1 4]   Forte SC 3-3

Set Q   Normal order {9 t 1}   ic vector [101100]
           prime form [0 1 4]   Forte SC 3-3

(1) How are sets M and L equivalent?

   M {7 t e}
 − L {5 8 9}
   T $\overline{2\ 2\ 2}$

   $M = T_2L$ or $L = T_2M$

(2) How are sets N and L equivalent?

      N {0 1 4}
    + L {9 8 5} (elements reversed)
   index $\overline{9\ 9\ 9}$

      $N = T_9IL$ or $L = T_9IN$

(3) How are sets O and L equivalent?

      O {2 3 6}
    − L {9 8 5} (elements reversed)
   index $\overline{e\ e\ e}$

      $O = T_eIL$ or $L = T_eIO$

(4) How are sets P and L equivalent?

      P {4 5 8}
    + L {9 8 5} (elements reversed)
   index $\overline{1\ 1\ 1}$

      $P = T_1IL$ or $L = T_1IP$

(5) How are sets Q and L equivalent?

      Q {9 t 1}
    + L {9 8 5} (elements reversed)
   index $\overline{6\ 6\ 6}$

      $Q = T_6IL$ or $L = T_6IQ$

Credits

Béla Bartók: *Mikrokosmos*, Vol. I, No. 2a. Copyright © 1940 by Hawkes & Son (London) Ltd. Reprinted by permission of Boosey & Hawkes, Inc.

Mikrokosmos, Vol. V, No. 128. Copyright © 1940 by Hawkes & Son (London) Ltd. Reprinted by permission of Boosey & Hawkes, Inc.

No. 39 from *44 Duets*. Copyright © 1933 by Universal Edition A.G., Wien/UE 10452 A/B. Copyright renewed 1960 by Boosey & Hawkes, Inc., New York. All rights in the USA owned and controlled by Boosey & Hawkes, Inc., New York.

Alban Berg: "Liebesode" ("Ode of Love"), from *Seven Early Songs*. Copyright © 1928 by Universal Edition. English version Copyright © 1955 by Universal Edition (London) Ltd., London. Copyright renewed 1956 by Helene Berg.

Violin Concerto, first movement. Copyright © 1936, 1996 by Universal Edition A.G. Wien.

Luigi Dallapiccola: *Goethe-Lieder*, No. 2. Copyright © 1953 by Edizioni Suvini Zerboni. Copyright © renewed. All rights reserved. Used by permission of European American Music Distributors Company, sole U.S. and Canadian agent for Edizioni Suvini Zerboni.

Quaderno musicale di Annalibera (*Musical Notebook of Annalibera*), No. 4. Copyright © 1952 by Edizioni Suvini Zerboni. Copyright © renewed. All rights reserved. Used by permission of European American Music Distributors Company, sole U.S. and Canadian agent for Edizioni Suvini Zerboni.

Sean Doyle: Excerpt from *Harlequin Redux*. Used by permission.

Excerpt from *Samaritan*. Used by permission.

Excerpt from *A Satire to Decay*. Used by permission.